Discovering

AMERICAN TRUTHS

Broken News and the Political World

★ ★ ★ ★ ★ ★ ★

Fleming J. Allen

<u>*Discovering* AMERICAN TRUTHS</u>
Broken News and the Political World

Copyright © 2018 by Fleming J. Allen

This book has been written as a source of information from some stories and news available via television media news outlets, newspapers, and Internet searches. It is as accurate as the articles and references used to create it. All opinions, remarks, and observations are based from the material gathered. The comments and opinions made from this known public information are *not* intended to give advice, incite illegal acts, purposefully libel, or threaten any one person, group of people, or business in order to cause loss or irreparable harm to that entity. The content is merely available public data mixed with some opinion, used with the notion that "freedom of speech" has been granted to each person as an inalienable right which can be exercised given the words written in the First Amendment of the United States Constitution.

Book and Cover design by Fleming J. Allen
ISBN-13: 978-1987431377
ISBN-10: 1987431375
First Edition: May 2018

CONTENTS

Acknowledgements ii
Preface.. iii

Title Page

Introduction ix

Chapter 1   Unfair and Unbalanced Journalism 1
Chapter 2   Creating an Impeachment Angle 16
Chapter 3   Fake and Ignorant News....................................25
Chapter 4   Hidden and Misrepresented Stories.......................40
Chapter 5   Immigration – Guns – Law Enforcement 60
Chapter 6   Presidential Criticisms and Insults........................77
Chapter 7   Identity Politics & Political Correctness 102
Chapter 8   Achievements by the President...........................128
Chapter 9   Inspirational Speeches....................................151
Chapter 10   Cries of Russia, Russia, Russia! 165
Chapter 11   The Real Obama Years: Failures.........................201
Chapter 12   The Real Obama Years: Scandals 221
Chapter 13   What Really Happened with Hillary? 241
Chapter 14   Falling Left: Stars and Activism.........................269
Chapter 15   Our Founding Fathers' Documents 287

Afterword 297
Historical Quotes to Ponder 301
Publications & Books to Consider Reading 303
References...304

ACKNOWLEDGEMENTS

First and foremost, the person I need to acknowledge is Nancy. She has been a source of strength for me and the love of my life. In moments of joy, inspiration, folly, disappointment, and grief, she has stood by me. With her support, I have been able to gain faith and fortitude to battle an unknown illness. If not for her unconditional love, continuous care, and advice this book may not have been possible. So, with an endless outpouring of love, I dedicate this book to her.

Of course, I must recognize my mother and deceased father, who had given me life. My parents supported all my dreams and aspirations. And, although my mother lives far away, she still exists in my heart, as I transmit my hugs and kisses to her over the many miles.

I revel in the remembrances of some wonderful moments which were shared with a brother I had grown up with as a child and adult. I send my love to him and his daughter, my niece.

Much peace, love, and happiness are wished for my other siblings and my step-mother in whatever they do.

My deepest gratitude and devoted endearment go to my uncle, who dwells in England, for his on-going guidance, love, and support.

I echo my fondest affections to my cousins, whom have always been in my thoughts and whose benevolence is unsurpassed.

Not to be forgotten are the thanks and love I must express to John and Charmaine for their unwavering friendship and support for nearly four decades. They will always be family to me. And, to Marc, Albert, and Eric, I recall the friendship we had in our youth and wish you well.

Of course, I send my best with love to Gene, Noreen, Ralph, Rita, Patricia, Martin, Amelia, Annamarie, Charlie, John, Nancy, Bernadette, Hugh, Elena, and all their relations. They are my extended family.

In addition, many prayers and blessings must be sent to my relatives, acquaintances, and friends' relations who have passed on. To name but a few, they are: Lydia, Vera, Gerald, Tom, Flora, Chester, Marie, Fannie, Anthony, Joanne, Alfred, Mary, as well as many others.

Lastly, I thank everyone on *Fox News* and *Fox Business* for giving me trustworthy news and laughter (i.e. The Five, Bret, Martha, Tucker, Sean, Laura, Shannon, Jeanine, Mark, Maria, Stuart, Lou, Trish, etc.).

PREFACE

America is being hoodwinked! But before explaining what brought me to this conclusion, I thought it was best to share some personal history.

I'm an American citizen who was born in Germany while my father served in the U.S. Army. When I was 2 years old, my parents, baby brother, and I moved to find a home in New York. Growing up, I worked as a newspaper boy, grocery bagger, file clerk and movie usher.

During my youth, through hard times, my parents collected public assistance (welfare) and foods stamps until they found jobs to better support me and my younger brother. But my parents used this program only when it was a necessity. They didn't want government dependency to hold them hostage. So, my parents struggled, skimped, and saved, while they found employment to once again became an integral part of society. Yet, as time passed on, when I was a teenager, the differences my parents had in marriage would inevitably end in divorce.

Despite the family split, I graduated high school and instead of enrolling in college decided to enter into the armed forces. Enrolling in the United States Air Force was one of the greatest honors of my life. I worked in the military as a Telecommunications Operations Specialist with a SCI (Sensitive Compartmented Information) Top Secret security clearance. Serving my country, I was able to visit many places in the U.S. and Europe, while also taking the opportunities to reacquaint myself with my uncle in England and grandfather in California.

After my four-year tenure in the military, I worked for years in several different jobs, such as a PC technician, computer supervisor, website designer, security guard, inventory control manager, accounts payable specialist, and bookkeeper. Then, as a 50-year old adult, I went to college and achieved an Associate Degree with a 4.0 GPA.

Regarding my family, it's diverse in ethnicity and heritage. My relatives are comprised of persons who have lived in or have descended from peoples in the Ukraine, Lithuania, Russia, England, Scotland, France, Germany, Italy, Spain, India (Bengal), and Puerto Rico. But my connections to different cultures doesn't end with my family relations.

In the springtime of life, the affinity I had for traveling the world was strong. I journeyed to commonplace and offbeat regions on our globe - in 25 countries and on seven continents. My youthful yearnings and military experiences had stirred my inquisitive nature to explore many: historical locations, religious sites, modern cities, ancient monuments, architectural masterpieces, famous museums, and places of natural wonder. I have been extremely fortunate in this respect. But from a humble background, I labored hard and long for many years to ensure enough resources were available to me so that I could embrace my heart's desires. Then, I fulfilled my dreams by experiencing the sights, sounds, tastes, and smells of many pleasurable places, as well as some impoverished regions on our globe. Whether it's karma, luck, God, or fate that gave me the opportunity to achieve my innate passion for travel, and the chance to visit other countries and cultures, is for others to decide. All I know is my yen to learn as much as I could first-hand about other peoples and places outside America was genuine.

The faiths of my family have included Judaism, Buddhism, Bahai, Islam, Christianity, Rosicrucianism, and Agnosticism. Myself, I was baptized a Catholic as a young adult. But this didn't prevent me from doing some soul searching. I have visited many churches, synagogues, mosques, and Buddhist temples around the world. During this spiritual journey I discovered a common central truth. That is, a good and honest soul lies at the core of most people. And, my belief is that there exists one thread of thought running through every religion. This century's old idea is "do to others as you would have them do to you" (Luke 6:31). Although it's a simple idea, which had been preached by Jesus, one can interpret much from the message. Kindness, honesty, compassion, and love can be encouraged, found, and lived when abiding by this phrase. In contrast, not giving any contemplation to embrace its meaning could lead to dishonesty, immorality, cruelty, or hate invading one's being. Unfortunately, these negative qualities are being expressed through word and action every day in our world, mostly because they oppose that fundamental precept which gives rise to humanity's better nature.

Regarding my political beliefs, I have never been affiliated with one political party. For me, it's best to think independently of ideological constraints which adhere to one political party. When I voted for a President, it was done so with the notion that this person would be the best option to protect my home, America, from threats abroad and within our country. And, I hoped this newly elected President would move America forward in some positive economic and social direction.

Before and during their presidency, I supported Carter, Reagan, Bush (Sr.), Clinton, Bush (Jr.), and Obama. Being that I had followed politics to some degree, much faith was placed in these leaders to do what was right for our nation. I trusted our politicians to make fair and just decisions and the news media to be truthful. But, unfortunately, through the decades, I and many other Americans were unknowingly misled on many occasions. It's why we must *live and learn.*

It's quite true that one grows wiser as one grows older. During this normal aging process, one's beliefs become clearer to them as well – whether they be social, moral, or political in nature. By visiting different parts of America and other countries, in addition to interacting with people of varied backgrounds and religions, life's experiences give one more clarity into what happiness, health, prosperity, freedom, and peace of mind means. Of course, this is subjective to everyone. And, what I have found is these positive aspects of life have been sometimes hindered by misunderstandings, a lack of courage to express oneself, and empowering some with trust who didn't deserve it in the first place. Unfortunately, in recent times, the negative aspects of empowerment have been exhibited in politicians we elect and then must endure.

I have always been a truth seeker about many things. So, if I am interested enough in a particular subject, whether it be literature, religion, philosophy, history, culture, science, or politics, and I find that something seems amiss, then I become very troubled. That's when I begin to engage in my own research and do my best trying to reconcile the inconsistencies I had found. While perusing through much data and different points of view, I use fair and rational analysis to come to an ultimate conclusion. There are undoubtedly many people just like me who are earnestly eager to discover the unfiltered truth.

My personal pursuit of seeking out the truth, however, has led me to sadly find that news we receive daily from most in the mainstream media has been undeniably misrepresented with extreme personal bias. The volume of this disinformation propagated into the public arena is extremely alarming. It may be unprecedented in American history. Maybe worse than this is some noteworthy stories are hidden from us.

As an American citizen, military veteran, and truth seeker, my conscience feels a duty to help. It's my want to inform those who aren't aware that the public is being bamboozled by unprincipled persons, and some alternative realities are being suppressed. The amount of biased opinions, misinformation, and vile accusations poisoning fair-minded people is staggering. The deceitful desire to undermine the values and morals of Americans, and many around the globe, should be exposed. Therefore, my hope is to set the record straight, in some way, and shine the light of positive truths through the darkness of negative falsehoods.

Why are my story and views relevant? Well, I wanted you to know: how I grew up; the diversity of my family background and religious beliefs; my vocational history; my education; my military service with top-secret security clearance; the desire I had to engage with other cultures and people; my non-affiliation with a political party; and my current thoughts. These life's experiences have allowed me to write poetry, short-stories and non-fiction. But more significantly, my history should give you a better idea about some conclusions made in this book.

With regard to the information soon-to-be shared with you, its sole purpose is to unfold truths that were misrepresented by garish opinions or sordid facts. Therefore, fairer data was viewed, noted, researched, compiled, and written over several arduous months. Once you read these facts one can accept them or not. It's up to you to decide.

So, why is America being hoodwinked? It's because there are blatant falsities, baseless opinions, and inexcusable hysteria being propagated to us regarding much in our present political landscape and about its affiliated history. Moreover, some truths have been carefully and purposefully concealed from the public. But these unconscionable deceptions must be confronted. The broken news should be picked up, reassembled, and re-examined through a new lens, while other hidden stories need to be exhibited. Yet given the countless number of news stories, only a fraction can be presented in this book. Of course, what will be divulged may or may not surprise you. Nonetheless, it's time to share this information I have gathered to, hopefully, let you discover, or reanalyze, some of the many known and unknown American truths.

Discovering

AMERICAN TRUTHS

Broken News and the Political World

★ ★ ★ ★ ★ ★ ★

From a great American author, words were spoken which arguably can be applied to much being told by the mainstream media today.

This quote remains timeless...

****

"Believe nothing you hear, only half that you see."

-*Edgar Allan Poe*

INTRODUCTION

This work has been written with the interest of America hanging in the balance. Our democracy is based on certain laws. For instance, every person has the right to express his or her opinion. Therefore, daily, *we the people* receive many diverse viewpoints regarding certain issues. The citizens of this nation, however, are entitled to obtain truthful and accurate information, not spin, opinion, slander, or gossip.

We gather, read, and examine this material transmitted to us by our news media, documentary film makers, institutions of learning (i.e. colleges and grade schools), politicians, health officials, pharmaceutical companies, and scientists. Yet what has been given to Americans over the passing decades is a decline and distortion of pertinent facts. There seems to be a fast and furious scramble to get out information, even if it's incorrect. Coupled with this is false, unsubstantiated, and biased stories being propagated in a leisurely manner. And, we are supposed to put our trust in those who are giving us this type of information?

These persons sometimes provide critical data to: young children, families, students, patients, the working class and impoverished, non-profits, corporations, political activists, immigrants who have become newly inducted American citizens, and colleagues in their fields of expertise. But those who may depend upon or retain this data being dispersed to them may act or speak out accordingly - sometimes in a most unfavorable way. So, if violence erupts, do we blame the receivers of data or those who pass on the skewed or illegitimate information?

Additionally, some information, mostly news, given to the public is provided with unverified hearsay or with obvious vindictiveness. It's done so without any conscience or contemplation that it may affect an individual or the well-being of a nation. Apparently, ratings, polls, and recognition about job performances have become more valuable to certain notables than serving the people with sincere and reliable data. Some even preach to us about the moral and ethical high grounds we should walk upon. Yet, ironically, these unsavory persons are the most untrustworthy and corrupt amongst us. They bury the truth or tell-half truths in the name of political, societal, and monetary gain.

Unfortunately, these are accurate depictions of the present world we live in. There are elite forces in our midst which wish to follow agendas that are not in the best interest of all people. These persons seek to be proven right to gain power and influence over the public. So, we should be skeptical about what is being portrayed as news.

Quite frankly and sadly, most in the mainstream media are being blinded by hatred and political bias, or both, when giving their so-called news stories about the President. Regarding OUR President, I will not use his name in this book. Instead, I will present him in other ways (i.e. the 45th American President). The reason for this is simple. Some get upset seeing or hearing about a President which they do not like. And, there is actually a very real name created for those who have been struck with a psychological affliction pertaining to this President. It's called *TDS (T.... Derangement Syndrome)*. Anyway, I will not write his name. But if I quote someone, his name may be mentioned.

But getting back to the mainstream media, a duplicitous crew at best, they are indifferent to the principles behind putting *GOD and Country first* before self. Without this patriotic concept in their minds, admittedly this a military term I've come to admire, their egos have overtaken their spirits of good conscience, and now a dark cloud follows them. They count on *group think*, which is an irrational psychological conformity to a desired way of thought. What this means is the media conspires and doesn't deviate from their group mindset. They push their thought on the public, wanting us to think as they do. It's their aim to only give us subjective views and sensationalized headlines. They desire that everyone conforms to their pompous demeanor without any introspection. The minds and hearts of the mainstream media want us to see, think, and align with their one-sided passions which inevitably tend to divide people rather than bond them. And, they feed upon and seek to wear down the emotions of the public.

But an independent thinker, not based on party lines, which I am, must remain steadfast when sifting through the muddied waters of the mainstream media's tiresome rhetoric. We must show them that some of us shall not remain silent in our displeasure of their cynical viewpoints. There are many people who are fair-minded, can think for themselves, and are not ignorant of what the media wants to twist into disturbing news. These slithering *serpents* should know that some of us Americans will not accept what they preach and peddle as gospel. We are well-aware of their game of spreading shade to cover for corrupt politicians, celebrities, activist groups, and others who share their ideologies. Therefore, it's almost paramount most of us resist their deceitful temptations from their many *fruits of their poisonous trees.*

Fortunately, what will be unfolded in this book will help to expose the unspoken truths, a disease of words, and outright propaganda that has been attacking our mental, physical, spiritual, and emotional states for far too long. To do so, the extreme biased perspectives from those who seek to dictate our way of life must be met with sincerity, honesty, and facts. Therefore, this work will mostly embody a resistance to their unjust resistance of not accepting political realities.

There will be unfettered truth and some history to the very best of the information collected. This work will provide many uncovered facts, quotes, and the disinformation about topics. Data and satirical opinion shall be given too; but this shall not lean toward conspiracy theories. Repetitive phrases and words will be used to emphasize points as this work unfolds. It will focus on the: journalism of yesterday and today; proliferation of fake news; impeachment angle floating around; hidden and misrepresented stories; usage of political correctness and identity politics; issues of guns, immigration, and law enforcement; untold Presidential achievements; unfounded Russia! Russia! Russia! cries; real Obama years and Clinton scandals; biased outbursts of celebrities and others, and laws we need to save us from catastrophe.

Hopefully, the facts within will eradicate some of the ugly darkness blinding us from seeing what is and was the light of reality. Therefore, the information to be shared aims to shine proven evidences upon the many who have been assaulted with negative biased news regarding our political world. Millions may know these facts, and others may not. Of course, not everything can be told (Note: This book will only provide information up to the first days of June 2018). It's impossible to do so. Yet with today's access to large chunks of data on the Internet and from honest news outlets, much can still be discovered. Most definitely the "truth is out there". But *we the people* must be willing to seek it.

"Each morning we are born again. What we do today is what matters most." – Buddha

<h1 style="text-align:center"><u>Chapter 1</u></h1>

UNFAIR AND UNBALANCED JOURNALISM

The news has been spread in many different forms over the millennia: on moistened clay slabs, stone tablets, papyrus, and scribed paper, or via horseman, smoke signal, carrier pigeon, printing press, telegraph, radio, television, fax machine, or computer. In this daily news, one can certainly discover: an allegiance to a preferred leader, organization, or locality; an affiliation with a specific religion, ethnicity, or race; and an adherence to one set of principles, philosophies, or ideologies. These listed allegiances, affiliations, and adherences have been present since civilization began. But how did modern day news begin in America?

The circulation of news in the New World (America) probably began in earnest after the first newspaper *Publick Occurrences, Both Foreign and Domestick* was published in Boston (September 25, 1690). As years passed, American journalism was spread even further through gazettes, posts, weekly journals, and newsletters. But reporters adapted biased commitments to persons, groups, places, and idealisms. This became so prevalent in the daily American news cycle that some news emerged as a *political force*. Actually, it sparked a notable fight for American independence by reinforcing patriotism through the new colonies, while simultaneously smearing Britain's King George III (more later).

By 1798, since journalism was becoming much more partial and politically motivated, the U.S. Congress decided to pass the *Alien and Sedition Acts*. These acts prohibited "false, scandalous, or malicious writing" against the government. Publishing such news or opposing any law or Presidential act was to be punishable by a crime. But in 1801, the acts expired as Thomas Jefferson became the 3rd U.S. President.

With no laws in place to stop them, journalists reverted back to reporting scandals, lies, and salacious news. Then, during the 1890's through the 1920's, a somewhat progressive mindset profoundly took hold in journalism. These reporters began attacking well-established leaders and institutions they felt had become corrupt and who were not involved with tackling tough issues of the era, including "urban poverty, unsafe working conditions, prostitution, and child labor." So, President Theodore Roosevelt labeled those journalists as *muckrakers*. These crusaders for truth and reform became the public watchdogs of that era.

The muckrakers were instrumental in shaping some American laws. Some of them were the 1) 1902 Newland Reclamation Act, which funded irrigation for 13 arid western states, 2) 1906 Pure Food and Drug Act, 3) 1908 Federal Employers Liability Act, protecting and compensating railroad workers who were injured on the job, 4) 1911 Mother's Pension Law, 5) eight-hour labor laws for women, and 6) adoption of child labor laws. But other reporters were involved with practicing another type of journalism. It was called *yellow journalism*.

The unethical and unprofessional sensationalism, scandal, and untruth of yellow journalism countered the reporting of muckrakers. This style of journalism developed a much bigger voice when publishing giants like William Randolph Hearst and Joseph Pulitzer distributed their newspapers to the public. Tabloid news had run amok.

As decades passed, journalists still would report scandalous and unsubstantiated news. But tabloid news was balanced by real news. In 1956, a poll was taken by the American National Election Study which showed 66% of Americans believed newspapers were fair (Democrats – 64% and Republicans – 78%). Then, by 1972, a popular news anchor of the time named Walter Cronkite (*CBS Evening News*) was found to be 72% trustworthy by Americans. But news began turning politically bias.

From the late 20th century through the 21st century, the public's confidence in the media has waned considerably. In 2013, a *Gallop Poll* found that Americans saw the mainstream media as 46% too liberal, 13% too conservative, and 36% just right. But by 2018, "only 27% feel very confident in their ability to distinguish factual news from opinion", as per the same polling group. Yet, really, the facts are worse than this.

The current American mainstream media

Through much research and invested time, what has been discovered is many individuals in the current mainstream media have not changed much from their predecessors. They still practice yellow journalism; and, it remains a *stain* on their profession. They have a political, moral, and ethical slant that is not in the best interest of their country – the United States of America. The animosity, jealousy, hate, and negative bias projected in the news by a clear majority of the American media toward the 45th U.S. President has been overwhelmingly apparent since his 2016 election. Their eager effort to present the reasons why the President should be impeached is transparent to anyone who has a fair mind and heart. They show their malice and how much they detest the results of a legitimate Presidential election via deceptive words.

These media types want nothing more than to have influence and control over susceptible persons who only desire to hear and read accurate news disseminated to them. Some receiving the daily news don't realize these anchors on television, hosts on radio, and writers in newspapers are intentionally misinforming them of the facts.

Most people in America have been receiving news from so-called journalists which is being echoed by political operatives, activists, and celebrities who are all in league with one another. They sensationalize news which is sometimes blatantly untrue. But because this President has bypassed the media's power through his social media twitter account to inform millions of noteworthy news, the media and its cohorts now conspire to be recognized via outrageous commentary. They need people to watch, read, and talk about the stories *they offer* to justify their existence. Their cunning methods of persuasion aim to pacify or infuriate people, depending on one's personal perspectives. Yet if the public could be more keenly aware of their tactics, it would only lend credence to how desperate and deranged they have become.

Their political motives are irrefutable, historically negative, and preconceived to prove they are correct. In truth, they are all fighting superiority complexes within themselves. Our democracy is being hijacked by elites who "think" they have privilege above the rest of us. They are modern day *Pied Pipers* who desire the people to be lured and hypnotized to follow their agendas. It's scary to see socialism and anti-capitalism pushed to the American people just to satisfy a political agenda. These individuals and groups don't seem to want to realize that socialism has spawned much malevolence in our world. Look no further than the Nazi Party in Germany, tyrannies and repressive regimes of Romania, Venezuela, Cambodia, North Korea, Syria, Somalia, and Iran, as well as Communism in Russia, Vietnam, Laos, China, and Cuba.

The mainstream media assumes that since they monopolize most of the viewership and readership in America, the people should stand silent and bow to them. They believe the public *must* listen to the conjectures, rants, and diatribes of men and women with predisposed opinions. But they are mistaken. Do these personalities know *we the people* are becoming more in-tune with the propaganda, untruths, and distorted facts being disseminated to us? Therefore, the mainstream media should take note that there are many of rational mind who shall not allow them to sully our eyes and ears with a barrage of garbage daily. These elites shall be shunned until such a time as they desire to awake from their slumber and begin to give us honesty and truth again.

The willingness on the media's part to lie, revel in half-truths, use phony anonymous sources, leak classified government information, and hide positive facts regarding the 45th American President is quite disturbing. They ignore the positive impacts he has made for America, and the world, as a direct result of his bold messaging and negotiations, coupled with his long-list of accomplishments (more later). Instead of transmitting these optimistic achievements to the people, most of the mainstream media circulates pessimistic views of our country and President to fit their narrative. They also support and don't discuss the intentional shutdown of conservative speech, which violates one of the constitution pillars of American society – the First Amendment. This media mob shows violence perpetrated by some hate groups while not showing other hate groups which are more violent and un-American. Moreover, the media unjustly tries to polarize those who are apolitical with intentional ideological banter, smut, righteousness, and falsities.

The mainstream media coordinates with all like-minded news outlets to get their talking points straight. Then, they echo the same messages, thinking the public will give credence to their opinions and news if they say them loud and long enough, repetitively. If one flips through the television channels, one can witness this first-hand. Of course, these personalities which have been spoken about infiltrate professions which were once respected and considered a worthy part of our society. But, most regrettably, in our present times, these persons apparently have earned and attained unfortunate titles of ill-repute given to them by their rival peers. They are labeled with a brand of their own making -- *biased hack journalists and reporters.*

It's quite apparent that some of these journalists and reporters are noticeably slanted toward one political party. The majority ally themselves with the Democratic party. This weakens any rationale indicating they are a fair and balanced press. The once well-respected anchors, writers, and editors have now given in to clear antagonistic animus and mockery. A fever and sickness have overcome them to a degree that is unparalleled. So much so, these media types have become utterly disingenuous and very opinionated in their reporting. As a result, the people are laughing at their absurdities, and their ratings have dropped significantly. But, actually, it's the people who suffer, because there is no objective reporting. Instead, subjective coverage casts a dark shadow over the news. Do they realize this? Do they care?

Given the mainstream media's approval ratings are lower or on par with the U.S. Congress, which is abysmally low (somewhere below 20%), why do they attempt to regain the public's confidence with lazy tabloid news? The people don't desire or deserve this. They create biased fictitious stories for shock value and seem unwilling to discover positive truths or real news in America. It's because the media's focus is to disparage the 45th American President every second of the day. Most of these media personalities use errant buzz words such as chaos, madness, racist, impeach, unfit, Watergate, collusion, authoritarian, and Russia, or phrases like *lack of empathy, obstruction of justice,* and *assault on the press* to amplify their derogatory messaging against the President. They display no guilt or shame for their injustices on air.

But here is a <u>news flash</u> for them! The American people are wise to their game of misinformation, sensationalism, and deflection from the facts. If this 45th American President has done anything, he has unveiled the true character and hidden beliefs about most of our so-called news anchors, journalists, and pundits. Unfortunately, the truth about these media elites and others associated with them would not have come to the surface if the other candidate for the presidency would have won the 2016 election. And, *his* presence in the White House has also led to uncovering mass corruption by the previous administration and about that other Presidential candidate. So, we are fortunate much is being exposed regarding the media and their cohorts in Congress.

As OUR President continues to move forward with an American agenda which will improve this country (and the globe), we must push back against the dreadful dishonesty of the mainstream media by *holding their feet to the fire.* Then, and maybe, only then, after they have been totally humiliated, can the truth live again, rising like a phoenix, from the ashes of a dead and hellacious press.

How much negative news was there during the 2016 Presidential election and since the inauguration of the 45th President of the United States? There are many articles of this biased and irrational news coverage. Only a few examples, however, shall be presented, such as 1) before the election, 2) comparing him to other Presidents, 3) the first 100 days, 4) the first year, and 5) the first two months in 2018.

Before the election: fall of 2016

On October 25, 2016, an article was written by Hadas Gold (*Politico*) entitled "Study: 91 percent of coverage on evening newscasts was negative to Donald Trump". It indicated that over "12 weeks" three of the nightly news broadcasts (*ABC, CBS,* and *NBC*) had "coverage (91%)" which had been "hostile" to the American President-to-be. This study taken by the *Media Research Center* consisted of "588 evening news stories". Only "29%" was focused on the campaign, while the rest of the time was spent on the absolute bias of correspondents, anchors, expert commentators, and voters on the street. Also, the networks spent little time on the Clinton email server, her Foundation, or *Wikileaks* emails.

Comparison to other Presidents: the first 60 days

In an article written October 2, 2017 by Peter Kafka *(Recode),* it shows the "positive" and "negative" assessments of the last four Presidents by the media through their first 60 days. The results compiled from 326 stories by *Pew Research Center* were predictable.

Positive:
Clinton (27%), Bush (22%), Obama (20%), OUR President (5%)
Negative
Clinton (28%), Bush (28%), Obama (42%), OUR President (62%)

The first 100 days: 2017

"Media Give Trump Most Negative Presidential Coverage in 25 Years" was an article written on October 13, 2017 by Jasper Fakkert (*The New York Times*). There was analysis of "3,000 stories" from "24 different media organizations" by *Pew Research Center (PRC)* over the first 100 days of his presidency. The 45th American President's assertions that the mainstream media was biased against him were true. PRC indicated "only 5 percent of news reports" were positive. So, in the last 25 years, it's undeniable that this President has had the most negative coverage.

Also, two-thirds of the news coverage consisted of five main topics: immigration, health care, Presidential appointments and nominations, his political skills, and U.S. Russia relations. Moreover, as per the same report, the media "sought to question the legitimacy of his presidency" with "anonymous sources" and "frequent erroneous reporting". During a Congressional inquiry, even FBI Director James Comey agreed with the assertions this article made about the mainstream media. He said regarding the reported stories about classified information, "people talking about it often don't really know what's going on."

The first year: 2017 – 2018

An article written by Rich Noyes and Mike Ciandella (*Newsbusters*) on January 16, 2018 entitled "2017: The Year the News Media Went to War Against a President" reported that one out of every three minutes of evening news airtime was about the President. During these evening broadcasts, 43% of the news about the 45th American President was centered on his "controversies" to do with the Russia investigation, not his policies. Additionally, the overall coverage was 90% negative.

From January 30 to December 31, 2017, the three evening news channels, *ABC*, *CBS*, and *NBC*, broadcasted "3,430 stories" which focused upon the President and his administration ("totaling 99 hours, 3 minutes of airtime"). Stories about him made up over 34% percent of the news. To put this in perspective, in 2015 and 2016 President Obama and his administration were covered only 10% by the evening news.

There were 5,883 comments made about OUR President and his administration, and only 617 (10%) were positive. As a matter of fact, there was only three months when the evening news had more than 10% positive news. It occurred in January (15%), when speaking about the reactions of the President's supporters; April (18%), when cruise missile strikes hit a Syrian airbase; and, December (15%), after the tax cut bill was passed.

But the negative media coverage dominated the broadcast networks in 2017. The issues which they mostly focused on were the: President's assertions that the Obama administration wire-tapped him, riots in Charlottesville, Virginia, temporary travel ban, and Russia collusion stories. From all the regular news being told, the Russian collusion stories consisted of "20 hours, 34 minutes of coverage" (21%) and the President's administration issues filled "42 hours, 37 minutes" (43%). And, then there were the President's policy issues.

There were five policies garnering 47% of the twisted news being spewed about the President. They were comprised of 1) the difficult North Korean nuclear issue, 2) repealing and replacing Obamacare, 3) travel ban and the wall 4) immigration and deportations, and 5) the tax reform bill. Only 9 hours, 17 minutes (9%) of the news was centered on important Presidential nominations, travel, and ceremonies.

There was no fair coverage on whether the Russian collusion story or investigation by Special Counsel Mueller's team was biased. The illegal "unmasking", wire-tapping, and surveillance by the Obama administration, as well as the Clinton campaign's involvement with the phony Russian (or Steele) dossier only got a total of 35 minutes of airtime. Only 11 minutes (in a year) or 1% of time was dedicated toward showing the text messages between FBI lawyer Lisa Page and FBI agent Peter Strzok that were biased against the 45th U.S. President or texts which implicated persons in the Obama administration (more later).

Moreover, a report showed Democrats having more confidence in the mainstream media, declaring that they "fully, accurately, and fairly" reported trustworthy news. The same report also indicated that just a year prior in 2016 only "51%" of Democrats trusted the news. Now, through 2017, "72%" Democrats trusted them. So, what changed? Someone sits in the White House Oval Office whom they abhor.

These Democratic politicians approve of the media because they are working in tandem with most news organizations to push negative narratives against the 45th United States President. Contrary to the Democrats, the Republicans believed "76%" of the mainstream media invented stories about the President and his administration. And, the President's supporters thought 85% of the news was inaccurate.

The first two months in 2018

On March 6, 2018 an article written by Rich Noyes (*Newsbusters*) which was entitled "TV vs. Trump in 2018: Lots of Russia, and 91% Negative Coverage (Again!)" highlights that the Media Research Center (MRC) found the same amount of negative analysis from ABC, CBS, and NBC over the first two months of 2018 as it did through 2017.

In January and February 2018, a study by MRC showed that a total of 505 stories from the evening news was about the 45th American President and his administration. From this, 204 minutes of coverage focused on "the Russia investigation" out of 851 total minutes spent on the President. The remaining minutes were split with discussions of the "economy, immigration reform, gun debate", and other issues.

In addition to the Russia stories, these two months also saw focus on domestic abuse problems with White House aide Rob Porter, the alleged closed-door meeting comments made by the President about African nations, and an attempt to validate the "Fire and Fury" book by Michael Wolff. This made up 63% of the news coverage.

The remaining 37% percent of the negative news coverage was

about immigration reform, gun control, and the government shutdown. But, of course, little, if any, news was said about the growth of the strong economy, number of jobs gained, great positive impact of the tax cut bill, or the gains and wins against ISIS and al-Qaeda.

Of all these researched articles, the following assertion can be concluded. The best portrayal of how the news was covered regarding the 45th American President is the article entitled, "2017: The Year the News Media Went to War Against a President". The only argument with most of this and other analyses is that other major contributors of untrue or negative news stories, such as *MSNBC, CNN, The New York Times*, and *The Washington Post* were not included. And, the amount of negative news seems higher than 91%, and closer to the 95% mark.

Of course, one of the reasons for this negative coverage by these news organizations is to provide the public with a dismal view of the President, and to keep his approval ratings at historic lows. These imitators of our news transparently despise him to the core and will do whatever it takes to try and help impeach the 45th President of the United States (more later). Remember, it was a businessman from Queens, New York who outsmarted them and a liberal career politician. They hate this fact and can't stomach that all their so-called analyses and fixed poll numbers were wrong. But, most of all, the mainstream media can't wrap their weary heads around the fact that even with their deceptively corrupt collaboration with each other, political activists, former politicians, the Clinton campaign, and the Democratic National Committee, *their* Presidential candidate still couldn't beat the populist movement of an unseasoned politician. It infuriates them to no end.

Just how corrupt are they? *Wikileaks* exposed just one example of this. The "proof is in the pudding", as they say. And, some of the ingredients of the pudding are not very sweet but rather sour. There undoubtedly was a conspired effort of collusion between the Clinton campaign, reporters, journalists, news anchors, and executives of the mainstream media outlets. The only exception is that representatives of the *Fox News* network were either not invited or blacklisted because of some of their conservative views. All is quite evident when one can examine the intercepted emails by *Wikileaks*.

1) On Apr 6, 2015, at 5:10 PM Jesse Ferguson, jesse@jesseferguson.com, wrote, "We wanted to make sure everyone on this email had the latest information on the two upcoming dinners with reporters. Both are off-the-record."

*2) Thursday night, April 9th at 7:00p.m. Dinner at the Home of John Podesta. His address is **** ********** St NW in Washington, DC. This will be with about 20 reporters who will closely cover the campaign (aka the bus).*

3) Friday night, April 10th at 6:30p.m. Cocktails and Hors D'oeuvres at the Home of Joel Benenson. His home address is (redacted for privacy) New York, 10128. This is with a broader universe of New York reporters. For those who have been asking, here is the ABC – Diane Sawyer YES

<u>*The invitees were 65 in total, including:*</u>

ABC – George Stephanoplous LIKELY
ABC – David Muir YES
Buzzfeed – Ben Smith NO/IN KOREA
CNN – Erin Burnett YES
CNN – Jeff Zucker YES
MSNBC – Ed Schultz TRYING
MSNBC – Phil Griffin YES
MSNBC – Beth Fouhy NO/IN PA
MSNBC – Thomas Roberts YES
New Yorker – Ryan Liza NO/IN LA
NPR – Mike Oreskes NO/OUT OF COUNTRY
NY Post – Geofe Earl YES
NYT – Amy Chozik YES
NYT – Maggie Haberman YES
NYT – Pat Healey YES
NYT – Jonathan Martin YES
NYT – Gail Collins YES
YAHOO – Matt Bai YES
PBS – Charlie Rose YES
VICE – Alyssa Mastramonoco YES

MSNBC – Joe Scarborough NO/IN PA
New Yorker – David Remnick YES

This is just a minor instance of collusion between a political party and the mainstream media. In this case, it's the Hillary Clinton campaign aligning themselves with the media. What makes it worse, however, is the Democrats and mainstream media seem to coordinate their *talking points* for the day. Moreover, they perpetuate the same message, albeit just in different formats. More distressing than this is the disheartening discovery that some of our law enforcement agencies, justice systems, local governments, state departments, and other high-ranking federal officials also have had biases not in the best interest of our nation. Their actions and thoughts seemed to have aligned with the mainstream media's vendetta aimed toward OUR President (more later). It's sad to note these types of partialities have been going on for years. The people are only beginning to be made more aware of these unjust and ethically unwise, and sometimes unlawful, practices.

Further proof of the American mainstream media's sentiments and reporting being unethically propagated is validated by a very biased website called *Media Matters for America*. This organization, founded by David Brock, is allegedly backed by many Democratic operatives, politicians, media organizations, big companies, and liberal activists, including the European billionaire socialist George Soros. And, they all wash each other's dirty little hands - figuratively speaking, of course.

Together, all these people are trying to feed a narrative that they have the answers and should be listened to without question. Not only is this occurring, but the brave individuals or groups who challenge and question the negative and false stories conceived in their transparent echo chambers are immediately discredited and demonized.

Most obviously, the media's desperate and ultimate objective is to delegitimize whatever the duly elected 45th American President does or says - as often and as best as possible. Regrettably, some who don't follow the news daily or are not politically savvy believe what they are being told by many in the mainstream media as truth. Those who fall into these traps don't realize the political motivations behind what they present to the public. Their unscrupulous bottom line is they hope most

Americans, and some in other nations, will end up despising the 45th President of the United States as much as they obviously do. And, they realize some are still very angry and disappointed about the election results. So, the mainstream media uses this to their utmost advantage. They succeed with their heightened negative rhetoric in some respects because some who align with their political ideologies want to believe OUR President is a malicious human being - just because the candidate they supported for President lost the 2016 election. So, these so-called purveyors of news, the mainstream media, use the emotions of these individuals and others to promote hatred toward the 45th United States President to dishonor and discredit him, minute after minute, hour after hour, day after day, month after month, and year after year.

Moreover, as was stated previously, the media focuses upon the innocent. They try to sow doubt in naive individuals, so they can pull them into their spider web and indiscriminately prey upon them. In the same breath, they blow winds of persuasion toward one of the most important groups in our society. These are the undecided who have independent and middle-of-the-road perspectives about our country. But these targeted citizens of our nation must be cautious, leery, examine the facts, and search for answers which seem hidden from them - for they have the power at voting machines to sway elections.

In addition to all of this, there are those who are trying to shut down *FOX News* by gladly smearing individuals on that network. It's because the other news channels are envious that *FOX News* has become the number one watched cable news network. Even though it's mostly a conservative news channel, it gives fair and balanced reporting. They have become 'modern-day muckrakers', and seekers of the truth.

When Shorenstein Center at Harvard University, *Newsbusters*, and others have determined that at least 90% or more of news coverage of the 45th American President is negative, the only news network which seems to have a fairly equal amount of negative and positive opinions and journalism is *FOX News*. The reporting on this channel is roughly 55% to 45% positive in favor of the President and his policies. Its motto is "Most Watched, Most Trusted". There has been no intentional or rampant fake news on this network. Most other networks have spewed misinformation about, not covered any positive accomplishments by, and spread lies regarding the 45th American President to the public.

The mainstream media scorn this President because he proved them all wrong about their predictions in the 2016 election. The media's polls were slanted toward Hillary Clinton, but the public didn't vote that way. The media's apparent collusion with her convinced them all that they were all ready to be richly rewarded. They were waiting to gloat about any minor achievement she would make and call it *wondrous*. But it didn't happen the way they envisioned. They were all shocked. Some cried while others had tantrums on air after Clinton's epic defeat.

Now, the public has begun to become wiser regarding their negative critiques and mantras. Many viewers and readers have fled to watching and reading more reputable and balanced reporting from news organizations such as *FOX News, The Washington Times, Wall Street Journal, The Hill,* and the *New York Post.* But if one wants a more conservative slant for news, then websites or publications which include *The Washington Examiner, National Review, The Weekly Standard, Townhall,* and the *Daily Caller* can be read. But, of course, the news most conveniently available to each one of us, however, should be chosen to make our own judgments about what is fair and objective.

It's very disconcerting, at minimum, that our *lame-stream media* (aka mainstream media) outlets have been crippled by prejudice and disgust. Ad nauseum, they want every person in America (and around the world) to adhere to their beliefs and ideologies. Also, they castigate and mock those who don't fall in-line with their very biased and warped commentary and opinions. It has become a dangerous time to be in the public arena because the feigned angst and predisposed reporting we watch, listen, or read from supposed reputable news outlets contribute to the way people react to certain situations. Mayhem, violence, twisted ideas, and even murder can arise from misinformation. Therefore, the indignant and continued rhetoric must be toned down.

Those in the mainstream media filled with jealousy and hatred must begin to embrace the fact that this 45th American President does want to do what is best for America. Their malicious criticisms are not helpful to the American people. If the mainstream media pauses to have a moment of reflection, they will find their views and stories have been counter-productive, inevitably only hurting themselves in the long run.

A quote by William Penn, the English philosopher, early Quaker, and founder of Pennsylvania, epitomizes the emotions and mindsets of most in the mainstream media.

"The jealous are troublesome to others, but torment to themselves."

The 45th President of the United States is undeserving of the daily wrath being cast at him by the mainstream media. He is not the evil incarnate they depict in their minds. His thoughts are those of a businessman, and one who has not been involved with the corrupt ways of politics. They are all very afraid of his bona fide candor and appeal to the American people. He openly unveils the truth regarding what is really happening behind the scenes in the political world. He is the most transparent President in modern-day history. Therefore, they want to see him impeached for his personality rather than his actions. But the mainstream media, progressively left Democratic Party, and those in law enforcement who continue to lay the foundation for impeachment, because they hate him, are doing so at their own peril. If it does occur, history shall remember their infamous and deceitful actions and words.

To begin legitimate impeachment proceedings against this 45th U.S. President would be an atrocity of justice. And, a revolt from the people may follow unlike anything in our lifetime. So, some should rethink their positions. To unjustly unseat a duly elected U.S. President under false pretenses because they don't like his vibrant personality, the policies he is implementing, or that their candidate lost an election will undermine America's democracy. At that point, the U.S. will have stooped to the level of a third world *banana republic* to satisfy the disdain certain individuals have for OUR President. Yet, with hope, 2018 and beyond will shed more light upon the vindictive motives and unprecedented negative agendas these detractors have in their spiteful bag of tricks. What very well may be exposed to the public in the coming months and years ahead is the accusers may become the accused.

Chapter 2

CREATING AN IMPEACHMENT ANGLE

I'm going to come right to the point. The primary reason for all the false rhetoric, disinformation, lies, and hidden truths is to intentionally undermine the will of the American people. The mainstream media, liberal pundits, progressively-left-wing Democratic Party members, those tangled up with the misdeeds of Obama's Administration and Hillary Clinton, and establishment Republicans, all want to do their utmost to provide evidence which leads to the *impeachment* of the duly elected 45th President of the United States. Their despicable rallying cry is "Impeach 45", which seems to be the motto of Democrats like Maxine Waters of California. But Americans have rights and must speak out against these individuals. The people's vote *trumps* their hate of him.

All those critics who are engaged in this impeachment crusade despise the 2016 Presidential election results because their agendas, and all which had been promised to them in way of favors, monetary gain, and power, went up in smoke on Nov. 8th, 2016. And, of course, most of all, they were made to look like fools. Now, they are trying to turn their images of shock, tears, grief, and discontent, as if a death had occurred in their lives, into a bearable happiness. They will do what they can, in all ways possible, to belittle, delegitimize, antagonize, and falsify news regarding OUR President. They can't stand that a businessman, neophyte politician, and ex-television star beat their shady politician.

They didn't count on the people realizing that a *vote for her* was not what the country really needed or wanted. Her flaws were extremely apparent. And, if justice is fair in America, those who voted for *him* will be vindicated because her misdeeds will finally be exposed to the fullest. There are already many verified facts about her collaboration with the highest levels of the Obama administration, Department of Justice (DOJ), Federal Bureau of Investigation (FBI), State department, as well as with the biased mainstream media outlets, the Democratic National Committee, and others during the 2016 primaries and general election.

This involved possible illegalities with a pay-for-play slush fund known as the Clinton Foundation, the sale of 20% of American uranium to a Russian backed firm, an improperly conducted classified email probe, and the purchase and distribution of a phony Russian dossier. But these unscrupulous activities by a former Presidential candidate, who lost "bigly", are being spoken about very little by the mainstream media. They are covering all this up for *her* and the past administration by distracting the public with wrongful rants of Presidential impeachment.

The media has focused on providing dim-witted remarks and creating ridiculous accusations about the President, his family and administration, as well as those who support him. They don't care the President is attempting to better the lives of American citizens, nor do they have *real concern* for other people whose countries are being threatened by terrorists and dictators. These haters and cynics who are opposed to the 45th American President may be trying to impeach him with the 25th Amendment. This specific constitutional amendment outlines the succession of the presidency if he declares to be unfit to serve the office, or others in the executive branch can conclude this. Obviously, if the President dies this amendment takes effect almost immediately and the Vice President is appointed President. This was the case when President John F. Kennedy was killed, and Vice President Lyndon B. Johnson became President. The 25th Amendment reads:

Section 1. *In case of the removal of the President from office or of his death or resignation, the Vice President shall become President.*

Section 2. *Whenever there is a vacancy in the office of the Vice President, the President shall nominate a Vice President who shall take office upon confirmation by a majority vote of both Houses of Congress.*

Section 3. *Whenever the President transmits to the President pro tempore of the Senate and the Speaker of the House of Representatives his written declaration that he is unable to discharge the powers and duties of his office, and until he transmits to them a written declaration to the contrary, such powers and duties shall be discharged by the Vice President as Acting President.*

__Section 4__. Whenever the Vice President and a majority of either the principal officers of the executive departments or of such other body as Congress may by law provide, transmit to the President pro tempore of the Senate and the Speaker of the House of Representatives their written declaration that the President is unable to discharge the powers and duties of his office, the Vice President shall immediately assume the powers and duties of the office as Acting President.

Interpreting Sections 1 and 2 seem straightforward. Section 3, however, exists under the condition the President provides a written declaration to the President pro tempore of the Senate and Speaker of the House of Representatives, depending which party has control, that he is unable to discharge his duties and power because of some temporary affliction. Then, the Vice President becomes acting President until the President has recovered. The President shall not be removed from office but is just temporarily unable to do his job during this time.

Section 4 is the only part of the amendment which has never been used. This gives the Vice President, and the majority of either the members of the executive branch cabinet or the body of Congress, the ability to declare that the President is unwilling or unable to discharge his powers or duties, under Section 3, to the President pro tempore of the Senate and Speaker of the House. Then, after being temporarily pushed out of office, the President resumes his duties when he sends a letter to the President pro tempore and Speaker of the House.

Still, Section 4 is more complex than this. In Section 4 of the 25th Amendment, it also states that if the Vice President and majority of the cabinet believe the President is still incapacitated to perform his duties or powers, then a two-thirds vote of the Congressional House and Senate must vote to discharge the President within 21 days. But the President can write a letter of declaration to the President pro tempore and Speaker of the House stating he is not incapacitated any longer to fulfill his duties or powers. So, this discharge and reinstatement could continue for an undetermined period. Again, this has never been tried.

The mainstream media, Democrats, celebrities, and liberal activists whom are calling OUR 45th American President "crazy" and "mentally unfit for office" are using Section 4 of the 25th Amendment as the basis for their impeachment. But their mental illness insinuations are a lie. Can someone 1) beat 16 political opponents in a Republican primary, 2) defeat a Clinton dynasty backed by the mainstream media, 3) overcome the tirades of Hollywood, liberal pundits, and Democrats, 4) travel through America and around the world for rallies, foreign diplomatic discussions, and speeches 5) have many televised cabinet meetings, and 6) approve more than a hundred executive orders, proclamations, and bills if he was indeed mentally unfit for office?

As proof of his fitness, the 45th U.S. President was even bold enough to take mental and physical tests in January 2018. He was examined at Walter Reed National Military Medical Center in Maryland by a highly respected physician, Admiral Ronny Jackson. This man was also the doctor for President Obama and George W. Bush. Regardless, OUR President passed his examination with flying colors, scoring 30 out of 30 on a mental test. But being a little overweight, he needs to take some cholesterol medication as a precaution. When questioned by reporters for nearly an hour in the White House press room the doctor jokingly remarked that if the President exercised and ate a little better he could live to be "200" years old. Moreover, the physician indicated this President's genes were a big contributor to his physical and mental health being so strong at his age. Of course, after the press conference, journalists, opinion reporters, and doctors who did not examine him all made ridiculous comments. Ken Dilanian of *NBC* tweeted,

"Seeing a lot of skepticism over the idea that @realDonaldTrump weighs only 239 pounds. Would he step on a scale in public to prove it?"

Then, Dr. Sanjay Gupta on *CNN* gave his very subjective and partial opinion. He stated the President is "borderline obese" and could have a heart attack in 3 to 5 years. One journalist even implied the President didn't undergo a real psychiatric examine so his mental fitness test proved nothing. These people are bent on describing the 45th American President in the worst possible terms. They may even be mentally unhinged themselves because of the unmitigated hate they have for this man. Why? Again, because their prides were hurt, they have lost credibility with the public, they were wrong to egg this businessman to run for the presidency of the United States, and he won.

Another impeachment angle some may try involves the phrase "Treason, Bribery, and or other high Crimes and Misdemeanors" which is mentioned in Article II Section 4 of the U.S. Constitution. Firstly, the word "high" in this phrase indicates someone in a high position; it doesn't mention a severe offense. The term *treason* is described under law by Article III, Section 3 of the U.S. Constitution as someone who stands against the United States and "consists only in levying war against them, or in adhering to their enemies, giving them aid and comfort." It's also part of legal 18 U.S. Code § 23821 (Treason) stating,

"Whoever, owing allegiance to the United States, levies war against them or adheres to their enemies, giving them aid and comfort within the United States or elsewhere, is guilty of treason and shall suffer death, or shall be imprisoned not less than five years and fined under this title but not less than $10,000; and shall be incapable of holding any office under the United States."

The 45th U.S. President has not in any way been guilty of treason in the legal sense, regardless of the made-up rhetoric unleashed toward him. In American history, there have only been a dozen who have been convicted of treason. So, this impeachment angle is highly improbable.

Of course, a *bribe* involves giving or receiving a gift in the form of money, property, emoluments, or objects of value for an advantage or gain, promise of action or influence or vote. In politics, it's called "pay-for-play." These details describing acts of bribery have not been in the news, and assuredly they will not be, as it relates to this President. That is because he wants to "drain the swamp", not become part of it. So, bribery also will not be a viable or likely impeachment angle that will be used to bring down the 45th President of the United States.

Then we have the incessant calls of the President colluding with Russia. The first thing to explain is the term *collusion* is not a federal crime, except in the case of a company violating an anti-trust law. But cooperation or conspiring to violate election laws, such as aiding, abetting, or advising Russian to hack or steal information from the opposing party is a crime. This type of conspiracy was like the infamous "Watergate" scandal in the early 1970's. It involved the pilfering of secret records from the Democratic Party, and the wiretapping of lines by FBI and CIA agents working for President Nixon administration during a Presidential re-election campaign. The actual articles of impeachment filed before President Nixon resigned were the following: Article I – Obstruction of Justice, Article II – Abuse of Power, and Article III, Defiance of Subpoenas. Regardless, to-date, by June 2018, there has been no known evidence to suggest there was unquestionable collusion or conspiracy between the then-candidate for the presidency of the United States, his campaign members, and Russia.

Ironically, there has been daily evidence coming out about the Hillary Clinton campaign that paid for a false Russian dossier and which may have begun this whole escapade of deception being launched against OUR President. Furthermore, to reiterate an earlier point, the FBI (Federal Bureau of Investigation), DOJ (Department of Justice), State Department, and other officials who worked under the Obama administration may have been involved in a massive partisan cover-up, spying operation, and conspiracy which has put the 45th United States President in jeopardy of being impeached. Again, if there is justice in America, those who were complicit in *deep state dealings*, including Clinton and some in the Obama administration, need to be interrogated and held accountable. Therefore, it's not the collusion of this President some should be focused on. They should be worried about their own collusion which has sought to undermine and obstruct the many daily agendas of a United States President, and, in turn, the American people.

So, since the "collusion" angle also may not be at their disposal, the mainstream media, Democratic Party, and others will try to use another angle for impeachment. It's regarding Article I Section 3 of the U.S. Constitution, and addresses an equivalent *obstruction of justice* that President Nixon was charged with during his impeachment.

The basis for their obstruction of justice inference, however, involves FBI James Comey. Those against the President will insist that

Comey was fired because the President wanted the Russian collusion investigation stopped. It's a preposterous assumption at best since the former Director of the FBI told the President three times he personally was not under investigation - only his campaign team would be under inquiry. Regardless, there is no legitimate case for OUR President to be charged with obstruction of justice in this instance. Article II of Constitution gives the President authority and responsibility over the entire executive branch of the government. Therefore, the President has the jurisdiction to *fire or hire* any person he so chooses within this constitutional article. That is why he had the right to fire FBI Director James Comey. But his detractors may purport that is not true, because there is a law, U.S. Code Title 18 Part I Chapter 73 § 1519 that reads:

"Whoever knowingly alters, destroys, mutilates, conceals, covers up, falsified, or makes a false entry in any record, document, or tangible object with the intent to impede, obstruct, or influence the investigation or proper administration of any matter within the jurisdiction of any department or agency of the United States or any case filed under Title 11, or in relation to or contemplation of any such matter or case, shall be fined under this title, imprisoned not more than 20 years, or both."

Yet although this law may be cited, Article II of the Constitution overrides this. Additionally, the prosecutors of such a crime must establish the accused "knowingly directed the obstructive act to affect an issue or matter within the jurisdiction of any U.S. department or agency" and "acted at least "in relation to" or "in contemplation"" of such issue or matter." Therefore, it will be extremely hard to prove an American President *knowingly* broke the law to obstruct justice when he had it in his power to fire or hire any person under his authority.

In 2017, out of prejudice and unjust ideology, some loathed the President so much that there was a premature call for impeachment proceedings to begin by Democrats Brad Sherman of California and Al Green of Texas. They cited some obscure obstruction of justice charge. Regrettably, these types of unwarranted accusations continue because most of the Democratic extremists, the mainstream media, and other haters, desire the ousting of OUR President from the oval office.

But some still wait for another obstruction of justice angle to emerge. For instance, in 2018, with the permission of Deputy Attorney General Rod Rosenstein, the Special Counsel Robert Mueller asked a NY Attorney General to obtain all documents from the President's personal lawyer, Michael Cohen, about the porn-star Stormy Daniels case, undermining attorney-client privilege. Many prayed the President would fire Mueller to trigger obstruction charges, so impeachment calls could begin. That didn't happen. Yet they are still hopeful of the President's fast removal from office before he succeeds keeping all the promises made on the campaign trail – which is already happening. Then, their greatest fear will arise. He will be elected to a second term.

Believe it or not, there is a website (*"Impeach Donald Trump"*) which exists calling for the impeachment of the 45th President of the United States. There was a petition sent to Congress on February 16, 2017, a month after the President took office, by *Free Speech for People* and *RootsAction.org*. There were 860,000 signatures on it. At the time, 1.2 million people joined their campaigns. Never has it been so very apparent that those who have lost power, money, and influence after the election are now hell-bent on pushing the idea of Presidential impeachment to the public. They too seek Congress to impeach him via 1) obstruction of justice, 2) violation of the Domestic Foreign Emoluments Clause, 3) conspiracy, 4) advocating illegal violence, 5) abuse of power, 6) recklessly threatening nuclear war, or 7) directing law enforcement to investigate and prosecute political opponents.

But those giving veracity to purported crimes leading to ultimate impeachment do so with serious folly. Concocting daily defamation to hurt anyone is beyond the pale of honorable reason. The promotion of fear, division, and hatred in the interest of self-gratification or to quench the thirst of assembled conspirators does not present citizens with a fair analysis of reality. The willingness to unseat a democratically elected U.S. President to heal wounds and enact revenge is insanity.

Those who perpetrate this malice of reason must realize that to impeach a President, first the House of Representative votes with a simple majority whether to charge the President with an offense. If the Democrats regain control in the House after elections in 2018, then impeaching the President will assuredly be first on their agenda. They will find some vague clause in our laws that will justify their reasoning for impeachment. Democrats seek revenge for the House Republicans impeachment of Bill Clinton in 1998 (which were for blatant crimes of perjury and obstruction of justice), dismantling of President Obama's legacy, and insufferable historic loss by Hillary Clinton in 2016.

Regardless, the U.S. Senate needs to vote to force the President completely out of office. Two thirds of the 100 Senators must vote "Yea" for impeachment. But as in the case of Bill Clinton, this will not happen in the Senate. If it does occur, woe be upon those who have wronged our country. For in time, they shall reap what they have sowed!

What is not obvious to the public, however, is those who openly oppose the 45th U.S. President play *wag the dog* with the American people. That is, they purposefully, continuously, and loudly bark unfounded allegations with anonymous sources, spout outlandish innuendos, and unleash falsehoods to divert us from the greater truth. It may be that individuals who shout negativities are complicit in wrongdoings and illegalities themselves, as well as protect others from crimes. They are running scared, and maybe they are thinking that *the best defense is a good offensive.* They use these rules of engagement, marching forward without pause, to disparage and mock OUR President lest they be ridiculed. For example, just look at all those former Obama Administration officials in high positions which are now declaring outrage in television interviews and tweets about this President. Their false allegations are a cover for their deceitful and possibly unlawful actions while in government. Some are undoubtedly petrified that a day of reckoning may be upon them. And, so they hide in the open, desperately praying they will not be discovered.

Maybe no words have rung truer about the propagators of forged political banter than those of Henry Field. He was an 18th century Englishman, author, playwright, and magistrate. He astutely said,

"Guilt has very quick ears to an accusation."

Chapter 3

FAKE AND IGNORANT NEWS

The term "fake news" has engulfed the world. It may be the most well-known phrase around the world today. It became very relevant during the 2016 primaries and general election for the Presidency of the United State. But fake news has been present through our television, radio, and, now, cable news broadcasts for a very long time. As a matter of fact, fake news has been around since the beginning of the civilized world. Although many examples exist, only seven will be shown.

Ancient and centuries old fake news

*1) Mark Antony's reputation was smeared by Augustus (or Octavian), the great-nephew of Julius Caesar. Because Augustus' sister was married to Antony, and at the same time having an affair with the Egyptian Queen Cleopatra VII, Augustus called Antony a drunkard and womanizer. Subsequently, a document was forged and pushed into the public as Marc Antony's legitimate will. It stated that Antony wished to be entombed in the mausoleum of the Ptolemaic pharaohs. This fake news enraged some Romans to rebel against Antony. But there was more fake news. After Marc Antony's defeat in the Battle of Actium, he was given grave news that Cleopatra had committed suicide. So, being distraught, Antony killed himself. But she was actually still alive. So, when Cleopatra heard of *his* death, this time, she did commit suicide.

*2) A document known as *The Donation of Constantine* was produced by the Church in the 8th century. It stated the 4th century Emperor Constantine had bestowed political power and land to the Church. But, in the 15th century, the paper was proven a fake. So, the Church then stated it was Charlemagne <u>not</u> Constantine who had given these gifts.

*3) During the 15th century, a false statement was spread in Trent (a part of the Hapsburg Empire in Austria) that the Jewish community had murdered a two-year-old Christian infant named Simonino. The effect of this fake news caused all the Jews in the city to be arrested and tortured. Some of these innocents were also burned alive at the stake.

*4) In 1761, Marc-Antoine Calais, the 22-year son of a French Protestant merchant, committed suicide. The Catholic Church sent out fake news indicating the father, Jean, had killed Marc-Antoine because his young son wanted to convert to Catholicism. The father was then tortured, wrongfully strangled, and thrown on a pyre. Voltaire, a well-known philosopher and historian, had the French government re-open the case. After three years of trial, Jean Calas, the father of the boy was acquitted posthumously. In this *Age of Reason*, Voltaire would keep the Enlightenment period of Europe lit to burn another day.

*5) To influence the public to favor a colonial revolt in the 18th century and spark the American Revolution, Benjamin Franklin spread fake news about King George III. Franklin created a phony newspaper in Boston indicating American forces had found bags filled with money and scalps of soldiers and civilians which were bound for the English king. This was done to imply the king conspired with the rival Native American Indians and outrage Americans fighting for independence.

*6) In June 1897, Mark Twain was reportedly "dying in poverty in London". This was news to the famous author since he was in good health. Twain said he wasn't quite sure if he should be "amused" or "annoyed" because he wasn't poor or sick. He indicated the rumor may have begun because his cousin had become ill while visiting London.

*7) In 1917, during World War I, in 1917, *The Times* and *Daily Mail*, two prominent London newspapers, reported that a large "Kadaver" factory existed in Germany. From anonymous sources, they purported that glycerin was extracted from the corpses of war victims so that soap and margarine could be produced. Obviously, this was false reporting.

It would be fun to go back to discover more historical fake news before the 21st century. The focus here, however, is to highlight the false stories that have been spread by the current mainstream media to cause civil unrest amongst our people, disrupt presidential agendas, deflect from his achievements, and provide reasons to disdain OUR President. The careless and intentional broadcasts of fake news by our media organizations should be an alarming indictor that they wish to build a rapport with those who may be uninformed and naïve in the ways of politics. Yet even these susceptible individuals are beginning to realize the news has become far too extreme in their analyses and opinions. It's because the mainstream media builds up their stories to reach a crescendo far too often. But because these far-fetched reports don't reach the heights they proclaim, they putter out until they are kaput. Doesn't the media discern that what they are doing hurts their credibility and undermines society's fundamental principles of gaining reputable and unbiased reports from news establishments? Therefore, this unruly and unfair proliferation of malicious and false information must stop. Otherwise, people will not know what to believe when reading newspapers, watching television, or listening to the radio.

Unfortunately, the speed of new technology and social media has become an excuse for journalists, opinion writers and anchors wanting to attempt to outdo each other. They rush to judgement to promote their latest propaganda. This is especially true if, as indicated, it has anything to do with furthering their ultimate goal of impeaching the President. To some in the press, it's almost paramount that this occurs.

Anyway, some of the many falsities from the past couple of years or so have been gathered. It would be impossible to show them all. But much of the fake news can be broken down into stories that are serious fake news, ignorant/idiotic news, or hateful hoaxes. They are somewhat similar but not the same - since they are related to the ridiculousness of partisan politics infiltrating our world. So, without further ado, some of the many news stories that have been reported are highlighted below.

Serious fake news

*1) On November 8, 2016, columnist and economist Paul Krugman of *The New York Times* predicted the "economy would never recover" because of the election result. Since then, he has been proven wrong. U.S. consumer confidence is at an all-time high. The Dow Jones broke numerous records. GDP had hit 3% for several quarters in a row. Many jobs are being created and coming back to the U.S. There are wage hikes and bonuses. And, unemployment in America has reached new lows.

*2) In November 2016, when the 45h President of the United States was elected, *Guardian* writer, Zach Stafford, purported that multiple transgender teenagers had killed themselves because of the election results. It was tweeted thousands of times and shared on *Facebook* by writer Dominic Preston (*PinkNews*) and Matthew Rodriguez (*Mic*). Only writer Elizabeth Nolan Brown (*Reason*) discovered that these allegations were indeed just rumor. But the damage was done.

*3) In November 2016, Gabriel Sherman (*New York Magazine*) said "a group of prominent computer scientists and election lawyers" wanted a recount in Wisconsin, Michigan, and Pennsylvania because there was evidence of hacking or manipulation of votes. Eric Geller (*Politico*), Dustin Volz (*Reuters*), Paul Krugman (*New York Times*), and other news outlets all shared the story. This went viral on *Facebook* and *Twitter*. The next day, Nate Silver (*FiveThirtyEight*) squashed this tale, saying the numbers were about demographics <u>not</u> hacking.

*4) In December 2016, a story was spread by Lorraine Woellert (*Politico*) indicating the Secretary of the Treasury nominee, Steve Mnuchin, had been involved with a company which had "foreclosed on a 90-year-old woman after a 27-cent payment error." Woellert said,

> *"After confusion over insurance coverage, a OneWest subsidiary sent [Ossie] Lofton a bill for $423.30. She sent a check for $423. The bank sent another bill, for 30 cents. Lofton, 90, sent a check for three cents. In November 2014, the bank foreclosed."*

Steven Ratner (*New York Times*), Brad Jaffy (*NBC*), *Huffington Post*, *New York Post*, *Vanity Fair*, *Facebook*, and others all shared the errant information. But, in truth, the Competitive Enterprise Institute's Ted Frank stated this woman never foreclosed on or lost her home.

*5) On January 20, 2017, the President's inauguration evening, he and his wife danced to the classic song *My Way*. But, *CNN* made a remark that Nancy Sinatra was "not happy" with this. She responded tweeting,

"That's not true. I never said that. Why do you lie, CNN?"

*6) In January 2017, Coral Davenport (*New York Times*) said on their website that the new President's administration had purged climate change references. But these were only minor deletions having to do with the transition of one administration to the other. The untrue story, however, was shared thousands of times on *Facebook*.

*7) In January 2017, reporter Zeke Miller *(Time)* wrote that the bust of Martin Luther King Jr. was removed from the White House. Obviously, this stirred racial fury from the media. It was false. The Presidential speech writer Steve Miller and others corrected this errant assumption.

*8) In January 2017, Betsy Devos, the Education Secretary was asked a simple question. Should schools have guns on their campuses? She stated, "best left to locales and states to decide." Devos added that since one school in Wyoming had a wire fence surrounding it, protecting it from wildlife, maybe there was "a gun in the school to protect it from potential grizzlies." So, the media fabricated a story with headlines like:

- "Citing grizzlies, education nominee says states should determine school gun policies" (CNN)

- "Betsy DeVos says guns shouldn't be banned in schools... because of grizzly bears" (Vox)

- "Trump's Education Pick Cites 'Potential Grizzlies' As Reason To Have Guns in School" (BuzzFeed).

*9) In January 2017, Josh Rogin (*Washington Post*) stated there was a sudden shake-up of the administration in the State Department. He said "the State Department's entire senior management team just resigned" because people wanted to leave the new administration. It was shared by *Facebook*, Anne Applebaum (*Washington Post*), *Wired*, *The Guardian*, *Bloomberg*, and *ABC*. But it was false. Only the lower-level staff members were asked to leave during to the new transition.

*10) In February 2017, there was an *Associated Press* (AP) report which *Yahoo News* published indicating that after a phone call with Mexican President Enrique Peña Nieto, the President now was considering sending troops in to address the "bad hombre" problem. Jon Favreau, speech writer for Obama, Jon Passantino at *BuzzFeed*, *Facebook*, *ABC News*, Judd Legum at *ThinkProgress*, Shane Goldmacher at *Politico*, Matt Tglesias at *Vox*, and Anthony Zurcher at *BBC* all shared the story. Not only was the story falsely contrived, but it exposed someone was either wire-tapping the President's phone call or leaking half-truths about the conversation between two world leaders.

*11) In February 2017, there was story indicating the new President was modifying sanctions the Obama Administration had imposed on Russia for interfering in our 2016 Presidential election process. But the 45th American President was <u>not</u> modifying sanctions. There was some sort of technical fix already in place which took place with the roll-over to the new administration in 2017. Peter Alexander of *NBC News* had perpetrated this falsehood and would issue a correction to his story.

*12) In February 2017, the media tried to play the race card again. The new President proclaimed February as National African American Month instead of the past Black History Month. *TMZ* professed the President renamed the month. Again, this was a false assumption because Obama, Clinton, and Bush all made the same proclamation.

*13) In February 2017, there were headlines stating "House GOP aims to scrap Obama rule on gun background check" by *CNBC* and "House votes to end rule that prevents people with mental illness from buying guns" by *The Independent*. Of course, *CNN*, *Politico*, *Associated Press*, *Washington Post*, and *NPR*, and others blew this out of proportion. The House GOP voted to repeal a small provision in the gun law by reinstating gun rights back to people who had trouble filling out their financial statements when applying for Social Security Disability and Supplemental Security Income. In Obamacare, these persons were placed on the National Instant *Criminal* Background Check System. Therefore, they were banned from having a firearm. Under our laws, this was unconstitutional, as were many laws imposed by Obama. The National Rifle Association (NRA), some disability organizations, and, even, the liberal *ACLU* (American Civil Liberties Union) agreed with the GOP law change. Again, the press misrepresented this to the people. This President doesn't want guns in the hands of the mentally ill.

*14) In June 2017, *CNN*'s Jack Tapper, Eric Lichtblau, and Gloria Borger said the President's tweet statements, regarding him being told three times by former FBI Director Comey that he was not personally under investigation for Russian collusion, would be refuted. But in a Congressional hearing, under oath, Comey would back up what the President had tweeted. Therefore, *CNN* was forced to retell the story.

*15) In June 2017, *CNN* reported the President's new advisor Anthony Scaramucci was under investigation because of ties to Russian bankers. This was false. *CNN* retracted the story, and three *CNN* employees Thomas Frank, Eric Lichtblau, and Lex Harris resigned the next day.

*16) In July 2017, *Newsweek* reported that the First Lady Agata Kornhauser-Duda of Poland didn't shake the hand of the American President. It was untrue. She bypassed the American President to shake the First Lady's hand. *Then*, she shook the President's hand.

*17) In October 2017, *CNN* had someone on its show stating the fake Russian dossier was first paid for by a Republican. But it was unveiled that *Fusion GPS* was paid by the *Washington Free Beacon* to discover opposition research against the then-Republican candidate for U.S. President. Yet nothing came of it. So, it was a *conservative publication* first hiring *Fusion GPS* not a Republican. And, they did <u>not</u> pay for the Russia dossier. That was paid for by the Clinton Campaign and DNC.

*18) In November 2017, during a Presidential trip to Asia, *CNN* spread false news indicating the President had poured out an entire box of fish food into koi fish pond in Japan. What really happened is the Japanese Prime Shinzo Abe was feeding the fish and dumped out the rest of his box into the pond. The President followed his lead. *CNN* made it seem as if the President did this out of disrespect and tried to kill the fish.

*19) In November 2017, during the same trip, *CNN* reported that the President asked Japan to build cars in America. They took his words out of context and portrayed him as not knowing Japan built cars in America. A dumb allegation, since he was a global businessman.

*20) In December 2017, *CNN* purported that the President's campaign and his son, Donald Jr., had received advanced access to stolen hacked emails from *Wikileaks*. This was debunked by the *Daily Caller*'s Chuck Ross. It was just another false accusation by the cable news network.

*21) In December 2017, Brian Ross of *ABC News* errantly asserted that Michael Flynn was going to testify against the President about Russia collusion. It caused the stock market to lose 350 points. But after his correction a few hours later, the market rallied back. Then, Ross was suspended for four weeks. Now, he will not be allowed to cover anything to do with this President again.

*22) In December 2017, Dave Weigel of the *Washington Post* falsely tweeted a picture that a Presidential rally in Pensacola, Florida had empty seats. But the photo posted all over the Internet was taken *before* the crowd had gathered for the event. Actually, the President drew his usual packed arena.

*23) In February 2018, after the horrific massacre of 17 people, mostly children, at Marjory Stoneman Douglas High in Parkland, Florida an anti-gun group called *Everytown for Gun Safety* sent out a tweet reading: "This is the 18th school shooting in the U.S. in 2018." The mainstream media and liberals echoed this message many times. But it was based on inaccurate data. Both pro-gun and anti-gun groups base their facts on skewed data. Ironically, the *Washington Post* corrected the false statements. They stated this anti-gun group has long inflated its totals by including incidents of gunfire that are not school shootings.

"For example, they counted suicides in a parking lot outside a school and accidental gunfire in the middle of the night in a school parking lot when no one was injured. The organization describes school shooting as "any time a firearm discharges a live round inside a school building or on a school campus or grounds."

Thank you, *Washington Post* for your honesty and research - this time.

*24) The assertion that mass shootings only happen in America is flat out wrong. Again, the taking of 17 lives by the Parkland Florida shooter was used as political fodder. This happens after every mass shooting in America. A Democrat, Senator Chris Murphy made this false statement.

"This happens nowhere else other than the United States of America."

It's utterly untrue to say mass shootings only happen in America. These types of incidents happen more times in other countries such as Africa, India, Pakistan, and Europe (more later).

*25) Again, regarding the Southern Florida high school shooting, a rumor was spread that the shooter, Nikolas Cruz, was a member of a White Nationalist group and participated in paramilitary drills. The police have concluded this was not true. It was another attempt to denigrate and lump certain types of people in society together.

*26) Many mocked the would-be-President for starting the so-called *birther movement*, which implied President Obama was not born in the U.S.A. This is unequivocally false. In 2008, during the President campaign, to smear her opposition, it was Hillary Clinton's ally Sidney Blumenthal who began the rumor that Obama was born in Kenya.

*27) As much as people want to believe everything in the book *Fire and Fury* by Michael Wolff, it seems to be full of errors and unsubstantiated stories. Even Katie Tur of *NBC News,* not exactly a supporter of the President, wrote,

"Wolff is likely to face some serious questions and criticism regarding his use of quotes......It does appear from the reading that he is in the room for many of the conversations he ends up quoting in the book but from the Author's Note it sounds like they are recreations. How can he be sure the characters said what they said?"

Other news outlets have blasted this book as well because many assertions in its pages have been disputed. For instance, they include:

I) Tony Blair, the former U.K. prime minister, warned the President's son-in-law Jared Kushner that the President was being spied on by British secret agents. Blair denied this.; II) Deceased Fox news chief Roger Ailes had allegedly proposed John Boener, the former Speaker of the House, be hired for Chief of Staff. Then, the President supposedly replied that he didn't know Boener. This was untrue since the President mentioned Boener's name in tweets and played golf with him in 2013; III) Katie Walsh, a White House advisor, reportedly said working with the President was "like trying to figure out what a child wants". Walsh refuted this; IV) Campaign advisor to the President, Sam Nunberg, said the President needed the constitution explained to him. Huh? V) The President supposedly has a long-time fear of being poisoned. Therefore, it's one of the reasons he likes premade food like McDonalds; Really? VI) Purportedly, Vogue editor Anna Wintour asked the President to be U.S. ambassador to the U.K. Of course, Wintour disputed this because she had endorsed Hillary Clinton for President.

*28) Glenn Simpson, owner of the smear firm *Fusion GPS* which produced the phony Russian dossier, Russian gun-rights activist Maria Butina and banker Alexander Torshin were "infiltrating the NRA". He said this insinuating Russia went through the NRA to collude with the billionaire Presidential candidate. But there are no links or financial transfers found to-date. This rumor was allegedly propagated by two Democrats Senator Ron Wyden and House Democrat Adam Schiff.

*29) Of course, the biggest FAKE NEWS that was and is still being spread by all the mainstream media outlets is the would-be-President and his campaign colluded with the Russians to win the 2016 election. Through 2018, there is no evidence of this ever-taking place. There is mounting evidence, however, that several members of the Obama Administration's Department of Justice (DOJ), Federal Bureau of Investigation (FBI), and State Department, as well as members of the Hillary Clinton campaign, Democratic Party, foreign nationals, and mainstream media may have been involved in an elaborate unlawful scheme to discredit the 45th United States President (more later).

Ignorant and idiotic news

There are many ignorant and idiotic samples of fake news reported to the public during 2017 and 2018. But only a few of them shall be presented below.

*1) When the President indicated he would be moving the U.S. embassy to Jerusalem, recognizing it as the capital of Israel, the Palestinian National Authority stated it would be recognizing Texas as part of Mexico. That is obviously a fabrication.

*2) During Thanksgiving in 2017 a story grew stating the new President would order the execution of Obama's pardoned turkeys. Idiotic!

*3) While the nation debated about removing Confederate statues from public places, because of their so-called racial implications, there was an article indicating Confederate soldier's bodies were being exhumed from their graves. This was false.

*4) There was a rumor alleging that the President called *Kentucky Fried Chicken*'s Colonel Sanders (because the President loves fast food) a Civil War hero. Apparently, the story stated Colonel Sanders saved the army in Valley Forge with his chickens. Preposterous!

*5) *ZeroHedge*, an Oregon news outlet, reported that 60% of protesters against the President were arrested and didn't vote. It was unverified.

*6) There was a rumor about voter ID laws being upheld, which gave the President a slim victory in the contentious state of Wisconsin – a state usually won by Democrats. This was refuted. He won outright.

*7) The *Now8News* website stated the First Lady was uncomfortable with her new role when her husband was elected President. So, it was reported that she "didn't sign up for this". Also, Melania was alleged to be "very upset" with her move to the White House because she was accustomed to the luxurious lifestyle at home. Of course, this news was spread by other media outlets. But the story was untrue. In actuality, it was Melania who *encouraged* her husband to run for President.

*8) Jeanne Moos of *CNN* falsely reported the President had used his executive privilege to get two scoops of ice cream for dessert. Supposedly, everyone else who dined with him only got one scoop. Of course, he may have had two scoops. But the President denying anyone else at the dinner table of two ice cream scoops was utterly ridiculous.

*9) *CNN* aired a segment that Jade Robinson, who resided in Tyneside, England, had a two-year old beagle with an weird ear resembling the President's side profile. Apparently, it was relevant news for the media.

*10) An 11-year old boy, Frank Xavier Giaccio, who had his own lawn-mowing business, wrote a letter to the President stating,

"Even though I'm only ten, I would like to show the nation what young people like me are ready for."

The kid said it would be an "honor" to mow the White House lawn. The President responded by allowing the boy to work with the White House gardening staff. Frank was seen mowing the lawn. When the President came out to greet and talk to Frank, being conscientious and wanting to impress, the boy kept mowing. So, the mainstream media went into a frenzy. They stated the boy had ignored the President on purpose. It was ridiculous because the boy, and his father, did stop to speak to the President *after* he finished his work. And, although the boy usually gets $8 per lawn for his services, he didn't want any money from the President. He said mowing the White House lawn was reward enough. White House press secretary Sarah Sanders told reporters,

"The President is committed to keeping the American dream alive for kids like Frank..."

*11) Valiant Sarah Sanders (White House Press Secretary) has been unfairly mocked about her appearance and speech numerous times by celebrities. But CNN's April Ryan went further, suggesting Sanders didn't bake her own Chocolate Pecan Pie during Thanksgiving in 2017.

*12) News anchor Anderson Cooper (*CNN*) interviewed 1998 Playboy Playmate Karen McDougal about her alleged 2006 sexual relations with the future President. He asked her a crude tabloid-like question on air,

"Did he ever use protection?"

McDougal seemed to be taken aback by this. But then cleared her throat, answering "No". But, uncouthly and unfazed, Cooper continued,

"Was that something you thought about, or didn't it concern you at the time?"

Sadly, this smut appears to be *dark yellow* journalism at its finest.

Hate story hoaxes

From 2016 through 2018, there have been hundreds of fake hate crimes promoted by the media or hidden from the public. Listed below are just a few of these hoaxes which wrongly stirred communities.

*1) In Texas, an openly gay black pastor, Jordan Brown, sued Whole Foods for adding a homophobic slur to the cake he ordered, which read "Love Wins Fag". But the cake's icing only read "Love Wins"; so, Whole Foods counter sued for $100,00. Brown saw *the light*, dropping his suit.

*2) A Muslim college student claimed supporters of the President attacked her in the New York subway. But, subsequently, after further investigation, *she was arrested* for making up the story.

*3) Lt. General Jay B. Silveria Air Force Academy in Colorado was told a black cadet was targeted by racist remarks written outside a dorm room. But it was later confirmed by Lt. Col. Allen Herritage that the black cadet admitted *he* had been responsible for this act.

*4) A racist note left on a black student's car sparked protests at St. Olaf College in Minnesota. The school admitted the *message was a fake.*

*5) There were bomb threats made to the U.S. Jewish community. This

was a hoax perpetrated *by an Israeli teenager* who was then arrested.

*6) In Oakland, it was reported a "noose" had been tied to the back of a company truck where African-Americans worked. It was a *media hoax.*

*7) Fake flyers portrayed a conservative student group as anti-Muslim for painting Nazi swastikas on his home. But an upstate New York *Jewish man* admitted he had painted the graffiti art on the man's home.

*8) At Elon University in North Carolina, a whiteboard read "Bye Bye Latinos Hasta La Vista." This set off a firestorm; and, yet, it was found that a *Latino student* had written this phrase to instigate an outrage.

*9) On Christmas Day, a mosque was set on fire in Houston, Texas. Of course, there were cries of racism and Islamophobia on the news. Ironically, it was a *Muslim* who committed the arson. Gary Nathaniel Moore looked to blame the local community for his actions.

*10) A woman from Ann Arbor, Michigan was supposedly attacked and scratched in the face with a pin because she wore a solidarity pin connected to the Brexit vote in the U.K. It turns out *she wasn't attacked* and pled guilty to making up a hate crime.

*11) A student from Bowling Green University in Ohio thought she saw a KKK rally about to take place. But it was actually just *lab equipment covered with a white sheet.*

*12) At Beloit College in Wisconsin, a student admitted spray painting a swastika and anti-Muslim / racial slurs on the walls *to incite hatred.*

*13) An Ottoson Middle School student in Boston, Massachusetts had said she received racist text messages from another 12-year old student. The story was fabricated. *But who put this scheme in the girl's head?*

*14) Hope Church in Kansas City, Missouri was subjected to racist graffiti and arson against blacks. But, it was a *black man* who did this to conceal the fact that he was stealing from the church.

It seems quite apparent that those who seek to knowingly deceive are doing so without contemplation. The moral implications these individuals had, through their words and actions, upon millions who heard or read about these false stories is unconscionable. To clutter the minds and emotions of many for some political self-gratification is unjust and unethical. The people have the right to be free from those who are very willing to bear "false witness against thy neighbor". They are fueling the fires of discontent and ignorance instead of instilling a sense of harmony and reason to others. Undoubtedly, these individuals are seeking attention and stirring unnecessary negative emotions in others around our nation. But those who are creating hoaxes, ignorant stories, and fake news are one day going to become answerable to their misdeeds. They may think it's humorous to do what they are doing. In truth, however, it's quite dangerous to do this. Their wretched bliss is spreading division amongst us. It's not the kind of bliss America needs or wants! So, the public should make a stand and resist the resistance of these willfully ignorant people by exposing their blatantly fallacious and wrongful words and actions, and use peaceful protests, if necessary.

Pope Francis struck the right words when preaching about the way today's news is being spread in our world. He said,

"Sometimes negative news does come out, but it is often exaggerated and manipulated to spread scandal. Journalists sometimes risk becoming ill from coprophilia and thus fomenting coprophagia: which is a sin that taints all men and women, that is, the tendency to focus on the negative rather than the positive aspects."

To be clear, "coprophilia" is an "abnormal interest and pleasure in feces and defecation, while "coprophagia" is the pleasure of "eating of feces." Another way of putting this is the Pope believes those giving us "negative news" are in danger of becoming sick with *pleasure from their interest in crap* and the *spreading of it.* God Bless You Holy Father. You certainly have a way with words!

Chapter 4

HIDDEN AND MISREPRESENTED STORIES

As was shown, purposefully spreading fake or ignorant news is deceitful and unethical. Doing the same with "anonymous sources" is just as bad. But what may be worse is hiding and mispresenting stories or reporting significant news so quickly that it seems irrelevant or unimportant.

In the new age of social media, local newspapers are not the primary sources of news. People gravitate toward headlines on the Internet because it's the quickest way to keep informed with the news cycle. So, some in the public may tend to believe that these one line sources of information are unequivocally true. They don't take the time, however, to actually read the articles fully, or read related articles elsewhere to assess their veracity. But if someone does opt to read a story, the truth may be placed near the end of the article; or, it's buried by opinion, rhetoric, or a distortion of facts. News media outlets are aware of these tricks of the trade. They want you to see, feel, and think what they do, and need your attention for their craft to succeed. So, one must be wary of sensationalized headlines from news outlets known to falsify stories.

Quite sadly, this present time in our history has brought out the hounds to prey on the very innocent. They laugh with their malevolent cohorts as they spread disinformation to the politically naïve. Most, but not all, of these people are the owners, anchors, journalists, pundits, talk show hosts, and others from the newspaper, television, and radio outlets that tend to have a liberal mindset. This is not fiction or opinion but, quite unfortunately, a noticeable fact. As exposed, fewer than ten percent of the mainstream media are seekers of truth. They are practicing yellow journalism. So, one must be leery of messaging which is over-the-top or scandalous. Furthermore, each us must try to turn a deaf ear to news that seems disingenuous and is being echoed as one voice by multiple voices. But how then does one get the news?

Everyone should feel an obligation to seek out media sources that legitimately desire to unfold the actual news. Sadly, one needs to sift through the *dirt of deceit* to discover the *jewels of integrity* within our news. Once identified, the sources of these stories can be discovered. Although few in number, they are very recognizable because they do not misinform us of the facts and share important stories that are buried by other media outlets. They are media sources like *Fox News*. So, some of the misrepresented and hidden stories mentioned below were from that trusted news source, some newspapers, or research on the Internet.

Oh! Canada

*1) Canada passed some crazy gender laws. A bill was passed in 2017 allowing the parents of infants not to identify their baby's gender. This way, after the *little baby* grows old enough, *it* (to be gender neutral) can identify its own gender and pronoun (arguably, over 50 genders exist). Moreover, if someone uses the wrong pronoun about a person's gender that individual can pay a fine and be jailed. Regarding this same line of thought, in February 2018, a woman was mocked at a conference by Canadian Prime Minister Justin Trudeau when she used the word "mankind". Trudeau corrected her, saying, "We like to say peoplekind."

*2) In 2017, Canada apologized and paid Omar Khadr, a convicted terrorist who spent 10 years in Guantanamo Bay, Cuba, a reported $8 million. Khadr pleaded guilty to having killed a Special Forces medic Sgt. Christopher Speer with a grenade. So why is he getting a reward?

California dreamin'

*1) In 2017, parents in Rocklin, California felt betrayed after a kindergarten teacher read two transgender books to their students without their knowledge. One parent said,

"My daughter came home crying and shaking, so afraid she could turn into a boy."

California has their own gender laws, with fines of up to $1,000 or a year in jail if one refuses to use a transgender's proper pronoun.

*2) In 2017, a girl attending a first-grade class in Rocklin used the incorrect pronoun when referring to her classmate who was apparently transitioning from a boy to a girl. It was said,

"...this innocent little first grader sees a classmate, calls him by the name she knew him last year and the boy reports it to a teacher, the little girl gets in trouble on the playground and then gets called out of class to the principal's office."

The parents stated their daughter was traumatized and "came home from school upset and crying," saying,

"Mommy, I got in trouble at school today."

*3) Fourteen California supporters of the 45th American President filed a civil lawsuit in July 2017 after the police failed to protect them from violent protestors after a campaign rally. They are defended by Harmeet Dhillon (vice chair of the California Republican Party).

*4) Joy Villa, a singer, received death threats by fuming leftists who were mad she had worn a dress which said "Make America Great Again" during The Grammys (2017). This has been happening to many of the celebrities or people who are willing to say they openly support the 45th American President. Because of these threats, and vile ridicule, some who back the President stay in the shadows. That is why when polls are posted regarding the President's approval ratings, they are wrong.

*5) In 2017, Tim Allen's *Last Man Standing*, which had conservative views, was cancelled after six seasons on ABC. It's allegedly being replaced by a new show called *Sanctuary Family*. It's based upon a married couple taking in an illegal immigrant nanny and her husband.

*6) In January 2018, Gregory Salcido, an El Rancho high school teacher in California went on an anti-military rant to his students. Oblivious

that he was being videotaped or to the fact his students may have had friends or family serving, or had served, our nation, he ignorantly said,

*"Think about the people you know who are over there. "Your freakin' stupid Uncle Louie or whatever. They're dumb sh*ts. They're not high-level bankers. They're not academic people. They're not intellectual people. They're the freakin' lowest of the low. Not morally, I'm not saying they make bad moral judgments."*

*7) In 2017, although later apologizing, Imam Ammar Shahin spewed anti-Semitism while conducting a sermon at a mosque in Northern California. He outrageously asked Allah to liberate his mosque from the "filth of the Jews" and added,

"Oh Allah, destroy them and do not spare their young or their elderly."

*8) In 2018, California ranked last amongst all 50 states for *quality of life* in the *U.S. News* publication. The air and water quality, toxins, pollution, voter participation, social support, the way people experience happiness, and mental and physical were examined. And, what surely demands scrutiny is California has amongst the wealthiest people in the world while also having one of the highest homeless populations. In turn, the U.S. middle-class people are fleeing from the Golden State.

A time for kneeling

Although there was much focus on the so-called righteousness and defiance of NFL players kneeling during the national anthem to oppose police brutality, they were incidents that have been missed. An example of this occurred is when a high school football coach, Joe Kennedy, from Washington was suspended for asking his players to kneel for a prayer at midfield before a game. The coach sued for religious discrimination.

Thumbs up with '*Down*'

*1) In August 2017, CBS News tweeted a headline for a news show:

"Iceland is on pace to virtually eliminate Down syndrome through abortion". So, actress Patricia Heaton, famous for her television role as Debra on *Everybody Loves Raymond*, rebutted them with a tweet:

> *"Iceland isn't actually eliminating Down syndrome. They're just killing everybody that has it. Big difference." #Downsyndrome #abortion https://t.co/gAONIzqRXW*

*2) In 2018, Gerber baby food elected its annual "spokesbaby". It was a Down syndrome child. But the parents of the child called this very "hypocritical". The sister company of this firm, Gerber Life, reportedly has denied insurance coverage to children with Down syndrome.

*3) The headline of Washington Post Deputy Editorial Page Editor Ruth Marcus's column read, "I would've aborted a fetus with Down syndrome. Women need that right." But Dr. Gina Loudin, media host, author, and conservative, responded with a column, partly stating,

> *"Now think about that for a minute – really think about it. How would you like to hear about someone saying you should never have been born? Saying you should not exist. How would you feel?"*

Dr. Gina Loudin had searched 10 years for a newborn with Down syndrome which she could adopt. She stopped a Latino man and Polish woman in Florida from aborting their Down syndrome son and adopted him. Now, her 12-year son Samuel can experience the life and affection from loving parents and 4 siblings he may never have known.

*4) In 2017, Mikayla Holmgren, a 23-old woman from Minnesota participated and competed in the Miss USA pageant. Having been an award-winning dancer and in the special Olympics as a gymnast, Holmgren said she desired to show "the world that people with Down syndrome have beauty that starts from the inside out." Then, referring to Iceland and other nations, she bravely stated "there are countries in the world that would like to get rid of people like me."

*5) In 2018, Pope Francis met with parents of children with Down syndrome at the United Nations. He spoke against disability-based abortion, and said it was "the greatest hate crime of this generation."

Women's March vs. March for Life

The evening news, consisting of *ABC*, *CBS*, and *NBC*, covered the *Women's March* in January 2018 three times more than the *March for Life* (pro-life group) as per *Media Research Center* (MRC). The March for Life was an historic event because it marked the first time a sitting President addressed the rally in person. The Women's March got 1 hour 15 minutes and 18 seconds of coverage while the March for Life was only broadcasted for 21 minutes and 52 seconds.

Then, in April 2018, *The Ingraham Angle* (*Fox News*) exposed that students from about 200 high schools and 80 colleges had a pro-life walkout to end abortion. But there was *zero* mainstream media coverage. It's just another case of how the media has a profound liberal bias with issues such as pro-life. They suppress what they want and complain about their *freedom of the press* rights. They're hypocrites.

Unplanning parenthood

The Planned Parenthood Federation of America was founded upon the ideologies of Margaret Sanger, an American nurse, sex educator, and birth control activist. Yet, in 1939, in a letter to an associate she stated,

"We do not want word to go out that we want to exterminate the Negro population."

Was this a racist remark? It has been speculated that this was one of the reasons Planned Parenthood aborted black babies in America "three times more often than white babies, and Hispanic preborns are killed 1 ½ more often than whites" (*The Washington Times*). But just why these racial abortions have occurred can't be proven. Sadly though, those words from Sanger are irrefutable, whether intentional or not.

Regardless, what has been undeniably proven is that Planned

Parenthood, funded by American tax dollars, is ending life prematurely. It seems they don't have any consideration for those who hold life to be sacred. The organization professes that they are a champion of women, especially for the poor. But they hadn't performed mammograms at their facilities and prenatal care was recommended elsewhere (i.e. Care Net). Rather, what has been found by undercover groups, such as The *CenterforMedicalProgress.org* and *LiveAction.org,* is it was trafficking human baby body parts, hadn't reported child-sex trafficking, provided birth control to underage girls, and executed abortions for illegal aliens.

One example of these practices can be attained by examining the $8 million settlement two bioscience companies received from California. These companies, DV Biologics LLC and sister company DaVinci Biosciences LLC illegally sold fetal tissue to companies around the globe. Some undercover videos have revealed these uncaring business objectives to sell and make millions off of baby parts. Furthermore, David Daeiden, who worked for The Center for Medical Progress, said,

"The fact that Novogenix, StemExpress, and ABR stationed their own workers inside Planned Parenthood abortion clinics to perform the harvesting, packaging, and transport of aborted baby body parts demonstrates that Planned Parenthood had no reimbursable costs under the law...The volume-based sums that Planned Parenthood charged these businesses for baby parts are criminal trafficking and profiteering in fetal body parts."

In addition to the undercover work, a former Clinic Director of Planned Parenthood, Abby Johnson, who had been pro-choice and worked in the organization for eight years, quit her job after what she witnessed in 2009. Johnson was asked to assist with an ultrasound-guide abortion but was horrified when a 13-week baby twitched and turned, fighting to stay alive during the procedure. When she spoke out in public against the organization, they put a gag order on her. But the lawsuit against her was thrown out of court almost immediately.

Lila Rose, President of *Live Action,* who founded the honorable organization when she was 15 years old, supports human rights in favor of pro-life principals. But, now, bravely, she and others also expose the falsehood of Planned Parenthood advocates and laws permitting abortions. Planned Parenthood doesn't recognize the scientific facts telling us that an unborn child feels pain 20 weeks after fertilization, or an unborn child can react to touch after just 8 weeks of being conceived. See the evidence by going to *doctorsonfetalpain.com.*

Live and let die

*1) The legalization of abortion up to 24 weeks, depending on state limits, enabled monsters such as Dr. Kermit Gosnell to abuse the law for profit. He was convicted of murdering three infants born alive during abortion procedures. Murder charges were also charged against him because a woman, Karnamaya Mongar, died after he performed an abortion on her. As if that wasn't enough, Gosnell was convicted of killing seven newborns by severing their spinal cords with scissors. Over the decades, he has performed hundreds of abortions, assuredly many of which may have been late-term abortions, in unlawful and ill-conceived manners. He was sentenced to three life terms in prison.

*2) Oregon has passed laws requiring insurers to cover abortions at no cost, co-pay, or deductible toward an individual's insurance policy. This taking of life can occur through nine months of pregnancy and includes illegal immigrant abortions. In addition, parents will be permitted to abort an unborn child if they don't like the gender which will be given life. Can you imagine a parent would desire to abort an unborn child and start over again just because he/she was not satisfied with what had been growing in the mother's womb as a boy or girl? Isn't that barbaric?

College campuses have no tolerance

A poll by *Pew Research Center* in 2015 indicates millennials are okay with limiting free speech. That may explain the reason why a growing number of college campuses, once a place where freedom of speech was strongly defended, are now running amok with the point of view that not all voices are created equal. Many leading, teaching, attending, or visiting our schools of higher education are thwarting the rights of others to express their opinions or perspectives. Schools seem not be educating anymore but rather indoctrinating students into seeing life through one small and narrow lens. Unfortunately, most colleges and other schools have adapted and proliferated extreme perspectives of liberalism, adhering to progressivism. One example of this is at the University of Wisconsin-Madison. The school spent $1,500,000 from student fees to support the funding of political organizations – 95% was spent on left-leaning groups and only 4.5% on conservative groups.

Conservative view is seen as hate speech instead of means for debate and open dialogue which would broaden minds in a meaningful way. Moderate liberal and conservative points of view through civil discussion are what this country and the world needs. It could settle differences with difficult issues, which may eventually bring an end to divisiveness and hate. The progressive left-wingers are, however, making it very tough for people in the middle of the spectrum and the right to even provide insight about other important alternative beliefs in America. Sadly, there are many instances of intolerance on display, especially in schools, where education is paid for at premium prices.

Three examples of intolerance on college campuses happened in 2017 at Berkeley College in California. The first instance occurred when Joy Villa and Kaya Jones received death threats over a free speech event at Berkeley. The second example involved this college not allowing Anne Coulter, a conservative author, to speak at an event. And, the last example arose when violent protests of radical *Antifa* and leftist anarchists shut down a speech of Milo Yiannopoulos, a conservative speaker. As a result, Berkeley College was being sued by the Berkeley College Republicans and the Young America's Foundation.

It's troubling to see that freedom of speech is frequently being shut down, mostly against conservative thought in colleges and high schools throughout our country. Our students are <u>not</u> being taught how to tolerate, debate, or share opinions with other students. Rather, they are taught that conservative speech is hate speech and should be opposed, threatened, and restricted without discussion. It's despicable when students can't peacefully discuss beliefs and opinions in the 21st century. These progressively liberal students will have to find out the hard way that life doesn't work this way. They will have a difficult time adapting to a work environment in the real world with others. There are no *safe spaces* at work where someone can cuddle stuffed animals, hug puppies, go into closets to cry, and get milk and cookies. The only refuge for these *snowflakes* is landing a job at a left-leaning business who will cater to their insecure demands and needs. Good luck with that!

More intolerance and craziness on campus

The ridiculousness and intolerance continued to occur at Berkeley. But it spread to other colleges nationwide. Here are a few examples of what has been occurring in schools where our children supposedly learn.

*1) Salisbury University in Maryland had <u>required</u> students to take a course teaching a *Pyramid of White Supremacy.* Courses of this nature are now being taught by colleges all over this country. They are adding to hate and division in our schools, communities, and workplaces.

*2) An Essex County College professor, Lisa Durden, from New Jersey appeared on *Tucker Carlson Tonight* (*Fox News*), defending the fact that *Black Lives Matter* had the right to ban whites at an event on Memorial Day. But the school fired her after appearing on the show. It's because when the opinion show's host confronted Durden about this apparent racism she supported, in a very demeaning tone she replied,

"Listen. What I say to that is boo-hoo-hoo! You white people are angry because you couldn't use your 'white privilege' card to get invited to the Black Lives Matter's all-black Memorial Day celebration! Wow!"

*3) California college professor, Olga Perez Stable Coxs, called the election of the 45th President of the United States an "act of terrorism". She also said the Vice President is "one of the most anti-gay humans in the country". But Coxs would later be absurdly honored by her school as faculty member of the year (and for exhibiting her group think hate).

*4) Cailin Jeffers, an English major at Northern Arizona University, got docked one point from a possible 50 by English professor Dr. Ann Scott. The reason? Jeffers used the word *"mankind"* in his paper, which was not a gender-neutral term her professor accepted in class.

*5) Professor Bret Weinstein disagreed with activists at Evergreen College in Olympia, Washington who demanded that *"all white people leave campus"* for a "day of absence". Because he opposed these racist remarks being upheld by the school, he was asked to resign.

*6) Michael Rectenwald, a liberal studies professor, had to sue New York University and several professors. He filed suit because he was put on paid leave and mocked by his peers after he was bold enough to express his dismay about political correctness on campus.

*7) There are many instances of gender rights exploding in schools, and throughout the country. Just two cases will be cited. In the first case, in the name of tolerance and support for transgender individuals, a Nobel prize-winning biologist who discovered DNA was *uninvited* from giving a lecture at NYU's School of Medicine. It's because he believes there is logically and physically *only two genders* on Earth. So much for science being taught at NYU! The second case shows students can choose their own name, gender and bathroom when they attend Michigan State, as per their Board of Education. But can't sexual abusers misuse this rule?

*8) A conservative student, Ryan Wolfe, of Wake Forest University was harassed continually prior to the election of OUR President. A photo of his head was placed on a *white cracker,* an obvious racial slur. So, being the college doesn't allow anything "motivated by race" or which seems "obscene, profane, or derogatory", this should have been addressed. Right? But instead, reportedly, Dean Adam Goldstein and the College Bias Response team made an exception here. The Dean informed Wolfe that they *refused* his case. The reason for their decision: "Trump won."

*9) Students are being brainwashed in colleges that all Caucasians have *white privilege.* Some want whites to feel guilty they are born white. It is racism spread by left-wingers to divide races. That's <u>identity politics!</u>

*10) A very strange ideology has spread on college campuses, and beyond. It's called *toxic masculinity*. Apparently, if a man or woman expresses too much masculinity it's a bad thing. A few examples of toxic masculinity are eating too much meat, playing violent sports, taking physical risks, driving recklessly, not using sexual protection, doing dangerous jobs, avoiding the doctor, and not expressing your feelings. To further emphasize the ridiculousness of this insulting belief, in 2016 Duke University (North Carolina) established a *safe space for male-identified students* so they could contemplate the topics of "male privilege, patriarchy, language dominance, rape culture, pornography, and machismo" as being part of toxic masculinity. So, being a man seems to be under attack by progressive left-wingers. And, if you are a *white man*, then it's even worse. But if you are a *white male Christian*, there will be a 'holy war' set against you. The most awful type of person on the planet, however, is one who confesses being a *white Christian conservative male* thinker. He should be shunned, spit-upon, and attacked because some very disturbed people see this as evil incarnate.

Changes in climate

Climate change is real. Let me repeat that. *The change in climate is real.* But despite all the hoopla, documentaries, and protests, there is no real concrete evidence produced, yet, indicating that the global warming patterns occurring are not cyclical in nature with the evolution of the Earth. Has man played a role in creating unneeded emissions of carbon dioxide, methane, and nitrous oxide into our atmosphere creating a slightly thinner ozone layer in some parts of our skies? Absolutely! But just how much is humankind contributing to this change in climate? Could climate change have begun well before the recorded industrial revolution? Is it a product of the Earth having come in or out of a cyclical Ice Age period? And, how do we *permanently* make changes to the warming of our globe without destroying businesses and people's livelihoods? Although most scientists, not all, believe in climate change, which is true because *changes in climate* have occurred for millions of years, to-date there has been no unanimous consensus by scientists on answers to the questions posed. Yet shouldn't there be 100% agreement regarding this presumptive dire subject?

China, the United States, the European Union, India, the Russian Federation, and Japan are top contributors to the carbon dioxide emissions. But the U.S. has reduced its emissions since 2007, beginning in the President Bush era, by about 12%. This trend will continue in the United States. So, why are these other nations not doing so as well?

Those countries listed as top carbon emissions contributors, and others, who signed the Paris Agreement (2015) to fund and reduce emissions have <u>not</u> been following the rules to this agreement nor funding it properly. Therefore, the U.S. pulled out of this ill-advised costly agreement in 2017. This was a financial burden which would have cost the U.S. tens of trillions of dollars in the coming decades. From the data, there will be a minimal effect on the global climate and weather at the current rate in the next couple of decades and beyond. It's not that the 45th President of the United States doesn't believe in the change in climate, but that America has been pulling its weight reducing our emissions into the atmosphere while other countries are not doing so - nor are they contributing enough financially.

The liberal hyperbole about increased hurricanes, earthquakes, tsunamis, and fires proving climate change is just unfounded. Many profess this under the guise of providing scientists with funds to promote this as they have financial and political stakes in *green* non-profit companies. Some protect this industry by unjustly condemning those who want America to be proficient in harvesting its own energy.

The public is told that scientists have proven climate change is dangerous and a major crisis. Unfortunately, this is false. What we need is real live televised and reported debate about climate change, and scientists to admit if they are liberal, conservative, or atheist for full disclosure. Scientists are supposed to regularly perform tests and be skeptical until there is undeniable proof about a subject matter. It's in their fundamental creed to have critical thinking, continued testable hypotheses, and challenges from others. This hasn't happened as of yet.

That is why in July 2017 the EPA Director encouraged an open televised debate by scientists take place so there can be clear proof that global warming is a serious threat. But pro-climate change scientists think this is a trap. Yet why should they feel threatened if the data they promote and subscribe to is accurate? If *all experts* who have studied this phenomenon can agree on the dangers of climate change, wouldn't that be beneficial to everyone? So, we need to hear all sides of the equation to learn how best to tackle it in the future. We shouldn't rashly accept such an issue that may be untrue just to fund green activists or sign exorbitant financial global pacts which may not better our world.

Unfortunately, the Democratic Party uses climate change as part of their ideology, which sees it almost as their religion to gain votes. But this is more than just obtaining votes. It's about discovering the facts which will enhance our world. The government should not dictate science and push for energy dependent business for green companies. So, a real debate should take place as suggested - maybe for one hour every six months on must-see television. Then, we can tell if its more beneficial for the climate to change politically, socially, or economically, or with the weather. Some will disagree on which will have a greater impact in the U.S. and on our globe. But let's have that debate.

Out of control tech companies

The age of computers is here! There are automated machines, drones, and robots. They all supplant people - and will continue to do so if we don't act fast. The companies building these machines are becoming more powerful by the day. But can they control what they invent?

In early 2017, two Facebook artificial intelligence (AI) robots were shut down because they exhibited some weird behavior. The robots called Bob and Alice began communicating in English but then stopped to speak an unrecognizable language. What happened is the robots quickly adapted their own language, in chatbots, so humans couldn't understand them. Frightening, huh? But this wasn't the first-time a robot acted under its own volition.

In a Washington, D.C. shopping mall, a robot decided to commit suicide by drowning itself in a street level water fountain. But others deduced that maybe the robot didn't detect the water below its feet, and accidentally roamed into the fountain. So, did the robot want to die?

Regardless of robots, tech companies are seemingly becoming more powerful than the government. They control what we can do on their software platforms; and, monitor the websites one visits on the Internet. Through algorithms and bots, our searches can be directed to sites that make them money. They can even allow or deny one access to communicate with others via text messages, tweets, personal profile pages, and pictures. Also, these companies pull services from users for not following specific rules - which mostly fit a liberal bias. Then, in 2018, we have the case of *Facebook* being caught gathering personal data from users, which they had given away or utilized for their own purposes. That's scary! And, yet, social media is the way in which most people converse and keep up-to-date with much in their daily lives?

We should become very self-aware about letting social media rule our way of life - 24-hours a day, 7 days a week. Some may want to abstain for hours or days at a time from it, like an ascetic practicing mindful meditation. To restrict use from these devices and vices of the modern age is in the end good for the soul. Becoming too reliant upon social media is not in our best interest because the constant need to use your phone to find out the latest post, tweet, text message, or voice mail can become an addiction. As a matter of fact, it has already been proven it can be dangerous to one's health. For example, cell phones could hinder sleep, raise heart problems, increase stress, impair hearing, cause poor vision, increase accident risk, enhance risk for brain cancer, and lead to spinal misalignment and pain. Also, did you realize your cell phone can be tracked and traced? Tracing your phone's whereabouts may be good if your cell phone was stolen or lost; but do you want a company tracking you? It's a double-edged sword. So, have we begun to live in an Orwellian dystopia? Is "BIG BROTHER" really watching?

Besides the technologies they produce, these companies seem to embrace another threat to society. It's called extreme liberalism. For example, Mark Zuckerberg (owner of *Facebook*) floated the idea of everyone in America getting a salary from the government. Isn't that socialism or even communism? And, yet, even with this progressive idealism, diversity in their workforce was lacking (In 2017: 3% black, 5% Hispanic, and 33% women). Then, there is the incident involving the *Facebook* censorship of two African-American women, *Diamond and Silk,* who are supporters of OUR 45th U.S. President. *Facebook* asserted that the two women were "*unsafe*" to the community. Rubbish!

Lastly, there was the high-profile case of a former *Google* engineer, James Damore, who was fired by the big tech company after he had written a memo criticizing their *lack* of diversity efforts. He filed a class-action lawsuit against this liberal tech giant because of their bias against conservative white men. It seems tech companies have too much power. They too need watching so freedoms of our democracy are not abused.

Cloverhill's hot topic

The Cloverhill bakery company, which sells products to supermarkets, fills vending machines, and manufactures buns for McDonalds, lost 800 workers late in 2017. These workers made up one third of their employees. The reason for their loss was an outside audit found that these employees were illegal immigrants and had either stolen or fake identifications. As reported, most were of Mexican descent and hired by a temporary employment agency. So, the company turned to another placement agency which hired many to replace the employees lost. This resulted in mostly African-American workers being employed in the company and being paid $14 an hour, as opposed to the $10 an hour the Hispanic employees were being paid. The remaining legal Hispanic workers were paid an extra $1 an hour to train the new black employees. Cloverhill had been paying less for more to illegal aliens. But, now, they hire and pay fair wages to citizens who want to work.

A moment of sunlight by a cable news host

In July 2017, Rolling Stone interviewed *CNN*'s Jake Tapper. He was honest about President Obama and the 45th U.S. President. Tapper said Obama benefited from "a media industry that was 'supportive' of him and reluctant to identify misleading information." He would explain that he was worried about confirmation bias, and stated,

"Look there's always going to be a place for ideological and even partisan journalism. That's been true as long as this nation has been around. I think that's great, but I think it's great as a supplement to more straight news."

Regarding falsehoods, Mr. Tapper gave a straight answer,

"A lot of people on the left didn't like it before, and now they like it…I don't want to compare President Obama and Trump on these issues because they're different, and the scale isn't even remotely the same. But President Obama said things that weren't true and got away with it more for a variety of reasons and one is the media was much more supportive of him. The Obama White House thought I was self-righteous and a huge pain in the ass."

Democratic National Committee (DNC) staffer scandals

On July 16, 2016, a DNC Staffer named Seth Rich was fatally shot in the Bloomingdale neighborhood of Washington, D.C. Nothing was taken from his person. So, why was he killed? Through 2018, the crime is still a mystery. Some implied he may have been connected to the DNC hack which exposed damaging emails from the Clinton Campaign that were given to *Wikileaks* during the Presidential election.

Another angle is he was killed because he knew too much about the Steele dossier, full of salacious and unsubstantiated data, which led to a Special Counsel investigation against the 45th American President. In a 2018 Congressional hearing, Glenn Simpson, the founder of *Fusion GPS*, the company where the Russian dossier came from, said that "someone's already been killed" because of the dossier. So, does this corroborate the theory that the dossier may have been involved with the Seth Rich shooting? That assumption has not yet been confirmed. Regardless, whether the unsolved murder was politically motivated or not, Rich's family stills suffer without any justice for this dastardly act.

There is also the case of Imran Awan, an IT staffer. Awan was banned by some Democratic Party members but still allowed by Debbie

Wasserman-Schultz, the then-head of the DNC (Democratic National Committee), to control and access their network server. But after many months, the DNC head finally terminated Awan's contract. Then, when trying to depart the U.S., authorities arrested Awan at the Washington, D.C. airport (Dulles International). He was arrested for embezzlement and fraud. Awan had wired $283,000 to two people in Faisalabad, Pakistan. He fraudulently received a large sum of $165,000 as a home equity loan from the Congressional Credit Union just prior to making wire transfers. Also, Awan's brothers and wife were reportedly involved in his shady dealings; and, he smashed hard drives with important information on them. But most troubling was that Debbie Wasserman-Schultz allegedly still had him on her payroll as he tried leaving the U.S. Moreover, he still had backdoor access to computers in the DNC. And, lastly, for some reason not yet disclosed, a laptop with a note on it was left so police could find it before he tried to exit the country. When the police seized the laptop, however, Wasserman-Schultz appeared to threaten a Capitol Policeman Chief Matthew Verderosa with some kind of "consequences" if he did not return it to her. Therefore, what had been so important on that laptop? Maybe, in the future, we'll find out.

Voting fraud denial

Despite what the *Brennan Center of NYU*, an ultra-liberal group, and others profess, there is definite proof that voter fraud exists during elections. People vote multiple times across state lines. Dead people are kept on voter rolls. People register on the honor system. That means they can just check a box and swear to be a citizen if they have a phony driver's license or stolen social security card. This is occurring all over America. It's how Democrats get extra votes in elections. It's not far-fetched because if there are 12.5 million *known* illegal immigrants in the U.S., isn't it logical some would vote with a false identification?

And, there are "more people registered" in "160 counties" than there are people in the counties, stated J. Christian Adams, on *Justice with Judge Jeanine* (*Fox News*) in March 2018. He was involved in a committee which checked voter rolls for the 45th U.S. President. So, he should know. But his committee's work was stymied because not all states were cooperating in their efforts to uncover illegal vote activities.

Popular vote loses in Presidential elections

Some want to change the U.S. Constitution because the electoral college decided the election of the 45th President of the United States. Many contend their candidate should have won because she had an edge in the popular vote. But it's not the first time someone lost and still won the popular vote in American Presidential election history.

In 1824, John Quincy Adams (Democratic-Republican Party) didn't have enough electoral college votes to win the election. Another candidate Andrew Jackson had more popular votes (38,000) but fewer electoral votes (99 to 84) than Adams. Regardless, the U.S. House of Representatives made the decision to elect Adams as the 6th President.

In 1876, Rutherford B. Hayes (Republican Party) lost the overall popular vote to Samuel J. Tilden by 250,000 votes. But Hayes won the electoral college by one vote. So, he became the 19th U.S. President.

In 1888, Benjamin Harrison (Republican Party) lost the popular vote to Grover Cleveland by 90,000 votes. But he won the electoral college (233 to 168). So, Harrison became the 23rd U.S. President.

In 2000, George W. Bush (Republican Party) won Florida; and, so, he won the electoral college: 271 to 266. Although he lost the popular vote by 540,000 votes to Al Gore, he became the 43rd U.S. President.

In 2016, a billionaire (Republican Party) won the electoral vote over Hillary Clinton (304 to 227). He also won the total number of states (30 - 20). But Clinton won the popular vote by 2.8 million votes (65,794,399 to 62,955,202). This higher popular vote count, however, really came down to one state - California. Out of an estimated 14 million people who live there, most voted in favor of Clinton (8,753,788 to 4,483,810). Why? It's the most liberal state in America. But, for fun, let's omit California from the election. Clinton would have lost the popular vote by about 1.4 million votes (58,471,392 to 57,041,611) and electoral college count 304 to 172. So, if California wants to secede from the U.S. and be its own country, many American citizens wouldn't object to it.

The Podesta Group

Two brothers, Tony Podesta and John Podesta, Hillary Clinton's 2016 campaign manager, formed the Podesta Group. It's a foreign lobbying firm which shutdown in 2017. It had pro-Russian ties in Ukraine's government. So, it should be scrutinized by Special Counsel Robert Mueller's investigation into Russian meddling in the 2016 elections. They purportedly didn't file under the Foreign Agents Registration Act. But the firm has not been penalized for it, yet. Also, they worked with Paul Manafort, a brief and early campaign aide of the President-to-be who was indicted for money laundering and other crimes. So, we shall wait to see if there is a *double-standard* when it comes to justice.

Wikileaks

Julian Assange, *Wikileaks* founder, has repeatedly stated for months that the leaked emails received from the Democratic National Party and Hillary Clinton's campaign during the 2016 election was <u>not</u> gathered by state actors or parties in foreign countries. Therefore, this tells us there were persons, possibly in the U.S., involved in obtaining the DNC data. But the mainstream media, and others, has been misrepresenting *Wikileaks* for years. It's because one moment the confused media is for full disclosure and the next day, they find whistleblowing treasonous. It depends on their political biases and narratives during the time of the major leaks. And, yet, the media has been involved with the gathering and leaking of classified information, or other crucial government data, recently, and for decades. It's just another example of their hypocrisy. To get more data on Julian Assange and *Wikileaks,* go watch some biographical movies about them, or visit the *Wikileaks.org* website.

There are many other misrepresented or buried stories in the news. But one ancient quote seems apt regarding the hidden stories.

"Three things cannot be long hidden: the sun, the moon, and the truth."
- Buddha

Chapter 5

IMMIGRATION -
GUNS - LAW ENFORCEMENT

This chapter is an extension of misrepresented and hidden stories. Once again, news stories which were either untold, briefly mentioned, or misinformed to the American public will be presented. But this news shall focus on the subjects of: DACA (Deferred Action for Childhood Arrivals), immigration, sanctuary cities, the gun debates, the lack of respect for our law enforcement, and botched investigations by the FBI.

The DACA issue

Several remarks President Obama made regarding illegal immigrants should be noted. In March 2011, on Univision TV, Obama stated,

"With respect to the notion that I can just suspend deportation through executive order, that's just not the case, because there are laws on the books that Congress has passed".

Then, in May 2011, President Obama gave a strict immigration reform speech at a park in sight of the U.S.-Mexican border. He said,

"Today, there are an estimated 11 million undocumented immigrants here in the United States. Some crossed the border illegally. Others avoid immigration laws by overstaying their visas. Regardless of how they came, the overwhelming majority of these folks are just trying to earn a living and provide for their families. But we must acknowledge that they have broken the laws. They've cut in front of the line. And what is also true is that the presence of so many illegal immigrants makes a mockery of all those who are trying to immigrate legally. Also, because undocumented immigrants live in the shadows, where they're vulnerable to unscrupulous businesses that skirt taxes, and pay workers less than the minimum wage, or cut corners with health and safety laws, this puts companies who follow the rules, and Americans who rightly demand the minimum wage or overtime or just a safe

place to work, it puts those businesses at a disadvantage."

"...And sometimes when I talk to immigration advocates, they wish I could just bypass Congress and change the law myself. But that's not how a democracy works."

"...First, we know that government has a threshold responsibility to secure our borders and enforce the law. And that's what Janet (Napolitano) and all her folks are doing. That's what they're doing. Second, businesses have to be held accountable if they exploit undocumented workers. Third, those who are here illegally, they have a responsibility as well. So, they broke the law, and that means they've got to pay their taxes, they've got to pay a fine, they've got to learn English. And they've got to undergo background checks and a lengthy process before they get in line for legalization. That's not too much to ask. And fourth, stopping illegal immigration also depends on reforming our outdated system of legal immigration."

Also, on July 20, 2011, Obama told radical La Raza activists,

"Now, I know some people want me to bypass Congress and change the laws on my own. And believe me, right now dealing with Congress...believe me, believe me, the idea of doing things on my own is very tempting. I promise you. Not just on immigration reform. But that's not how – that's not how our system works."

But even after all the preaching President Obama made about the way illegal immigrants are breaking the law, and that he can't just decide to change the laws by himself, he did so. He passed the so-called DREAM Act as part of a DACA (Deferred Action Childhood Arrivals) executive order. This order would need to be reinstated every two years. In his speech in the White House Rose Garden, Obama said,

"Now, let's be clear. This is not amnesty. This is not immunity. This is not a path to citizenship. It's not a permanent fix. This is a temporary, stopgap measure..."

President Obama made a unilateral decision to give 600,000 illegal immigrants new social security cards so they could legally get some benefits Americans receive as citizens. These people were brought to America as children by their parents who either broke the law by sneaking into the country illegally or overstaying their visas while in the U.S. Subsequently, a federal judge indicated that the executive order President Obama had signed to allow thousands of DACA people into America, even temporarily, was unconstitutional. Also, the statute for this temporary DACA order would expire sometime in 2018. Even a fierce Democrat, Senator Diane Feinstein of California, was asked on cable network *MSNBC* whether DACA was illegal. She admitted in September 2017 that the DACA executive order was upon *shaky-legal* ground and Congressional action would be needed to fix the problem.

Through January 2018, there was thought to be 800,000 DACA individuals in the U.S. But these people are considered and spoken of as the "DACA kids." This is an incorrect label for this group of individuals because they have an average age of 24 years old with some being up to the age or 36 years of age. It has also been reported, however, in January 2018, by the *Associated Press,* that the original numbers of these DACA persons was grossly distorted. The *Associated Press* alleged the real number to be up to 3.6 million, not the 800,000 as was previously thought. Not only was this uncovered, but Democrats keep making false accusations which indicate DACA recipients serve in the military and go to colleges. The truth is only about 900 DACA enrollees are in the military and only 5% are in school. And, then, there are an estimated 2,000 criminals in their midst's from the original 800,000. There could be more criminals given the new numbers. This is bad if there are more, and good if less. But, regardless, like any ethnic or cultural group, there will always be some bad apples in a bunch.

In 2017, the 45th U.S. President ended the illegal executive order by Obama. But in 2018, inevitably, the Supreme Court will need to revisit DACA; or, Congress can pass a *lawful* immigration reform bill.

OUR President has four pillars he wants tackled before signing an immigration package: 1) funds for a secure northern and southern border, including walls, fences, electronic surveillance, and many more border control agents, 2) a fix to extended family chain migration, 3) a stoppage of the visa lottery program, and 4) allowing 1.8 immigrants to gain citizenship in 10 – 12 years. That's three times more than Obama.

In January 2018, there was a government budget shutdown, led by Senator Chuck Schumer and minority leader representative Nancy Pelosi, because of a dispute about immigration reform. The budget bill at that time, however, had nothing to with immigration reform. The purpose of this bill was for Congress to approve funding for several key government agencies, including giving payments to our military and healthcare for our children. Eventually, within 48 hours, the Democrats gave in to public pressure. But they were criticized for both shutting down the government in the first place and not holding out long enough to try to get a deal for DACA. Some of the hyperbole and rhetoric used by Pelosi regarding the immigration issue was infamously memorable. She stated, "lady liberty is crying" and there were "five white guys" trying to settle this deal. Then, later, Pelosi had an 8-hour filibuster speech on the Congressional floor in support of DACA in which she said something over-the-top, even for a seasoned politician:

"I'm reminded of my own grandson. He is Irish, English, whatever, whatever, and Italian-American, he is a mix. But he looks more the other [Italian] side of the family, shall we say…And when he had his sixth birthday… he had a very close friend whose name is Antonio, he's from Guatemala. And he has beautiful tan skinned, beautiful brown eyes, and this was a proud day for me, because when my grandson blew out the candles on his cake, they said did you make a wish? He said yes, he made a wish. What is your wish? I wish I had brown skin and brown eyes like Antonio."

Obviously to partially confront the illegal immigration issue in the U.S., the President has been asking for border security and "the wall". Many Democrats are opposed to it. But, ironically, in 2006, Democrats such as Senators Barack Obama, Hillary Clinton, and Chuck Schumer all voted <u>in favor of</u> a bill authorizing 700 miles of secure fencing, more vehicle barriers, checkpoints, lighting, and some advanced technology on the U.S. and Mexican border. So, why are they opposed to border security now? In the same year, Senator Barack Obama famously said,

"When I see Mexican flags waved at pro-immigration demonstrations, I sometimes feel a flush of patriotic resentment. When I'm forced to use a

translator to communicate with the guy fixing my car, I feel a certain frustration."

Also, back then, a liberal columnist from *The New York Times*, Paul Krugman, remarked that "immigration reduces the wages of domestic workers who compete with immigrants" and "the fiscal burden of low-wage immigrants is also pretty clear." Then, his article concluded that "we'll need to reduce the flow of low-skilled workers." Interesting!

In 2012, the Democratic National Party platform stated,

"We cannot continue to allow people to enter the U.S. undetected, undocumented, and unchecked. The American people are a welcoming and generous people, but those who enter our country's borders illegally, and those who employ them, disrespect the rule of the law. We need to secure our borders, and support additional personnel, infrastructure, and technology on the border and at our ports of entry. We need additional Customs and Border Protection agents equipped with better technology and real-time intelligence. We need to dismantle human smuggling organizations, combating the crime associated with this trade. We also need to do more to promote economic development in migrant-sending nations, to reduce incentives to come to the United States illegally. And we need to crack down on employers who hire undocumented immigrants."

So, why have all the prominent liberally-minded people and the Democratic Party altered their viewpoints? It's because they want to oppose everything the 45th President of the United States thinks and wants to do to make America better. They are just shameless hypocrites.

Regardless of the media rhetoric, the 45th U.S. President desires to approve lasting immigration reform. He doesn't want the corrupt ways of Washington, D.C. (the so-named "Swamp") hindering this important issue. The President wants to fix DACA, not keep the issues in Congress for years so they have something to argue about. But this scares the crap out of many politicians, lobbyists, activists, and the mainstream media. It's because he wants to take a top-executive-like approach toward ending all the Tom-foolery, time-consuming methods of legislation, corrupt lobbying, and wasteful spending which has been going on for years inside the U.S. government. So, those who have the most to lose and must adapt to him - instead of the other way around – hate him for his bold agendas and a change which is long overdue.

In January 2018, a Harvard-Harris poll was taken indicating 65% of those polled would support a DACA deal if a wall was funded, there was an end to chain migration, and the visa lottery program was stopped. Furthermore, 53% supported the building of a wall to secure our borders, while 79% wanted a merit-based immigration system.

Then, in March 2018, the 45th U.S. President spoke to a group of Hispanics business leaders at the Latino Coalition's Legislative Summit in Washington, D.C. about the change tax cuts have had on many Latino Americans. He also stated the following:

"…We're trying to have a DACA victory for everybody . . . and the Democrats are nowhere to be found...The Latino community embodies the pioneering spirit of America..."

Sanctuary cities

NOT ALL illegal immigrants are to be demonized. Some did break the law by overstaying their visas or crossing our borders unlawfully. But sometimes these people sneak back and forth across our borders many times without much penalty. Because of *sanctuary city* policies, which defy our federal laws in California and many other cities throughout our nation, preventable crimes were committed by illegal aliens. Instead of these criminals being imprisoned or permanently deported from America, they were set free. Below are some examples.

*1) In 2018, San Francisco ridiculously acquitted an illegal immigrant, Garcia Zarate of murdering 21-year-old Kate Steinle in 2015. She had been walking on Pier 14 with her father and was shot by Zarate. The defense attorney argued the gun had accidentally gone off, and the biased jury agreed. But Zarate was deported and had returned five times to the U.S. and had committed other criminalities. This is one of many cases American citizens have faced because our politicians have not acted to reform illegal immigration. And, many citizens have died unnecessarily because of the political lunacy of sanctuary cities.

*2) In 2017, an undocumented immigrant, Sergio Jose Martinez, was deported from the U.S. 20 times. But he was allowed safe entrance into the U.S., again, to attack two women in Portland, Oregon. He faced illegal immigration, probation violation, kidnapping, robbery, assault, and sodomy charges. Yet, he was only sentenced to 35 years in prison.

*3) In 2017, Border Patrol Agent Rogelio Martinez was smashed in the head multiple times with a rock - by a group of illegals he was tracking.

*4) In 2018, Deputy Oliver and Detective Davis Jr. were shot by an illegal alien, Luis Brachamontes. During his trial, the criminal said,

"I'm going to kill more cops soon."

*5) In 2018, Edwin Jackson, a star player of pro-football's Indianapolis Colts, and another man were killed by a drunk driver. The perpetrator was an illegal alien which came into the U.S. after being deported twice.

As if the harboring of illegal immigrant criminals isn't bad enough, sanctuary cites also placate to illegal immigrants. Two prime examples are: 1) San Francisco paid an illegal immigrant from El Salvador, Pedro Figueroa-Zarceno, $190,000 because he was previously turned over to immigration authorities. His defense lawyer insisted this had been in violation of San Francisco's sanctuary city policies; 2) Brown University in Providence, Rhode Island, granted illegal immigrants financial aid. But students who are foreign born and live in the country legally are not being given the same privilege. Isn't it shameful that illegal immigrants are given more leniency in our schools and health care systems than *legal immigrants* and our *less privileged citizens?*

Illegal immigrant gangs and crime

Once again, it should be made clear that not every illegal immigrant commits crimes, and not all are part of dangerous gangs like MS-13. But non-citizen federal crime had been measured by the United States Department of Justice in December in 2017. Those results were quite shocking. One in five federal prisoners was foreign-born, and 94% of these were illegal aliens. But what is not included in the study is the number of foreign-born or illegal aliens that may be present in *state or local jails*. Moreover, the U.S. Sentencing Commission in December of 2017 released new statistics which concluded that non-citizens are far more likely to commit serious crimes than Americans. The statistics showed that 22% of murders, 33% of money laundering schemes, 29% of drug trafficking, 72% of drug possession convictions, and 18% of frauds had been committed by non-citizens. And, given all the crimes outlined, illegal immigrants comprise *only* 7% of the U.S. population.

A *Crime Prevention Research Center* study revealed detailed data about prisoners in Arizona state prisons from 1985 to 2017.

"Undocumented immigrants are at least 142% more likely to be convicted of a crime than other Arizonans. They also tend to commit more serious crimes and serve 10.5% longer sentences, more likely to be classified as dangerous, and 45% more likely to be gang members than U.S. citizens. Yet, there are several reasons that these numbers are likely to underestimate the share of crime committed by undocumented immigrants. There are dramatic differences between in the criminal histories of convicts who are U.S. citizens and undocumented immigrants. Young convicts are especially likely to be undocumented immigrants. While undocumented immigrants from 15 to 35 years of age make up slightly over 2 percent of the Arizona population, they make up almost 8% of the prison population. Even after adjusting for the fact that young people commit crime at higher rates, young undocumented immigrants commit crime at twice the rate of young U.S. citizens. These undocumented immigrants also tend to commit more serious crimes."

Meanwhile, gangs like Mara Salvatrucha, better known as MS-13, who originated in El Salvador and also has a presence in Mexico and Guatemala, are thriving in over 40 states in America. Yes, there are dozens of other groups of hooligans and thugs roaming around causing havoc throughout this country, such as Crips, Bloods, 18th Street Gang, Gangster Disciplines, Barrio Azteca, Florencia 13, Trinitarios, Mongols,

Latin Kings, and Aryan Brotherhood. But MS-13 is one of the most dangerous gangs in America which mostly prey on minority and Latino communities. They commit murder, rape, work with Mexican drug cartels, and are involved in sex trafficking. So, to keep Americans safe, the new President's administration has begun locating, incarcerating, and deporting thousands of these gang members.

Unfortunately, there are many who believe that MS-13 is not a grave concern to our nation, although many families have had to suffer the pain and dire consequences this gang, and others like it, inflicted upon them. In an extremely well-received State of the Union speech, the 45th American President addressed this issue by having families of those that had been affected by this terrible gang present. After the speech, however, their stories were diminished. For example, *MSNBC's* Joy Reid proposed that nobody had "ever heard of" MS-13, except for viewers watching *FOX News*. She was sadly mistaken and should visit the AVIAC (Advocates for Victims of Illegal Alien Crime) website.

The gun debates

There is an old saying that "guns don't kill people, people kill people." Okay, before someone takes a *shot* at me, just hear me out first. Guns, just like knifes, swords, hatchets, axes, spears, arrows, rocks, bombs, hand grenades, deadly gases, poison, and now cars or trucks, can't be used without a person or persons having the *intention* to maim, injure, or murder. For centuries, this has been the case. Unfortunately, it will not change now. For example, London has strict gun laws but has seen a rise in crime from 2017 - 2018, especially with knife murders. The murder rate in that city had surpassed New York City in early 2018. This flies in the face of Mayor Khan's 2017 declaration that his city was "the safest global city in the world". So, this proves that even with strict gun laws enforced if some people are bent on committing unspeakable acts, their weapon of choice doesn't matter. But how can we stop those who are mentally ill or acting in a moment of anger from causing harm or death? And, how do we specifically address gun violence in America?

To tackle this last question without infringing on the rights of

American citizens, there should be *limits*. We must be rational in our thinking. First, we could reasonably limit the number of guns someone can purchase or possess. Second, we can limit semi-automatic style weapons from being purchased by the public. In reality, these weapons should only be used by the military and law enforcement. In addition to these limits, guns should not be sold to the mentally-ill, people who seem to be a bit off-center, or ex-convicts. But, unfortunately, there is a problem when doing mental or physical health background checks as a person attempts to purchase a gun. It's called HIPAA (Health Insurance Portability and Accountability Act). This organization has health privacy acts hindering thorough background checks. So, a law must be made to override some of these privacy acts when someone buys a gun. This will protect the seller from being liable for the actions of a buyer. But if someone doesn't do a thorough background check and knowingly sells a gun to the wrong person just to make money, that person should be punished. That is just intentional immoral carelessness and greed.

There are preventative measures that could be taken as well. If one sees another person from their neighborhood, or in Internet videos, cruelly killing small animals or has remarks about killing people in the future, that person has an obligation to tell a law enforcement agency. Also, it's imperative we protect ourselves, especially our children, in public domains which are soft targets. That means hiring and arming retired military, law enforcement officials, or unemployed veterans at schools and libraries. Security is already in some airports, hospitals, sporting arenas, malls, and government buildings. Why not schools? Some smart schools do have police or armed guards. But they are few. The presence of an armed security guard or guards will change schools from soft to hard targets for those wanting to plan attacks. Trained dogs which have been retired from war zones could also be used to sniff out weapons and bad people. Of course, there could be identification checks, metal detectors, x-ray machines, and check points in places our children go to visit. Maybe there should be gun drills, so people know what to do in the instance there is a shooter, just like there are fire drills or, in the 1950's, bomb drills? And, lastly, people who own guns should be trained and renew their licenses at reasonable intervals, depending on the type of firearm. Then, after renewals, some, depending on recent crimes or mental health issues, may need a background check again.

Unquestionably, the American people and businesses do have the right to protect themselves. Unfortunately, no matter how hard we try, if someone has the evil intent and careful devious planning to commit horrific carnage, we can't stop it. The unlawful will always find ways to steal or buy weapons, no matter what form of weaponry they use to cause injury or death. But, again, we can prevent it as best as we can with reinforced protection, and by abiding by a well-known cliché - if we *see something*, then we should *say something*. Nonetheless, local and federal authorities must *do something* as well before massacres happen. And, yet, the shooting at a high school in Parkland, Florida did not abide by this, because four law enforcement officers stood outside the learning facility while many children and adults were being killed and injured. These officers and their commander should live in shame and seek forgiveness for the rest of their lives for these cowardice acts.

Regarding this terrible shooting and others like it, when they do occur it seems as though there will always be those who will rush to judgement and condemn all Republicans and the NRA (National Rifle Association) for the atrocities. It was appalling to see a televised *CNN* town hall meeting be stacked with bias individuals who aimed to ban guns just for the sake of notoriety. Even Broward County Sheriff Israel, a Democrat who had overseen the actions of the deputies at this horrific mass shooting, defended banning guns. The Sherriff arrogantly argued against a member of the NRA (Dana Loesh) and a Republican (Senator Marco Rubio) while attending this town hall meeting. But this Sheriff ordered his subordinates not to go into the school to confront the killer of many innocents as per his protocol. The Sheriff had rules in place to set-up a perimeter outside the school rather than going in to stop the shooter, while the shooting was known to be taking place. To make matters worse, the emergency medical technicians (EMT) were held off from going inside the school as well. All this, coupled with the fact that the law enforcement office in his county had been warned about two dozen times and officers went to the mentally disturbed shooter's house 39 times, is an utter disgrace to that sheriff and his department.

Nonetheless, the unconscionable and distorted televised *CNN* town hall meeting by this biased cable channel was all about trying to overshadow the good message the 45th U.S. President had given hours earlier. The President had opened the White House doors to a *listening session* with the survivors of this shooting and other shootings from the past. The President had showed everyone, in a televised sit-down, what a civil and rational exchange of thoughts, feelings, and suggestions about gun violence looked like for the future. But that town hall meeting was "deplorable". Only one viewpoint was being shown to the public.

Blaming members of the NRA, Republicans, and others who support them on gun violence is shameful. These people are demonized and addressed as if they don't care about our country or people. This is false. *They do* want certain laws to be fixed to better society. They can't change the laws - Congress does that. The NRA does <u>not</u> sell guns. It *only* has 4 million members. The NRA just upholds the rights of all citizens to "bear arms" which is written in the 2nd Amendment of our Constitution. It's akin to the *ACLU,* who upholds our 1st Amendment rights regarding freedoms of speech, press, expression, and assembly. Furthermore, government funding and lobbying for the NRA are nowhere near Democratic backed Planned Parenthood, which receives about half billion from Washington, D.C. each year. This organization takes more lives through abortions than gun violence does every year.

If we must cast blame, it should be on Congress, and as a matter of fact, the inaction of Democrats. They have as much fault with tweaking the laws as do Republicans. Does one really think that some Democrats do not receive money in their coffers from the *NRA* as well? We must remember the shootings at Columbine High School (1999), Fort Hood military base (2009), Aurora Theater (2012), Sandy Hook Elementary School (2012), Washington Navy Yard (2013), South Carolina Church (2015), San Bernardino Health Company (2015), Pulse Nightclub (2016), Dallas Police attack (2016) took place under Democrats (Clinton and Obama). Why hadn't they acted on gun issues back then, especially in Obama's case, when they had control of Congress? But, to be fair, the shootings at the Virginia Tech College (2007), First Baptist Church (2017), Las Vegas concert (2017), and Parkland High School

(2018) happened under a Republican President. Unfortunately, there are many more incidents not mentioned when a Republican or a Democrat President was in office. Therefore, in actuality, this is not a politically partisan issue. It's an issue of our humanity and morality.

The gun issue is probably one of the most difficult decisions for lawmakers from both political parties to agree upon. But they should not be given a free pass for inaction. Each state has its own laws on long guns, hand guns, assault weapons, concealed carry permits, open carry permits, magazine rounds, background checks, licenses and renewals, the right to defend oneself at home or in a vehicle (Castle Doctrine), and restrictions on carrying over state lines (Peaceable Journey Law). And, we have federal laws in place too. It's one very complex issue lawmakers scream about but never really tackle to the satisfaction of all Americans.

But again, how do we address gun laws? First, there must never be a rush to judge those who support the 2nd amendment after a tragic shooting. Also, Congress should propose *sensible* limitations on some laws, and who gets them, which will be beneficial to the American people. Of course, there will be disagreement about how to modify the laws to keep people safer. Yet besides Congress, there are many others in our society which must take responsibility. These individuals are more complicit with promoting and de-sensitizing the public toward gun violence than anyone in America. Look no further than to those who create and depict violence, destruction, and murder in Hollywood movies, documentaries, video games, music lyrics, and plays, or on the news, billboards, and social media. Scenes and words of violence have been ingrained in our societies. So, this is at the crux of the gun issue. Children, teenagers, and some unbalanced people can see this daily. This must not be overlooked. Those involved with sensationalizing and creating violence for monetary gain must admit this to themselves. We have become stoic to the violence shown. So, how do we curb it now?

There is also much misrepresentation to do with guns in America. Some statistics prove when more citizens are armed, violent crime tends to go down. Others show that increases in the right-to-carry guns will increase violent crimes. It all depends on the specific areas of America, the types of shootings, times of the data, and more, being evaluated. But what we do know is from 1982 to 2012 that 66% of the mass shootings in America were done by handguns and only 14% by assault weapons. This study was reported by *Mother Jones*, a liberal news outlet. Also, if one visits the FBI website then one can see most Active Shooter Incidents between 2000 and 2016 involved handguns.

Then we have the rhetoric that other countries have lower "annual death rates from mass public shootings" than does the U.S. Although that is true, it's also false. The U.S. is in the middle of the pack in this analysis. Information from the *Crime Prevention Research Center* proves this through a chart called "Comparing European Countries to US and Canada from January 2009 to December 2015 with the Annual Death from Mass Public Shootings". The research provides ranking for the "Death Rate per million people from Mass Public Shootings from 2009 to 2015" for the top nations involved in the study. It shows the following: (1) Norway: 1.888, (2) Serbia: .381, (3) France: .347, (4) Macedonia: .337, (5) Albania: .206), (6) Slovakia: .185, (7) Switzerland: .142, (8) Finland: .132, (9) Belgium: .128, (10) Czech Republic: .123, (11) U.S.: .089, (12) Austria: .068, (13) Holland: .051, (14) Canada: .032, (15) England: .027, (16) Germany: .023, (17) Russia: .012, (18) Italy: less than .012. Believe it or not!

The gun debate will always stir feelings on the right, on the left, and in the middle. It is not too late to embark upon fixing the problem. As mentioned, it's a complex issue. So, it will not be easy. Limitation, not elimination, and normal use, not abuse, is needed. We must hold steady, aim, and shoot in the middle of the target to ultimately execute the solving of this most difficult dilemma in America. Let's take a shot!

No respect

Over recent years, the anti-police protests and sentiments have grown from the fabrication and misrepresentations of news reports. Hundreds of police officers have been targeted, injured, maimed, or killed as a result by those wanting to believe the mainstream media rather than the facts. Such a case occurred in July 2016. An African-American sniper killed five police officers in Dallas during peaceful protests. But this wasn't the only instance of anti-police sentiments that year. In

2016, there were 143 police officers who lost their lives, an increase of nearly by 56 percent over the previous year. Although the total police officer death toll dropped in 2017 to 128 officers killed, the 2nd lowest in 50 years, it is still a lot to fathom. They are the people who protect us. There would be chaos and anarchy without them. So, we should honor our brave police, not commit violence against them. Sadly, there are those who do attack our police; but the media barely shows this.

*1) In 2014, the anti-police chants and sentiments adopted by several activist groups were influential in the slaying of two police officers, Rafael Ramos and Wenjian Liu, in New York City. But there was a lack of support exhibited by Mayor Bill Deblasio for NYC police departments before the murders. It was a good reason for police officers attending their colleague's funeral to turn their backs on the mayor. But it wasn't the last time this would happen to De Blasio. In 2017, Miosotis Familia was slain by a cop hating madman. Yet the abhorrent Mayor decided to join protests against OUR President in Hamburg, Germany rather than attend a memorial service for the fallen officer. Again, the police rightly turned their backs on him when he returned to speak at her funeral.

For those disrespectful acts toward the New York police, and more, including: I) allowing the homeless population to reach record highs, II) letting the NYC streets to become filthy again, III) reneging on his promise (saying he was overbudget) to rebuild homes for Hurricane Sandy victims, and IV) removing security from some NYC schools and mental health facilities, DeBlasio should join the ranks of mayors like Chicago's Rahm Emanuel as one of the worst mayors in recent U.S. history. To support the NYC police, go to *bluelivesmatternyc.org*.

*2) In 2017, a hate crime against police occurred when a black police officer, Quincy Smith, of South Carolina was shot eight times at point blank range for stopping another black assailant from possible robbery. Somehow, miraculously, he survived after bullets broke two bones in his arm, severed a vein his neck, and passed through his upper torso.

*3) In 2018, Chicago Police Commander Paul Bauer was absurdly and fatally shot six times by a four-time felon Shomari Legghette. Chicago has been identified as amongst America's top 25 murder capitols.

*4) In 2018, two sheriff deputies, Sgt. Noel Ramirez and Deputy Sheriff Taylor Lindsey were ambushed and killed at a restaurant in Trenton, Florida by gunman John Hubert Highnote. Then, he shot himself.

*5) In 2018, Officer William Gentry responded to a neighbor shooting a cat in Florida. Gentry was shot in the head by Joseph Edward Abeles, who was a convicted felon and had a violent history toward the police.

These are only a fraction of the tragic incidents suffered by police. Even though their lives are risked daily to keep us safe, they get <u>no respect</u>.

Federal botched investigations

I admire the work most are involved with in our intelligence agencies, including the FBI. But the FBI has missed many warning signs that led to several tragic shooting events in America. Here are a few high-profile mistakes by the FBI resulting in the mass murder of innocent people.

*1) In November 2009, there were 13 fatally shot and 30 others injured when U.S. Army Major Nidal Hasan opened fire at Fort Hood, near Killeen, Texas. The FBI was aware this individual had been dealing with known terrorists, including Yemen-based Imam Anwar al-awlaki. Hasan had begun to show signs of radicalization. But out of political correctness for his religious belief, he was never questioned. One of his classmates, Lt. Col. Val Finnell said,

"There were all sorts of … comments made throughout the year that made me question his loyalty to the United States, but nothing was done…The issue here is that there's a political correctness climate in the military. They don't want to say anything because it would be considered questioning somebody's religious belief, or they're afraid of an equal opportunity lawsuit."

The blame should fall on the FBI and military for their inaction.

*2) The FBI received a tip from the Russians that Dzhokhar Tsarnaev and Tamerlan Tsarnaev were being radicalized and trained for an attack. While investigating them for about two years, and then closing the case, the FBI didn't visit their mosques, friends, family, or tell local law enforcement. In April 2013, these two brothers would set bombs at the Boston Marathon and killed three, while injuring several hundred.

*3) In June 2015, nine people died, and others injured, at the Emanuel AME Church in Charleston, South Carolina. The FBI failed to acquire the proper information from police when doing a background check. It would have revealed the shooter, Dylann Roof, had a previous criminal record. This data could have prevented him from purchasing a firearm.

*4) In June 2016, another person, Omar Mateen, declaring allegiance to terrorism, slaughtered 49 people and injured over 50 others at the Pulse Nightclub in Orlando, Florida. Although the FBI investigated him for 10 months before the attack, the agency stated he never broke the law. Therefore, he wasn't pursued, and grave consequences followed.

*5) As mentioned, in 2018, there was a mass shooting in Marjory Stoneman Douglas High School in Parkland, Florida resulting in the deaths of 17, mostly children. The shooter, Nikolas Cruz, had many warning signs before the killing spree. There were two tips sent to the FBI. The first tip was that Cruz posted a *Youtube* message, "I'm going to be a professional school shooter." The second tip indicated that Cruz wanted to kill people; and he exhibited erratic behavior. If those weren't enough warning signs, Cruz had lost both his parents, posted his guns on-line, and killed small animals.

So, all of these tragic situations, and others, were preventable if the FBI had done a better job investigating, followed up on leads, and staked out persons that they knew had the potential for committing crimes. But the unfortunate truth had been that some FBI cases were hindered by the politically correct bureaucracy being instituted by some in the U.S. government, legal systems, schools, and companies.

Chapter 6

PRESIDENTIAL CRITICISMS AND INSULTS

As unveiled in the last chapter, many misleading or untold stories exist in our news world today. We know some news is either quite dodgy, ignorant, or just outrageous. Then, there is the disturbing reality that persons with unsavory agendas aim to wave their ideological stances in our faces. Some believe they have carte blanche to do so. But in a time of division and strife, partly because of what is being presenting to us by the media, we need to be given the truth. Couple all of this with the simple fact that the mainstream media detests the 45th U.S. President, and we have a combustible situation on air and in the newspapers.

The President who currently resides in the White House has been treated quite unfairly and more negatively than any other President in the last 25 years. Outlandish opinion is seen as truth toward him. Facts are misrepresented, hidden, or just falsified. Receiving this type of so-called news about OUR President puts people into two camps. Those who want to believe the ill-will against the President and those who do not. So, to find the truth one must be careful not to jump to unjust conclusions without first having the data, evidence, and, in some cases the history. Daily, we must be like a one-person jury in our minds. There should be a deliberate approach to analyzing the facts before a deciding verdict is reached.

But even with the mainstream media as primary judge, jury, and executioner, OUR President moves forward to make progress for our country. He aims to expel the corrupt persons and organizations in Washington, D.C. who make shady donations and under-the-table deals. The President realizes establishment politicians are in bed, literally and figuratively, with unseemly foreign and domestic lobbyists. And, he knows that when these politician's term limits are up, they go work for those same lobbyists. This funny business amongst politicians is what the 45th President of the U.S. wants to eliminate. He has started to clean this up. But still, he has a long way to go to "drain the swamp". Yet one would think the mainstream media and all Americans would be happy about this cleansing of Washington, D.C. But, no! Instead of embracing the opportunity to wash away the sins of the few, the media whines and goes into frenzies about fallacies and half-truths involving OUR President. It's because the mainstream is actually an integral part of the sleazy establishment "Inside the Beltway" - an area encircling Washington, D.C. which includes parts of Virginia and Maryland. Also, media outlets in New York and California are part of the corruption too. It's also the reason why the media misreports, embellishes, and will not give ample time about any pertinent story favoring OUR U.S. President.

These media outlets working in tandem with political operatives will not give credit to the President or anyone affiliated with him. They seek to demean the President, his family, his administration, or anyone who supports him at every turn. If he succeeds, they fail. So, they must be fully engaged in an unabashed flurry of slander which will degrade this President. There must be no remorse or they will be seen as weak.

To criticize and insult him means some reporters, anchors, opinion writers, and editors can wear a badge of honor amongst their peers. But what the media doesn't realize is some of us understand why they are setting negative narratives for the day. The *'lame'*-stream media doesn't tell us that many important policies and decisions spoken about or made by this President had already been addressed by other Presidents before him. And they don't inform us "the wall" is <u>not</u> something new.

The mainstream media hides or revels in many shadowy issues concerning the President. They indulge in vice Presidential snubs. They attack the First Lady and President's family. And, they don't recognize or show the hateful tweets toward Republicans. So, these disingenuous, dishonorable, and hypocritical issues will be the focus in this chapter.

It's happened before

Jerusalem:
There have been many who have previously supported Jerusalem being Israel's capital. In 1992, Bill Clinton, during the Democratic primaries

and Presidential election, had passionately acknowledged,

"Jerusalem as the capital of the State of Israel."

There were others who recognized Jerusalem as Israel's capital too. In 1999, while campaigning for the U.S. Senate, Hillary Clinton said Jerusalem was the "eternal and indivisible capital of Israel", and if elected to the New York Senate she would help to "move the U.S. embassy to Jerusalem." In 2000, during the election campaign, George W. Bush attacked Bill Clinton because he had not delivered on his promise to move the U.S. embassy to Jerusalem. So, in front of a Jewish audience Bush said he would "start the process as soon as I'm sworn in." Lastly, in 2008, during a campaign speech, Barack Obama said,

"Jerusalem will remain the capital of Israel, and, I have said it before, and I will say it again."

The one glaring fact is these individuals who emphatically stated Jerusalem was the capital of Israel, or the U.S. embassy will be moved to Jerusalem, had mostly done so on the campaign trail. The 45th U.S. President also promised this during his Presidential campaign. The difference is these politicians would talk a good game to get elected. But it took a businessman, OUR President, to begin the process of moving the U.S. embassy to Israel and declare Jerusalem as Israel's capital (opening on 5/14/18 and under budget for only about $300,000). Yet the detractors will always criticize the President, while they ignore the fact that those whom they fawned over and supported for years failed in keeping their promises about Jerusalem.

North Korea:
Resolving the North Korean matter dealing with nuclear disarmament has been evasive for the U.S. and the world. American involvement with the affairs of North Korean regimes has been going on since the Korean War in the 1950's. But the issues got progressively worse when nuclear weapons started coming into play.

On October 21, 1994, President Bill Clinton entered into a bad deal

(Agreed Framework) with North Korea dictator, Kim Jung Il. The U.S. gave $4 billion to the N.K. regime so they could build two light-water reactors in exchange for stopping their nuclear program. Clinton said,

"North Korea will freeze and then dismantle its nuclear program. South Korea and our other allies will be better protected. The entire world will be safer as we slow the spread of nuclear weapons."

"...The United States and international inspectors will carefully monitor North Korea to make sure it keeps its commitments. Only as it does so will North Korea fully join the community of nations."

Yet, in 1998, North Korea ignored President Clinton and conducted its first nuclear missile test.

After President Bush took office, in his State of the Union address, President Bush criticized North Korea for "arming with missiles and weapons of mass destruction, while starving its citizens". Bush said he would not certify the Clinton era *Agreed Framework*. Then, he found nuclear tests were being performed by North Korea. So, the *Six-Part Talks*, which included China, North Korea, South Korea, Japan, Russia, and the U.S. took place in 2003. They continued until President Obama took office. But, again, North Korea completed a nuclear test in 2006. In 2007, Bush sent $400 million worth of fuel, food, and other aid in exchange for the shutdown of North Korean's main nuclear reactor. Yet North Korea would continue to defy America.

In 2009, when Obama was elected as President, the U.N. Security Council adopted some sanctions on North Korea. In April 2014, while visiting South Korea, President Obama stated he would "not hesitate to use our military might" when it came to defending allies. North Korea followed with 11 missile launches and 2 nuclear tests while Obama sat in the oval office. Not only that, but Obama gave Iran, a terrorist enabling country and ally of North Korea, about $1.7 billion.

In August 2017, the 45th President of the United States changed that. Tired of the *passive inaction* prior presidential administrations had taken against the grave threat North Korea posed, he spoke out.

After North Korea launched test missiles, which could potentially carry nuclear warheads to the U.S., the President dubbed Kim Jung-Un, the North Korean leader, "rocket man". And, he sternly warned,

"North Korea best not make any more threats to the United States."

"They will be met with fire and fury like the world has never seen...He has been very threatening -- beyond a normal statement...As I said, they will be met with fire, fury and frankly power the likes of which this world has never seen before."

The mainstream media went into their usual tailspin and feigned outrage. Yet this new President's so-called harsh rhetoric and strategies to deal with the North Korea situation, including talks, resulted in massive sanctions and a unanimous decision at the U.N. to confront the development of nuclear weapons by North Korea.

Then, in March 2018, a South Korean representative addressed America, stating North Korea dictator Kim Jong-un was willing to speak face-to-face with the 45th U.S. President about denuclearization. The President responded by indicating he was willing to meet Jong-un in 2018. A meeting was set for June 12th in Singapore. But the President cancelled it in late May because North Korea was still showing hostility and playing games. Sickly, the mainstream media was overjoyed with the news. However, to their chagrin, talks continued and the summit was back on. It was the <u>first time</u> *a sitting President* (Carter and Clinton met as ex-Presidents) met with a North Korean leader.

Will North Korea end its building of nuclear weapons or will they continue to undermine the U.S. and its allies by building its own nuclear arsenal? Who knows? But even as he took a more pro-active approach with North Korea than three previous Presidents, the mainstream media and Democrats still ridiculed the President's on-going efforts on this critical issue. They don't want him to succeed - even though this helps the U.S. and world. It's because past Presidents and politicians the media supported had miserably failed in their efforts with N. Korea.

Military Parade:

In February 2018, the 45th President of the United States indicated he may want to have a military parade to honor our military on the streets of Washington, D.C. The mainstream media, pundits, and members of the Democratic Party went bonkers, and relentlessly criticized the President. The so-called news anchors stated he was acting like a "dictator" or a leader of the old "Soviet Union". They sarcastically said he should wear "shoulder epaulettes" to show his power.

But had the media forgotten the President didn't just come up with this idea out of thin air? Were they just trying to push a negative narrative to the American people about OUR President? Most probably, the latter was the case because when the U.S. President visited France (2017) he was impressed by the annual Bastille Day parade and told President Emmanuel Macron this. The President indicated the French parade showed a sense of patriotism. And, so, the idea of an American military parade had its roots in France. The President thought it would be nice to show some pride in this country too. That was the President's intentions when he mentioned a military parade in the U.S.

The people can have protests, women's marches, and gay, ethnic, or holiday parades. But we shouldn't have a parade to show the country's patriotism to honor the men and women in our military? Why? In the past, even Democratic Mayor Bill DeBlasio (N.Y.) and Senator Charles Ellis Schumer (N.Y.) wanted a military parade. In 2014, Schumer said,

"...these men risked their lives to protect us."

"...they experienced terrible trial and tragedy along the way."

"...a grand event at the Canyon of Heroes that would include military brass, color guards, military bands, and fly-overs."

Then, N.Y. Mayor DeBlasio (born Warren Wilhelm Jr.) echoed this.

"The brave men and women who have selflessly served our nation with courage and skill in Iraq and Afghanistan deserve recognition for their sacrifice. I stand with Sen. Schumer in his call for a parade to honor our

veteran heroes, and NYC would be proud to host this important event."

As usual, those who are now against the President's proposal for a military parade were for it several years ago. The hypocrisy is thick.

Disaster Relief:
The 45th President admirably and quickly responded to three major hurricanes in the span of a month, for people in Puerto Rico, Texas, Louisiana, and the U.S. Virgin Islands. His reactions were excellent and consistent with what was needed at the time of these horrific disasters. Of course, the mainstream media had all kinds of foolish things to say about him, his administration, and the First Lady.

Yet maybe those who had spoken poorly about the President's efforts should recall Obama hesitated before implementing plans for the 2010 BP oil spill in the Gulf of Mexico. *The New York Times* wrote,

"The reports also say that about two weeks after the BP rig exploded, the National Oceanic and Atmospheric Administration asked the White House for permission to make public its worst-case models for the accident. The White House Office of Management and Budget initially denied the request..."

"...government officials have acknowledged that they miscalculated the amount of oil pouring into the gulf..."

Frustrated with the situation, President Obama reportedly said in a White Meeting,

"...just plug the damn hole."

In 2005 President George W. Bush's response to Hurricane Katrina was less than emphatic. The brunt of the disaster had decimated Louisiana, with major damage in New Orleans and Mississippi. Bush even admitted to the failed governmental response by saying,

"Katrina exposed serious problems in our response capability at all levels of government...To the extent the federal government didn't fully do its job right, I take responsibility."

Of course, many in the biased mainstream media equated what happened to Bush to the 45th American President. But President Bush didn't have to face three enormous back-to-back-to-back storms hitting the U.S. Regardless, the media did their best to mislead the American people about the planning, response, rescue efforts, and clean-up of the President's administration. But many officials at the disaster zones debunked the media, saying that all was "outstanding" considering the unprecedented disasters which had occurred within a month's time.

Presidential Website:

The 45th President of the United States used his own *Facebook* page to produce *real news* and show the administration's progress during his presidency. So, the mainstream media accused him of having a "state run" news outlet. They asserted the website shows he had "given up on the free media and now he's making his own media"; and he wants to "replace the news". Unfortunately, the President has to do this to by-pass all the fake, misrepresented, and hidden news stories.

But President Obama launched his own website in 2008 to "debunk rumors" during his Presidential campaign. Of course, like little obedient lapdogs, the mainstream media followed Obama's lead to confirm his narrative. Then, after being elected, Obama produced the *change.gov* website, which promised it would be "your source for the latest news, events and announcements so that you can follow the setting up of the Obama administration." The difference with Obama's website was it was a government website which was paid for by us - the taxpayers. The 45th American President's *Facebook* page, however, is free to the taxpayers. So, what's the beef with the President's website? Of course, all Presidents have the *whitehouse.gov* website too.

What's all the fuss about building a wall?

"The wall" is a symbol associated with the 45th President of the United States. Those who support him are obviously in favor of it, while the people who oppose him abhor it. The reason is simple. This was one of the biggest promises the President made on the campaign trail. If the opposition can prevent building a wall on the southern border it will be a major accomplishment for them. They contend the idea of a wall is racist. But the reality is a wall is not about prejudices toward certain people but about protecting our nation from terrorists, drug smugglers, those who make money from bringing innocent people over our border illegally and stopping foreign-born criminals. It's a national security issue in addition to an immigration one. Of course, immigrants should be permitted into the U.S. to better their lives, if possible. This must be done, however, on a limited basis. We can't have open borders. Strict security background checks and limiting the amount of people coming into America each year will benefit our nation from mass population explosion and criminal threats. Therefore, rather than having a huge influx of people entering the U.S., a point or merit-based system should streamline our immigration problem. This is not racist. There are many countries using these systems, such as Australia, Canada, Germany, Hong Kong, New Zealand, and Scandinavian nations.

Those who come into the country illegally should be sent back to their country but be allowed to re-enter if they apply for citizenship at the border. They should go through a process just like every other immigrant coming into the country. Why should people going through the immigration process *legally* for years have others cut in front of them to gain citizenship in a shorter period than they do? Logically, to any rational person, this is not fair. But many in the mainstream media and irrational liberals desire amnesty for illegal aliens - so millions of immigrants will vote for Democrats and their power can be regained.

In addition to the immigration issue, "the wall' is needed to combat terrorists and criminals, as was stated. It makes sense. Would you like people entering *your* house or apartment unannounced and then staying for years to *freeload* off of you? Then, we hear from all those hypocrites, the millionaires and celebrities who preach to us that it's "cruel" and "racist" to build a wall. Meanwhile, they have guarded gates preventing criminals or anyone else from entering their property.

Hey, does any other country have walls to secure their borders? Well, Israel has a wall on the West Bank, and building one in the Gaza

Strip. Saudi Arabia has a 560-mile fence against Iraq. Turkey has a 90-mile wall against Iran, a 500-mile barrier against Syria. Hungary has a 110-mile wall against Serbia. There is a massive 2,500-mile barbed wire fence between India and Pakistan. There are 99 Peace walls in Belfast. Jerusalem has a wall surrounding its city. Oh! And, of course, the nation state of Vatican City has a wall protecting itself. Actually, 65 countries have walls completed or under construction (as per Quebec University expert E. Vallet). So, BUILD THAT WALL! There is nothing wrong with securing our borders and keeping out those wanting to break our laws.

Casting shadows on the White House

Leaks:
When the 45th U.S. President took office, within the first 4 months or so, the administration faced seven times more leaks of information to the press than the previous two administrations. Some of it was done to discredit the President and his administration. But other news which was leaked out endangered America's national security and persons in the field trying to protect us. There were about 125 leaks in the first 126 days. Some were punishable by fines or jail time. Those leakers violated the statues of the *Espionage Act,* which prohibits the communication of classified information retrieved from a computer if the information could be used to the injury of the United States. This also is related to the *unmasking* of U.S. citizens to discover information about a person. This was nefariously done to General Michael Flynn and many others involved in the President's campaign in 2016 (more on this later). Nobody has been held accountable for this, yet. But maybe, hopefully, some will face the consequences of their unlawful actions soon.

Health Test:
Doctor Admiral Ronny Jackson, also the physician for past President's Obama and Bush, said during a press conference that the 45th U.S. President passed all physical and mental tests. He scored 30 out of 30 on his mental test. The only physical issue the tests showed was the President had been slightly overweight and needed to take some

cholesterol medication. The doctor said his genetics were outstanding. But this didn't stop the White House press core from questioning the doctor for nearly an hour with insane questions. They asked,

Reporter: "Can you explain to me how a guy who eats McDonald's and KFC and drinks all those diet cokes and never exercises is in as good a shape as you say he's in?"

Reporter: "Is a cognitive exam the same as a psychiatric one?"

Reporter: "Is he limited to one scoop of ice cream now?"

Reporter: "Are you ruling out things like early-onset Alzheimer's?" and "Are you looking at dementia-like symptoms?"

Reporter: "Given the President's age, he's somewhere like where President Reagan was. Can you say that there's scrutiny of what was overlooked at the time with President Reagan in terms of A.L.S. and things he was then known to — Alzheimer's and things he was known to suffer from?"

These people obviously were looking for any reason to confirm their narrative that the President was either mentally or physically unfit to serve as the 45th President of the United States. Of course, their unscrupulous agenda was, and remains to be, to provide any evidence they can find for impeachment to begin or to discredit him.

Then, May 2018, the President wanted Admiral Jackson to become head of the Veterans Administration (VA). But bureaucrats, and specifically, Democrat Jon Tester, alleged that Jackson was caught drinking on duty. The allegations were completely unfounded. Many Democrats and the media continued their deception. They wanted the President's pick to be ridiculed. So, Jackson withdrew his candidacy.

The 2016 Campaign Smear:
When the 45th President-to-be was campaigning in 2016, all kinds of assertions swirled about his sexual misconduct with women after the famous *NBC* video tape was shown to the world. Some of these sexual

allegations have been debunked. And, before 2016, American political history has had many examples of an opposition party falsely accusing innocent politicians through smear campaigns during elections.

Then, in 2017, it was reported by *The Hill* news outlet that Lisa Bloom, a prominent California lawyer, who is an advocate for woman, had purportedly offered compensation to women if they told a story about alleged sexual misconduct between them and the President-to-be. One woman received a payment to end her mortgage. But another woman, who wanted to remain anonymous, was offered a donation to her church, relocation fees, and, eventually, up to "$750,000". This woman also revealed texts between her and the lawyer. Since she didn't want to commit to unseemly allegations, one of her texts read,

"What does time have to do with this? Time to bury Trump??? You want my story to bury trump for what? Personal gain?..."

Then, days before the election (11/5/16), the lawyer allegedly said,

"I begged you not to jerk me around after what I had just gone through..."

Also, Bloom had initially defended the accused sex offender and Hollywood elite producer Harvey Weinstein. He frequently donated to Democrats and was friends with many in the government, including the Obamas and Clintons. So, being Weinstein was a high-profile celebrity, Bloom allegedly investigated and tried to kill the story given from the first sexual accuser of the Hollywood producer, Rose McGowan, and then Ambra Battilana Gutierrez. But as more sex and rape allegations arose Bloom retreated from defending Weinstein. Yet why didn't Bloom believe the first Weinstein accusers if she was an advocate for women?

So, now, given this, how can the public believe, without any doubt, the myriad of sexual accusations against the 45th U.S. President?

Losing Hope:
When Communications Director, Hope Hicks, announced she would be leaving the White House the mainstream media went into another

meltdown. They insisted that Hicks was forced out or left because she had testified to Congress that everyone tells "white lies". Her exit, however, had already been planned internally for weeks. She had been by the President's side for nearly three years, when he first declared his Presidential candidacy. But being only 29 years old, Hicks will have many grand opportunities outside of government. Regardless, as Hicks' departure was looming liberal comedienne Chelsea Handler sent out a nasty tweet. She referenced *Anne Frank,* a Dutch holocaust victim who had made a diary while hiding from the Nazis during WWII, texting,

"Hope Hicks reportedly kept a detailed diary about her time in the White House. So, this will be the second time a woman wrote a diary about Nazis."

Mixing Guns with Healthcare:
The same old anti-gun rhetoric was spoken by many after the tragic high school shooting of many children and adults in Parkland, Florida. The President addressed the nation, giving condolences, speaking to children, and mentioning mental illness. This was an excellent speech.

"My fellow Americans, today I speak to a nation in grief. Yesterday, a school filled with innocent children and caring teachers became the scene of terrible violence, hatred and evil.

Around 2:30 yesterday afternoon, police responded to reports of gunfire at Marjory Stoneman Douglas High School in Parkland, Florida -- a great and safe community. There, a shooter, who is now in custody, opened fire on defenseless students and teachers. He murdered 17 people and badly wounded at least 14 others.

Our entire nation, with one heavy heart, is praying for the victims and their families. To every parent, teacher, and child who is hurting so badly, we are here for you -- whatever you need, whatever we can do, to ease your pain. We are all joined together as one American family, and your suffering is our burden also.

No child, no teacher, should ever be in danger in an American school. No parent should ever have to fear for their sons and daughters when they kiss them goodbye in the morning.

Each person who was stolen from us yesterday had a full life ahead of them -- a life filled with wondrous beauty and unlimited potential and promise. Each one had dreams to pursue, love to give, and talents to share with the world. And each one had a family to whom they meant everything in the world.

Today, we mourn for all of those who lost their lives. We comfort the grieving and the wounded. And we hurt for the entire community of Parkland, Florida, that is now in shock, in pain, and searching for answers.

To law enforcement, first responders, and teachers who responded so bravely in the face of danger: We thank you for your courage. Soon after the shooting, I spoke with Gov. Scott to convey our deepest sympathies to the people of Florida and our determination to assist in any way that we can. I also spoke with Florida Attorney General Pam Bondi and Broward County Sheriff Scott Israel.

I'm making plans to visit Parkland to meet with families and local officials, and to continue coordinating the federal response.

In these moments of heartache and darkness, we hold on to God's word in scripture: 'I have heard your prayer and seen your tears. I will heal you.'

We trust in that promise, and we hold fast to our fellow Americans in their time of sorrow.

I want to speak now directly to America's children, especially those who feel lost, alone, confused or even scared: I want you to know that you are never alone and you never will be. You have people who care about you, who love you, and who will do anything at all to protect you. If you need help, turn to a teacher, a family member, a local police officer, or a faith leader. Answer hate with love; answer cruelty with kindness.

We must also work together to create a culture in our country that embraces the dignity of life, that creates deep and meaningful human connections and that turns classmates and colleagues into friends and neighbors.

Our administration is working closely with local authorities to investigate the shooting and learn everything we can. We are committed to working with state and local leaders to help secure our schools and tackle the difficult issue of mental health.

Later this month, I will be meeting with the nation's governors and attorney generals, where making our schools and our children safer will be our top priority. It is not enough to simply take actions that make us feel like we are making a difference. We must actually make that difference.

In times of tragedy, the bonds that sustain us are those of family, faith, community, and country. These bonds are stronger than the forces of hatred and evil, and these bonds grow even stronger in the hours of our greatest need.

And so always, but especially today, let us hold our loved ones close, let us pray for healing and for peace, and let us come together as one nation to wipe away the tears and strive for a much better tomorrow.

But, of course, many liberal detractors who are just filled with anger and acrimony toward the President did their usual spin. For example, *MSNBC's Morning Joe* news anchor Joe Scarborough made outlandish comments, as he does often with his co-host on the show.

"He's letting Christians that go to church get slaughtered, like Pontius Pilate."

"...just washing their hands of it, like Pontius Pilate, letting Christians get slaughtered in pews, letting country fans get slaughtered at concerts."

Another instance of ire was when late night talk show host Jimmy Kimmel gave his recurring spiel of ridiculously exaggerated offbeat criticism. In his monologue, he said the President is "mentally ill", and,

"...he also signed a bill that made it easier for people with severe mental illness to buy guns legally."

But Kimmel's latter statement was just fallacious banter. This issue was mentioned previously. But to reiterate, the President's new bill actually upheld the rights of those receiving Social Security benefits. Under an Obamacare mandate, the SS recipients were deemed mentally unfit because they needed help filling out their financial applications under the program. Therefore, they couldn't purchase or own guns. That was unlawful. It was even opposed by the *ACLU*, a mostly liberal group, because it violates the Americans for Disabilities Act.

Vice Presidential snubs

When Omarosa Manigault-Newman left the White House, from her position in the President's administration, she decided to jump back into television. On an episode of a show called *Celebrity Big Brother,* Omarosa made news after mocking Vice President Mike Pence about his religious beliefs, amongst other things, when saying,

"I'm Christian, I love Jesus, but (Pence) thinks Jesus tells him to say things. I'm like, 'Jesus didn't say that.'"

Well, that opened the floodgates. Christian conservatives, such as V.P. Pence, are a target for liberals. So, Joy Behar of *The View* eagerly took advantage. She insulted OUR Vice President with nasty remarks.

"It's one thing to talk to Jesus. It's another thing when Jesus talks to you."

"Can he talk to Mary Magdalene without his wife in the room?"

The problem with liberal celebrities, like those on *The View* and elsewhere on television, is they always get away with this. They profess to be comedians; and, so, it's their right to tell a joke. But the jokes are getting very old. They offend millions of people in the process with their bigoted and biased views, without having any remorse for their words.

So, Pence was not hesitant to respond to Behar's blatant lack of dignity toward many who had similar beliefs to his in America. He said:

"I actually heard that ABC has a program that compared my Christianity to mental illness. And I'd like to laugh about it, but I really can't. Tens of millions of Americans today will have ash on their foreheads to mark the beginning of Lent. The overwhelming majority of Americans cherishes their faith. And we've all different types of faith in this country. But I have to tell you, to have ABC maintain a broadcast forum that compared Christianity to

mental illness is just wrong."

Good for V.P. Pence. He stood up for the sanctity of Christianity, and the freedom to have religious beliefs in America. Thanks be to God!

Then, Oprah Winfrey talked on a *CBS* show called *"60 Minutes Overtime"* and was asked about possibly running for President in 2020.

"If God actually wanted me to run, wouldn't God kinda tell me? And I haven't heard that."

Did Joy Behar attack Oprah with the same sarcasm and distaste she delivered against V.P. Pence? Of course not! But, ironically, what was found on *YouTube* three months before Behar's ridiculous remarks against the Vice President was very typical of a person who is filled with much hate for conservative thought. While interviewed about her new comedic book (it's about surviving the world with OUR President in office), Behar states it was written because she was being,

"...told by God to save the country."

It's laughable what celebrities like her preach when they don't do or say it themselves. Of course, eventually, Behar would have to apologize to Pence. Being a forgiving Christian, the Vice President accepted her apology. Whether the apology was at the behest of the television station or on her own is unknown. Nevertheless, Pence also encouraged Behar to apologize to the millions of Christians she insulted. She did so.

Then, when Vice President Pence visited South Korea during the 2018 Winter Olympics Vice, he was criticized for not standing when the North Korean/South Korean assembly of athletes marched together during the Opening Ceremonies. David Meeks of *USA Today* wrote it was an embarrassment Pence came to the Olympics, adding,

"Pence couldn't stand for it and opted for disrespect instead, and that is all the world will remember about his appearance at the Pyeongchang Olympics."

All the haters in the media of this administration followed suit with their own headlines. They compared his not standing at the Olympic opening ceremony to that of the NFL players not standing during OUR national anthem at the beginning of football games. It's not the same thing! When football players don't stand as our national anthem is sung and American flag is shown, they disrespect all who served, defended, or gave their life for the United States of America.

V.P. Pence did not stand to protest North Korea's brutal regime because they imprison and kill many, starve half their people, and defy America and many nations of the world. He was right to do so!

The mainstream media, however, continued to show their contempt for the U.S. Vice President. And, so, they honored Kim Yo-Jung, the North Korean dictator's sister, with praises in headlines, like:

"Kim Jong-Un's Sister is stealing the show at the Winter Olympics"

"Kim Jong-Un's Sister Turns on the Charm, Taking Pence's Spotlight"

The media used words like "captivating" to describe her. They even compared Yo-Jung to Ivanka, the President's daughter - ironically and unwittingly, since they loathe her too. But did they realize Kim Yo-Jung, the sister of the dictator, was the *Director of the Propaganda and Agitation Department* in North Korea? Did these media types even contemplate the father of Otto Warmbier, who was tortured to the brink of death for years, was present with Pence as a symbol to oppose the oppressive regime? The mainstream media has no morals or scruples!

Fortunately, there was some honest reporting present in South Korea. Such is the case with Michael Graham of *CBS News* who wrote,

"If the murder of Kim Yo Jong's brother occurred as believed, it's likely the 'captivating' Ms. Kim knew about it. When she's not being celebrated by the press for giving a 'deadly side eye' to Vice President Mike Pence (a Twitter comment by the Washington Post's Philip Bump he later deleted), Kim Yo Jong oversees propaganda for the public executioners of the North Korean government. 'A key part of the North Korean system of enslaving people is total control of the media, of the information people are allowed to consume

there,' says Korea expert Ethan Epstein. She is the director of the department that oversees it. If there is the perfect poster person for the war on the North Korean people's psyche being waged by the Kim regime, it's Kim Yo Jong."

The news reporter Graham also added in the article that,

"Everyone knows the press hates President Trump. But who knew they hated him enough to make a hero out of the most deadly dictators in history."

Surprisingly, even *MSNBC's* Willie Geist was forthright about the situation in South Korea when he tweeted out,

"I can report South Koreans here in Pyeongchang are not as enthralled with Kim Yo Jong and the North Korean cheerleaders as it seems some media are back home. Something about N.K. killing, starving, & imprisoning its people while threatening South Korea with nuclear annihilation."

Attacking the President's family

Many instances of celebrities, the media, and others disparaging the President's family exist. But only a few shall be presented here.

*1) In March 2017, Eric, the President's son, and wife, Lara announced they were pregnant, and expected a boy. Many congratulated them. But less than funny comedienne Chelsea Handler tweeted,

"I guess one of @realDonaldTrump's sons is expecting a new baby. Just what we need. Another person with those jeans. Let's hope for a girl."

Handler's hate toward anyone related to the President blinded her from seeing she should have said "genes" instead of "jeans".

*2) When the President pulled out of the Paris Accord Agreement, the media blamed Ivanka because she is one of his White House advisors. They stated she should have stopped her father from doing this. The media and others thought since Ivanka believed in climate change she could influence her father's mind in the White House. The media was

apathetic toward Ivanka's staunch advocacy for women, or the fact that she had supported gay, bisexual, and transgender rights for years. They didn't acknowledge Ivanka had been celebrated around the globe by leaders such as German Chancellor Angela Merkel. And, they had no respect for Ivanka's 2017 brilliant speech in India for women's rights and the economic empowerment of women. Her critics are indifferent to these facts because the 45th United States President is her father.

*3) In May 2017, late night Bill Maher disgustingly spoke about how the President and his daughter, Ivanka, acted toward one another. He said,

"Oh, Ivanka is gonna be our saving grace.' When he's about to f--king nuke Finland or something, she's gonna walk into the bedroom and you know...'Daddy, Daddy. Don't do it, Daddy.'"

Then he made a crude gesture, as if implying that Ivanka was attempting to stop the President by incestuously masturbating him. But people like this should know this sickness is rejected by *true* Americans.

*4) In 2016, ex-comedienne Rosie O'Donnell speculated that Barron, the 10-year son of the President, is autistic (below). But this drew much criticism. To bully a child or dehumanize autistics is quite appalling.

"Barron Trump autistic? If so - what an amazing opportunity to bring attention to the AUTISM epidemic."

*5) In 2016, comedian Steven Spinola said more awful things about the President's innocent young son, Barron. Spinola said Barron was a:

"...handsome date rapist to be.......I don't want my Mom to get raped, but if she does I hope it's by Barron.....Small pp [sic] would be painless and we'd win lots of money in court."

*6) In February 2018, Vanessa, the wife of the President's son Donald Jr., opened a letter which was addressed to him. When opening the envelope, white power flew out at her. The letter itself read,

"You are getting what you deserve...You are an awful, awful person. I am surprised that your father lets you speak on TV. You're the family idiot. Eric looks smart."

Vanessa felt ill and was taken to the hospital. Thankfully, she was released without any incident. The madman, from Boston, who sent the letter, had called the President, "Adolf Hitler". But being that he worked at Catholic Charities Archdiocese, did he a*tone for his sins*?

*7) Then, you have ludicrous remarks by anchors like *MSNBC*'s Chris Matthews. He compared the President's family to a ruling Russian royal dynasty called the "Romanovs". But they were captured and executed by the Bolsheviks. Was he implying the media would be the Bolsheviks?

Bashing the First Lady

Lastly, there are brazen attacks on OUR First Lady of the United States of America, Melania, from the mainstream media, pundits, haters of the President, and even Hollywood. Although she was born in Slovenia, and English is not her first language, she speaks five languages (Slovenian Serbo-Croatian, French, Italian, German, and English). How many first ladies of America have spoken five languages? None. Not only does she have these linguistic skills, but Melania is a beautiful woman who evokes elegance and grace. She is a caring individual who is eager to help children. Melania has gone to many hospitals, children's libraries, schools in America, while on Presidential visits, and abroad on her own. She has had many children to the White House on numerous occasions.

In addition, Melania is an advocate for cyber bullying, gender equality, and has engaged in Presidential rallies and speeches, such as addressing the opioid crisis. In May 2018, she launched a "Be Best" campaign. But, expectedly, the slogan drew criticism from many haters in the media. They denigrate anything Melania does because she is the wife of the 45th U.S. President. Examples of their hatred of her follow.

*1) There was a brief rumor on the Internet indicating the First Lady, Melania, had a secret decoy double. This was ridiculous.

*2) The removal of a 200-year old tree on the White House lawn was said to have been ordered by the First Lady. It was false. The U.S. National Arboretum recommended this historic Jackson Magnolia be removed because it had been decaying, and then its saplings could be preserved and replanted in the future.

*3) In August 2017, on a visit to Texas after the damage of Hurricane Harvey, the First Lady left the White House in high heels. Reporters went crazy saying Melania was being pretentious and insensitive as she left to board Air Force One with the President. The story was debunked because she had a change of shoes on the plane. She arrived at the disaster area with sneakers and a FLOTUS hat on ready to pitch in.

*4) After the high heel story from the hurricane disaster, a *Newsweek* writer wrote something very disrespectful about the First Lady,

"When women wear high heels at work, they send sexual signals that should be avoided if they want to be taken seriously." Then, she added that *"shoe historians say the first women to wear heels were Italian prostitutes in the 17th century, when they adopted them, along with smoking, from their male friends. From there it became a sexual symbol. The high heel was a staple of Victorian porn."*

*5) To shame OUR First Lady, a *New York Times* reporter Jacob Bernstein printed nude photo shoots of Melania when she was a model. Allegedly, he called her a "hooker" which was <u>not</u> defended by any so-called feminists. There seems to be a double standard when it comes to much in this country. But what if this happened to a liberal woman?

*6) Melania was mocked about her ethnicity by many comedians even though these celebrities insist they are pro-immigrant supporters. For example, a so-called model, Gigi Hadid, gave a terrible impersonation of the First Lady, with a bad accent on the American Music Awards.

*7) Melania wore a Gucci ensemble with flowers and birds when visiting China. But the *Elite Daily* suggested the First Lady was committing "cultural appropriation" to wear something of that nature in China. Of course, this was an idiotic statement because what Melania had been doing was showing respect for the Chinese culture.

*8) During the Christmas season of 2017, the First Lady oversaw the decorations for the White House. She did a spectacular job with trees and holiday decorations everywhere, including having wreaths put on all the White House windows. Many of the decorations had a white theme to them, instead of the traditional red and green theme. Of course, media outlets called the outstanding displays set-up by many volunteers "creepy", "horrific" and "a nightmare before Christmas."

*9) In April 2018, Jimmy Kimmel, late night talk show host, went after Melania's accent when she was reading to children at the White House. Sean Hannity of *Fox News* bravely confronted Kimmel, showing how this *#MeToo* supporter had degraded women on his past shows. After a few days of feuding, Kimmel realized he was wrong and apologized.

Not so kind tweets against Republicans

On the morning of June 14, 2017, a Republican softball team practicing, in Alexandria, Virginia, for their annual game against the Democrats, came under fire by an Illinois madman. The shooter, a Bernie Sanders supporter, James Hodgkinson, unloaded his firearm. He sought to take out as many conservative politicians as possible. The heroics of armed security officers and Alexandria police brought down this hateful perpetrator. As Hodgkinson died at the hospital, many other injured congressmen were rushed to get treatment for their wounds. But none had been more seriously injured than House Majority Whip Steve Scalise. While many visited him, including the President and First Lady, others sent him cards, prayers, and well-wishes. Some ugly people, however, responded to the shooting with sickening tweets.

"It's a shame more Republicans weren't shot — what to heck?"

"Republicans created this hate-filled rhetoric & now bitching about one

of their own getting shot. Oh PLEASE!"

"No, I don't feel bad republicans were shot at don't @ me I don't feel bad for people that think I should die."

Thank God Scalise recovered from his critical state of being. But, unfortunately, he is still being treated for his injuries.

In November 2017, Republican Senator Rand Paul's neighbor, Rene Boucher, assaulted him. Paul had suffered multiple fractured ribs and subsequently contracted pneumonia. Then, after having recovered, in 2018, he objected to a spending budget which briefly shut down the government. But for some reason Bette Midler, the singer, tweeted,

"Where's Rand Paul's neighbor when we need him?"

Others followed with more idiotic tweets that read:

"Rand Paul's neighbor didn't hit him hard enough."

"Lots of lawmakers pissed at @RandPaul right now for holding this budget deal up. Someone needs to fly his neighbor up here."

But Scalise, Paul, and other Republicans kept getting a barrage of tweets, even through the holidays. A prime example of this happened after the Republican Party managed to pass one of the best tax cuts and reforms since Ronald Reagan was President in the 1980's. When House Majority Leader Paul Ryan released a holiday video to our country and to those in the U.S. military across the globe, wishing everyone, their family, and friends a very Merry Christmas, an irritatingly bitter Rosie O'Donnell, former actress, sent a nasty tweet reading:

"paul ryan - don't talk about Jesus after what u just did to our nation - u will go straight to hell u screwed up fake altar boy."

And, to release the intensity of her rage, she is making artwork to mock the President. It's been reported she is using this as therapy.

Pooper story

With blatant animosity in the air toward the 45th American President, *CNN* Host, Anderson Cooper made one of the most ignorant jokes of 2017. Prior to the 2016 election campaign, he seemed to be fair and balanced. But since then, Cooper and others in the mainstream media have gone off the rails with their criticisms toward the President.

The incident involved Mr. Jeffrey Lord, a politically conservative commentator and supporter of the President. When he appeared on the *CNN* show *Anderson Cooper 360*, the host, Cooper, asked Lord about some comments the President had made to a Russian ambassador regarding former FBI Director James Comey. Lord said he didn't care what the President said to the Russian ambassador because he had the right to do so. In a very cheeky tone, Cooper interrupted the President's supporter saying that Lord would defend the President even

"...if he took a dump on his desk."

Cooper would *wipe* his answer clean to Lord by apologizing for his remarks. But through 2018, there is still a stench coming from that network because it has been reported they said "shith*le" on the air about 192 times in 24 hours. Because of these crude remarks, there were reportedly over 160 public complaints to the U.S. FCC (Federal Communications Commission). There were no reports about fines yet.

"In war, you can only be killed once, but in politics many times."
– W. Churchill

Chapter 7

IDENTITY POLITICS &
POLITICAL CORRECTNESS

With unfair and unbalanced journalism, fake news, hidden stories, and calls for impeachment of the 45th President of the United States swirling around our country, tactics are used to prop them up. These tactics have been around for years. But over the last two decades or so, they have been cooked up to reach a boiling point in our nation. In the past, politicians and some activists would have used these tactics for their underhanded gains during elections. Yet, now, they are used daily.

These politically motivated methods of persuasion have been pushed and spread into the public sphere to willingly cause division in communities, schools, courtrooms, and businesses. The different sector elites of America yearn for people to question what is morally and ethically right or wrong. They greatly desire confusion so that distorted ideals are accepted as gospel by the masses. As a result, many have now begun to think and act in extreme terms because what they hear, read, or see through the mainstream media has radicalized their political ideologies into ways of life. What once was a small discussion or minor conversation about a political point of view has become an argument, or in some cases a culmination of hatred leading to unthinkable actions of violence and tragedy. Sadly, these ugly strategies are mostly being disseminated by one political party to gain supporters and voters, while at the same time creating schisms in society. These sharp political tools being utilized are known as <u>identity politics</u> and <u>political correctness</u>.

Identity politics is defined by the Merriam-Webster dictionary as "politics in which groups of people having a particular racial, religious, ethnic, social, or cultural identity tend to promote their own specific interests or concerns without regard to the interests or concerns of any larger political group". Also, this same dictionary has aptly described *political correctness* as "conforming to a belief that language and practices which could offend political sensibilities (as in matters of sex or race) should be eliminated". Both of these political ideas are being used daily to divide America and other countries around the globe.

Brazenly, both tactics are utilized by the mainstream media and Democratic Party politicians, activists, and, even celebrities (of which 90 percent support the Democratic Party). They stoke the fires of resentment against those, mostly conservatives, who support American morality, prosperity, security, laws, and the U.S. Constitution. These people seeking to ignite division and gain power have begun to spread a hardline progressive response. They are promoting the demonization of 1) capitalism in favor of socialism, 2) the right to life in favor of choosing to prematurely end life, 3) stopping conservative dialogue and debate in favor of extreme liberal disruptive discourse, and 4) a right to choose healthcare in favor of being forced to buy healthcare one can't afford. Also, the desire to help many poor people strive and work their way out of poverty, so they can be a success in society, is downplayed. Some want to keep these less privileged and prosperous on government dependency. It's all tangled in identity politics and political correctness to segregate Americans by race, color, creed, religion, and gender.

When someone calls another person a racist, sexist, xenophobe, or homophobe, they are implementing identity politics. For example, Hillary Clinton's slogan was "I'm With Her." She used sexism to influence women to vote for her. California Representative Maxine Waters will throw around the word *racist* like candy when speaking about white people, our 45th American President, and the President's supporters. It's done to gain respect from the black community, people like Louis Farrakhan, and the progressive constituents in her district.

On the other hand, political correctness is sort of an offshoot of identity politics. It means advertisements, dialogues, and expressions of belief used in society are scrutinized so the race, ethnicity, religion, gender, or sexuality of a person or group is not offended. This political correctness is currently most prevalent in college campuses (and is used on twitter). This was once a place where tolerance for another person's points of view had been upheld and appreciated, so honest debate took place. Now, if a conservative viewpoint or an opposite thought of a college student or teacher is observed, it's seen with disdain. Different individual thought and free-speech, not one-sided *group think*, is not to be shut down. Students shouldn't need to go to *safe spaces* because they can't handle an alternative perspective on life. They are taught to think this way at home or at school, and are pampered by their school's teachers, principals, and fellow students. Therefore, they shall be known as *snowflakes* until they experience the other sides of life and, hopefully, one day, become pillars of society with individual thought.

It's a very sad situation. Our children are being fed the notion that one political view is better than another, without first discovering this for themselves through lessons, discourse, debate, business, and more. Political correctness is taking over. Prime examples are not being able to dress up like a Mexican bandit on Halloween or a sports franchise being castigated for having a caricature of a Native American Indian (i.e. Washington Redskins). Political correctness has gone so far that if one uses an incorrect pronoun against a transgender person some states and countries punish the one making the errant remark through fines or even jail time. And, then you have atheists who are offended because the word "God" is on a document or plaque. It has come to an almost irreversible point in which political correctness has evolved into a form of brainwash. It convinces our children what and how to think, say, or do without having their own freedom of will.

The political correctness and identity politics being propagated by many *do not alleviate* hate, bigotry, and division in our country. They promote it. The proliferation of these tactics and ideas can be best seen in news, and through the omission of news daily in our mainstream media outlets. We are engaged in very troubling times where dominant news organizations have failed us. What people are receiving is very biased information and opinion that pits the American public and countries around the world against each other for the sake of sensationalism, ratings, and a sick sense of righteousness. Identity politics is utilized to its utmost. It's done because the elites harbor a very apparent hatred toward the 45th President of the United States, and aligned with this, a strong detestation for conservative thought.

Some blatant examples which have the stench of identity politics and political correctness on them will be shown shortly. Those wishing to engage in these amoral methods will distract, distort, and demonize. The modern Democratic Party, quite unfortunately, has much more to offer in this negative regard. Democrats play the race and gender cards often to gain votes. They race bait! But, ironically, some of them supported segregation years ago. It's why some of them are in favor of whitewashing history, including alleviating statues and monuments. They want to wipe away <u>their history</u>. So, there is much hypocrisy when examining this political party's actions and thoughts over the decades.

The new progressive liberal movement has taken things further than this by using the mottos from *Rules for Radicals* by Saul Alinsky, including an equivalent meaning to "resist, insist, persist, and enlist." Hillary Clinton, the modern Democratic Party, liberal activists, and the mainstream media are in lock-step with this un-American strain of thought. Even some of the American intelligence agencies, judges, FBI, and DOJ have become corrupted with this virally infectious thought pattern against the 45th American President. It's one of the most troubling aspects in modern-day America. If our U.S. law enforcement and intelligence agencies are not politically neutral, then how do we trust them to justly uphold our nation's laws and security?

Unfortunately, we have much division in our great country instead of unity because false ideologies and injustices are not being addressed or held at bay. Some eagerly encourage hostility and antagonize with discontent. But at the same time, they want to convince those ignorant of their political motivations that their actions and words have more meaning than others with the opposite viewpoint. It's all in the name of four of the seven deadly sins – wrath, greed, pride, and envy. These are some of the great sins that humanity has been subjected to throughout the centuries, everywhere around the globe. And, now America, a once just nation, has allowed its democracy to be hijacked by persons and organizations with less than honorable intentions.

Bill Murray, long-time actor and comedian said it best when interviewed on *CNBC* in 2018. He spoke about another comedienne,

"How can Kristen Wiig (comedienne) make everyone laugh?...She's not thinking about being political, she's thinking about what resonates and what is common to all of us, and I think that's harder and harder to do because

people are trying to win their point of view as opposed to saying 'What if I spoke to everyone?'"

Then, Murray commented about comedy writer Jim Downey.

"He's saying: 'No, I just think the way the Democrats handle things is poor where they try to pick out little pieces of a population…We represent the Hispanics, we represent the LGBT or something.' And they're not speaking to everyone all at once. And it's almost demeaning to say, 'I'm choosing you because you're a splinter group, or a certain minority group.' There's almost resentment that some how you're separated, again, by a politician."

Murray correctly points out that Democrats believe they have a hold over certain groups and individuals in America, when saying,

"'You're my people. I'm in control of you, I represent you,' instead of thinking that each citizen has a right to be respected as a citizen first, under the laws of the country."

Anyway, facts and stories shall be unveiled which are linked to the biased instigations of identity politics and political correctness. They will be shown through some examples of disdain and prejudice. Also, some history lessons will be given to set the record straight about what has been assumed and told as truth to the public for many years.

Examples of disdain and prejudice

Over many months, there has been much in the way of false remarks, distorted facts, and hateful rhetoric in the news. The mainstream media used identity politics to the fullest whenever they deemed it necessary. Their goal was to put the 45th U.S. President in harm's way of attacks, demonization, and identity politics through tragedy and divisive times.

The Hurricanes:
The mainstream liberal media portrayed the 45th American President as having no sympathy after the brunt of the category 4 hurricanes of Harvey, Irma, and Marie hit Texas, Louisiana, Florida, Puerto Rico, and

U.S. Virgin Islands. It cost many lives, homes, infrastructure, and billions of dollars. The relief efforts were miraculous; and, the camaraderie and will of the people that had been affected in the wake of those disasters were spectacular. But the media focused upon the President, and the many involved with his efforts who were aiding those that had lost much. The media's criticisms were cynical and vicious.

The President sent out tweets on August 30, 2017, such as:

"After witnessing firsthand, the horror & destruction caused by Hurricane Harvey, my heart goes out even more to the great state of Texas!"

"We are w/you today, we are w/you tomorrow, & we will be w/you EVERY SINGLE DAY AFTER, to restore, recover, & REBUILD!"

He responded quickly with implementing the rescue work and clean-up of those affected areas. The President did much to contribute. He 1) donated a million dollars of his own money to the hurricane relief efforts, 2) visited the areas in Texas, Louisiana, Florida, and Puerto Rico, 3) pitched in by distributing food & supplies, 4) spoke and comforted many adults and children (including African-Americans and Latinos), and 5) met with first responders and leaders of the localities to praise what they had done in the aftermath of those hurricanes. But the pictures shown, and stories told, by the liberal mainstream media were negatively biased; and, the public was misinformed of the truth.

Then, there were cartoons related to the Hurricanes which were sickening. For instance, after the hurricane of Harvey, *Charlie Hebdo*, a controversial French weekly magazine, depicted drowning people in Texas with Nazi flags with the headline "Dieu Existo! – God Exists." This symbolism insinuates that those affected by the hurricane in Texas deserved to be hit by the storm because they were racist, and the overwhelming majority of the state voted for the 45th U.S. President.

Again, after hurricane Harvey, *Politico*, posted a cartoon that showed a hurricane victim being rescued from a helicopter by a federal emergency responder. The person being rescued from a flooded house was depicted with a confederate flag on his shirt, and a secessionist sign next to him stating "Don't Tread on Me." The caption over the rescued man's head said "Angels! Sent by God". The rescuer says, "Er, Actually Coast Guard...Sent by the Government". The meaning of this cartoon was to chastise the victims of the flood in Texas. They were mocked for their belief in God and conservative views of limited government. The cartoon implied the Texan hurricane victims should have asked God to help them out of their situation, not the government. Of course, when many people objected, the cartoon was deleted immediately.

But the miscellaneous cases of hatred continued. A University of Tampa ex-professor, Kenneth Storey was fired for tweeting,

"I don't believe in instant karma but this kinda feels like it for Texas. Hopefully this will help them realize the GOP doesn't care about them."

Linda Sasour, formerly with the Arab American Association of New York, tweeted that people should donate to the "Harvey Hurricane Relief Fund." The link she put in the tweet, however, didn't go to a relief fund organization but to the Texas Organizing Project Education Fund. This is a nonprofit dedicated to "advancing racial and economic justice through community and electoral organizing." It's not a group that provides relief funds for food and shelter. Their *Facebook* page read,

"All donations made here will only be used to organize in the aftermath of Hurricane Harvey. Together we will organize and advocate for our devastated communities, shining a spotlight on inequalities that emerge in the restoration of lives, livelihoods, and homes, amplifying the needs of hard-hit communities, and providing legal assistance for residents wrongfully denied government support."

Many criticized her for using this tragedy as a political tool and pilfering funds from hurricane victims. But you can decide for yourself.

Lastly is the case of the well-known televangelist Joel Osteen. He was condemned by social media mobs and the mainstream media for not allowing victims of the Hurricane into his parish in Houston, Texas while the storm raged. When interviewed, he rightly defended himself.

"There were safety issues that people didn't see. They see this building sitting up on a high hill, looks like a high hill, but behind the building is where the water comes in. And so, our flood gates were keeping the water out until, I'm told, Sunday night or maybe even early Monday."

He added, there is "so much misinformation about the church this week." Then, Osteen argued to support his actions by saying,

"Had we opened the building sooner and someone got injured, or perhaps the building flooded and someone lost their lives, that would have been a very different story. Now I don't mind taking the heat for being precautious. But I don't want to take the heat for being foolish. This is not just an attack on me, it's an attack on what we stand for—for faith, for hope, for love. Jesus even said, 'When the world hates you, remember: it hated me first.'"

Obviously, this is an attack on Christian religious values, which some in American also see as connected to conservatism, or Republican thought, and, ultimately, to the 45th President of the United States.

David Duke and the President-to-be:
The mainstream media, haters in the Democratic Party, and those who support them, have continually tried to paint OUR President as a racist. They continuously contend he hasn't fully denounced the former Grand Wizard of the Klu Klux Klan, David Duke. This is utterly untrue. Here are excerpts of interviews the 45th American President had years before or just prior to being elected to the highest office in the nation.

In 2000, the President-to-be considered running for a Reform Party nomination, an independent party. But in a statement, he said,

"The Reform Party now includes a Klansman, Mr. Duke, a neo-Nazi, Mr. [Patrick] Buchanan, and a communist, Ms. [Lenora] Fulani. This is not company I wish to keep."

Then, in an interview with *NBC's* Matt Lauer, he remarked,

"Well, you've got David Duke who just joined − a bigot, a racist, a problem. I mean, this is not exactly the people you want in your party."

In 2015, when the would-be President announced his candidacy he was asked by John Heilemann of Bloomberg,

Heilemann: "How d'ya feel about David Duke quasi-endorsement?"

Trump: "I don't need his endorsement; I certainly wouldn't want his endorsement. I don't need anyone's endorsement."

Heilemann: "Would you repudiate David Duke?"

Trump: "Sure, I would do that, if it made you feel better. I don't know anything about him. Somebody told me yesterday, whoever he is, he did endorse me. Actually, I don't think it was an endorsement. He said I was absolutely the best of all of the candidates."

In 2016, at a news conference the candidate was asked,

Question: "How do you feel about the recent endorsement from David Duke?"

Trump: "I didn't even know he endorsed me. David Duke endorsed me? Okay, all right. I disavow, okay?"

Then, the Presidential candidate said on *NBC*'s *"Today Show"*,

"I'm sitting in a house in Florida, with a very bad earpiece that they gave me, and you could hardly hear what he was saying. But what I heard was 'various groups.' And I don't mind disavowing anybody and I disavowed David Duke. And I disavowed him the day before at a major news conference…. I have no problem disavowing groups, but I'd at least like to know who they are. It would be very unfair to disavow a group if the group shouldn't be disavowed. I have to know who the groups are. But I disavowed David Duke."

Finally, after disavowing the KKK and David Duke so many times, on March 1, 2016, the President-to-be addressed the press again.

"We had a news conference and they asked me the exact same question. I

said I disavow. Now, right after the program that we're talking about — and I thought it was clear, but you know, we're talking about groups, groups, groups. I do have to know the name of the group because, who knows? I mean, they have to give me the name of the group. But right after, when I reviewed it, I put out a tweet and I put out on Facebook that I totally disavow. Now everybody knew I did that, but the press refused to look at that. It was right after. And I disavowed then; I disavowed today on ABC with George Stephanopoulos, I disavowed again. I mean, how many times are you supposed to disavow? But I disavow and hopefully it's the final time I have to do it."

Charlottesville:
Before the uproar of racial tension ensued in Charlottesville, in June of 2017 Bill Maher, the late-night *HBO* host, interviewed Republican Bob Sasse from Nebraska. Sasse had been saying that some people mature faster than others and some people still feel as if they need to be young again by dressing up at Halloween. Maher stupidly replied.

Maher: "I've got to get to Nebraska more."

Sasse: "You're welcome. We'd love to have you work in the fields with us."

*Maher: "Work in the fields? Senator, I'm a house n*gger. No, it's a joke."*

Expectedly, many were not amused. Maher had to apologize. But why wasn't he temporarily suspended for this? Double-standards?

Then, when the Charlottesville incident occurred in Virginia it set off a firestorm of negative commentary and media coverage which basically echoed the same message repeatedly. The unfounded outcry was the President was a "racist" and "white supremacist." But, actually, the governor, mayor, and local officials in August of 2017 should have been blamed for this ugly incident which occurred in Charlottesville. These government officials had known white supremacists would be gathering as a *Unite to Right* protest to defend the taking down of Robert E. Lee's statue (a confederate general during the civil war) in Emancipation Park. These protestors arrived on a Friday night;

however, the high-ranking government notables <u>also were informed</u> that busloads of fiery antagonist groups like *Black Lives Matter*, *Antifa*, and others were being brought to the site to aggressively confront the white supremacist protestors on Saturday. These combative anti-protest groups far outnumbered the white supremacists present.

But, on Saturday afternoon, more protestors from "both sides" showed up. Those government officials were well-aware of the disaster waiting to happen and should have anticipated the events.

After the protestors and anti-protestors engaged in free speech, it got out of hand. Riots and violence erupted. It resulted in a woman being run down, and killed, by a Nazi sympathizer who was driving a car. It was an abhorrent act. And, yet, the police had been advised <u>not</u> to enforce the law or keep these groups separated from each other. The <u>state and local government inaction</u> led to the tragedy and injuries then.

Unfortunately, the mainstream media was all too complicit when calling out the actions of right-wing groups, while at the same time not condemning the acts of the left-wing groups who were just as wrong and violent. Then, the media backed up Governor Terry McAuliffe, a Democrat, who had made a false statement that there were guns in the city planted by militia. He stated, the reason local police didn't act to break up riots was he didn't want them to get hurt. Huh? It' their job!

"They had battering rams and, you know, we had picked up different weapons they had stashed around the city. This was a powder keg. This was a very volatile situation. And I'll once again say, I am very proud of our team on the ground. Nobody hurt except for those people hit by the car and you couldn't stop that."

The local police disputed the statement that their guns stashed in the city. If the governor was so concerned about guns being used why didn't he bring in the National Guard? It's because he wanted to make guns an issue, deflect from his incompetence, and allow violence to occur so the 45th U.S. President could ultimately be blamed for the Charlottesville incident. Of course, the mainstream media and their minions ignored the governmental blunders. They shifted their focus squarely on the President, as he tweeted about the horrible incident.

The first message of the President via twitter stated,

"We ALL must be united to condemn all that hate stands for. There is no place for this kind of violence in America. Let's come together as one!"

The second message of the President via twitter then said,

"We must remember this truth: NO matter our color, creed, religion or political. We are ALL AMERICANS FIRST."

This wasn't good enough for the mainstream media and all the critics of this President. So, the President sent out a third tweet.

"We condemn in the strongest terms the egregious displays of hatred, bigotry, and violence on many sides."

The third statement still didn't appease the critics and haters because they wanted him to name names and groups, and immediately denounce white supremacists and others. But it was apparent left-wing radicals were undeniably present and instigated the violence as well.

So, the President sent out a fourth message via twitter, saying,

"Racism is evil and those who cause violence in its name are criminals and thugs including the KKK, Neo-Nazis, and White Supremacists and other hate groups that are repugnant to everything we hold dear as Americans."

Still the mainstream liberal media and others wouldn't let up. They were bent on making him into a racist, bigot, and white supremacist. Therefore, only a few days later, after the President and some in his administration had an infrastructure meeting, the media pursued him until he was cornered in the Trump Tower lobby. Then, they asked him about the Charlottesville incident again. He responded with,

"You had a group on one side that was bad and you had a group on the other side that was also very violent, and nobody wants to say it, but I'll say it right now. You had a group on the other side that came charging in without a permit and they were very, very violent....I think there's blame on both sides. And I don't have any doubt about it."

A reporter questioned him about what he meant by "both sides?" The President responded by saying the media should refer to his third statement about Charlottesville. He added that the alt-left and *Antifa* were to blame as well. Of course, the press didn't like it when they were challenged and asked, "why did you wait so long to respond?" They are fools because he sent the first two messages about the incident immediately. So, again the President answered,

"I didn't wait long, I didn't wait long. I wanted to make sure, unlike most politicians, that what I said was correct. Not make a quick statement. The statement I made on Saturday, the first statement, was a fine statement. But you don't make statements that direct unless you know the facts. It takes a while to get the facts. You still don't know the facts. And it's a very, very, important process to me, and it's a very important statement. So, I don't want to go quickly and just make a statement for the sake of making a political statement. I want to know the facts."

The President then took out the statements he had made prior to this one and re-stated them. Then, he continued,

"Here's the thing. When I make a statement, I like to be correct. I want the facts. This event just happened. In fact, a lot of the event didn't even happen yet as we were speaking. This event just happened. Before I make the statement, I need the facts. So, I don't want to rush into a statement. So, making a statement when I made it was excellent. In fact, the young woman, who I hear is a fantastic woman, her mother wrote me and said ... the nicest things. And I very much appreciated that. I hear she was a fine, really actually incredible young woman. But her mother on Twitter thanked me for what I said. And honestly, if the press were not fake, and it was honest, the press would have said what I said was very nice. But unlike you, and unlike the media, before I make a statement, I like to know the facts."

Then, he made some remarks about the economy. But the reporters still came after him about Charlottesville. He stated again,

"I had to see the facts, unlike a lot of reporters. I didn't know David Duke was there. I wanted to see the facts. And the facts as they started to come out were very well stated. In fact, everybody said his 'statement was beautiful,' if he would've made it sooner that would've been good, I couldn't have made it

sooner because I didn't know all the facts. Frankly, people still don't know all of the facts. It was very important … to me to get the facts out and correctly. Because if I would've made a fast statement, and the first statement was made without knowing much other than what we were seeing. The second statement was made after with knowledge, with great knowledge. There are still things that people don't know. I want to make a statement with knowledge; I wanted to know the facts."

Then, the President was asked if a man driving a car into a crowd was an act of terrorism. He replied,

"Well I think the driver of the car is a disgrace to himself, his family and this country. And that is, you can call it terrorism, you can call it murder, you can call it whatever you want. I would just call it as the fastest one to come up with a good verdict. Because there is a question, is it murder? Is it terrorism? And then you get into legal semantics. The driver of the car is a murderer and what he did was a horrible, horrible, inexcusable thing."

Then the President was asked about then-senior adviser Steve Bannon, and the alt-right movement. He responded,

"When you say the alt-right, define alt-right to me, you define it. Go ahead, no define it for me, come on, let's go. What about the alt-left that came charging at the, as you say, alt-right. Do they have any semblance of guilt? Let me ask you this, what about the fact they came charging with clubs in their hands, swinging clubs, do they have any problem? I think they do. As far as I'm concerned, that was a horrible, horrible day…You had a group on one side that was bad and you had a group on the other side that was also very violent, and nobody wants to say it, but I'll say it right now. You had a group on the other side that came charging in without a permit and they were very, very violent."

Then, President spoke about Neo-Nazis and the protesters,

"Those people, all of those people, excuse me, I've condemned neo-Nazis, I've condemned many different groups, but not all of those people were neo-Nazis, believe me. Not all of those people were white supremacists by any stretch. Those people were also there because they wanted to protest the taking down of a statue, Robert E. Lee. And you take a look at some of the groups, and you see, and you'd know it if you were honest reporters, which

in many cases you're not, but many of those people were there to protest the taking down of the statue of Robert E. Lee. This week it's Robert E. Lee, I noticed that Stonewall Jackson is coming down, I wonder is it George Washington next week? And is it Thomas Jefferson the week after? You really do have to ask yourself where does it stop? They were there to protest, excuse me, you take a look the night before, they were there to protest the taking down of the statue of Robert E. Lee."

Again, he was asked if the white supremacists and the counter-protesters were equal, and the President replied,

"I'm not putting anybody on a moral plane, what I'm saying is this, you had a group on one-side and you had a group on the other and they came at each other with clubs and it was vicious and it was horrible and it was a horrible thing to watch. But there is another side. There was a group on this side, you can call them the left...you just called them the left...that came violently attacking the other group. So, you can say what you want, but that's the way it is...I think there's blame on both sides. And I don't have any doubt about it. And you don't have any doubt about it. And, if you reported it accurately, you would say it."

The President compared removing the Robert E. Lee statue with taking down other statues of significant importance to the country.

"George Washington was a slave owner, so will George Washington now lose his status? Are we going to take down statues of George Washington? How about Thomas Jefferson? Do you like him? OK good, are we going to take the down the statue...because he was a major slave owner? Are we going to take down his statue? You're changing history, you're changing culture, and you had people, and I'm not talking about the neo-Nazis and the white supremacists, because they should be condemned totally, but you had many people in that group other than neo-Nazis and white nationalists. And the press has treated them absolutely unfairly...In the other group, also you had some fine people, but you also had troublemakers. And you see them come with the black outfits, and with the helmets and with the baseball bats, you had a lot of bad people in the other group."

He said the *Unite the Right* group was protesting quietly while carrying Tiki torches on Friday night before the craziness happened on Saturday. The President continued with,

"I'm sure in that group there were some bad ones. The following day it looked like they had some rough, bad people. Neo-Nazis, white nationalists whatever you want to call them. But you had a lot of people in that group who were there to innocently protest, and very legally protest, because I don't know if you know, they had a permit, the other group didn't have a permit, so I only tell you this. There are two sides to a story. I thought what took place was a horrible moment for our country. A horrible moment! But there are two sides."

The President pulled out a letter he had received, and said,

"The mother's statement I thought was a beautiful statement...It was something I really appreciated. I thought it was terrific. And under the kind of stress that she's under and the heartache she's under, I thought that putting out that statement to me was really something I won't forget...It read, "Thank you, President Trump, for those words of comfort and for denouncing those who promote violence and hatred. My condolences, also, to the grieving families of the two state troopers and quick recovery for those injured."

Finally, the biased media ended by asking how he would combat racism. The President ended with,

"Well I really think jobs can help. I think if we continue to create jobs, over a million, substantially more than a million," Trump said. "I think that if we continue to create jobs at levels that I'm creating jobs. I think that's going to have a tremendous impact, positive impact, on race relations. ... People are going to be working, they're going to be making a lot of money, much more money than they ever thought possible. And the other thing, very important, I believe wages will start going up. ... I think that will have a tremendously positive impact on race relations."

If one is a reasonable and rational person, without bias, it can easily be surmised that the President had been quick in his response to the Charlottesville incident after being fully informed and having examined the evidence available to him. Initially, and rightfully, he didn't want to answer the ignorant race-baiting reporters who already had a hateful predisposition about the incident. And, although the President was confronted in Trump Tower by a relentlessly prejudiced press, he answered their rapid-fire questions without filter. Moreover, he was

100% correct that 1) *both sides* were at fault, 2) this would lead to other statues being torn down, 3) some founding fathers were slave owners, and 4) economic stability will have a great impact on race relations.

Sadly, the mainstream media and many others supporting their partisan perspectives, just hear what they want to hear. Their minds are made up, and there is no fair analysis or contemplation - only negative reaction. It's because some envision one unconstitutional and unjust goal - to impeach the 45th President of the United States. No matter how wrong they are, false allegations and disinformation are spread to achieve their amoral objective. The Charlottesville incident epitomizes the nonsense they have been preaching. It's *sick* identity politics.

Then, after the Charlottesville incident there was continued backlash. In August 2017, Chanelle Helm a *Black Lives Matter* leader, requested white people to follow these ridiculous and racist rules:

1. White people, if you don't have any descendants, will your property to a black or brown family. Preferably one that lives in generational poverty.

2. White people, if you're inheriting property you intend to sell upon acceptance, give it to a black or brown family. You're bound to make that money in some other white privileged way.

3. If you are a developer or realty owner of multi-family housing, build a sustainable complex in a black or brown blighted neighborhood and let black and brown people live in it for free.

4. White people, if you can afford to downsize, give up the home you own to a black or brown family. Preferably a family from generational poverty.

5. White people, if any of the people you intend to leave your property to are racists assholes, change the will, and will your property to a black or brown family. Preferably a family from generational poverty.

6. White people, re-budget your monthly so you can donate to black funds for land purchasing.

7. White people, especially white women (because this is yaw specialty — Nosey Jenny and Meddling Kathy), get a racist fired. Yaw know what the fuck they be saying. You are complicit when you ignore them. Get your boss fired cause they racist too.

8. Backing up No. 7, this should be easy but all those sheet-less Klan, Nazi's and Other lil' dick-white men will all be returning to work. Get they ass fired. Call the police even: they look suspicious.

9. OK, backing up No. 8, if any white person at your work, or as you enter in spaces and you overhear a white person praising the actions from yesterday, first, get a pic. Get their name and more info. Hell, find out where they work — Get Them Fired. But, certainly, address them, and, if you need to, you got hands: use them.

10. Commit to two things: Fighting white supremacy where and how you can (this doesn't mean taking up knitting, unless you're making scarves for black and brown kids in need), and funding black and brown people and their work.

In 2017, *ESPN* moved Robert Lee, a commentator for Virginia football games, to Pittsburgh. The network feared people would be offended because his name was close to Robert E. Lee – the Confederate General. But that was ludicrous because he was an <u>Asian-American</u>.

A few weeks later, also on *ESPN*, anchor Jemele Hill ridiculed the President who called out NFL player protests. She tweeted,

"Donald Trump is a white supremacist who has largely surrounded himself w/ other white supremacists."

Hill was not removed from her position because she was supposedly just responding to the President being against *NFL* players not kneeling for the national anthem. Personally, being a military veteran, I find this stance by *NFL* players, and others, to be non-productive. Nobody in a normal workplace environment would be allowed to make political protests on the job. Those who do so disrespect our country, flag, and the military men and women willing to protect America. So, why are the *NFL* players, who make millions, permitted to do this on their jobs?

When NFL quarterback Colin Kaepernick (San Francisco 49ers) took a knee during the national anthem of a game in 2016, he should have been reprimanded or fined. This started the uproar of political protests against police brutality. So, why aren't players protesting outside police departments? It's because they then will not be protected by police. Yet, now, this foolish stance of some in the NFL, and *ESPN,* is being countered through dismal ratings, viewership, and attendance.

Regardless, Jemele Hill was removed from *ESPN* Sportscenter in 2018 to bury her opinions at *The Undefeated.* But it took her a long time to be relocated. That was not the case with Curt Schilling in 2015. He was removed quickly from *ESPN* broadcasts because he made reference to Muslim extremists being equal to Nazis. Was this similar to what Jemele Hill did? Is there another double standard here? It's obvious.

Then, Democrat Nancy Pelosi remarked that Confederate Statues should be removed from the halls of Congress. But her father, the late Thomas D'Alesandro Jr., had spoken at a dedication ceremony, years ago, honoring the monuments of Confederate generals Robert E. Lee and Thomas "Stonewall" Jackson. Isn't that being hypocritical?

Lastly, Joy Reid on *MSNBC,* who has made opinionated remarks and had to apologize for anti-gay comments, made a very inaccurate comment, like many do on that cable network, after Charlottesville.

"I've said that this is probably the worst time to be a journalist, and the worst time to be a human."

Huh? The worst time to be a human? As co-host Greg Gutfeld on *The Five* (*Fox News*) stated, there are other times in history worse than now. These include "the Dark Ages, the Black Death, the Mongols, Nazi concentration camps, the atrocities of the Aztecs, famine in the Ukraine, the Khmer Rouge". But I'll add the Roman Empire's slaughter of Christians, Hundred Years' War, Salem Witch Trials, Spanish Civil War, Spanish Inquisition, Cholera Pandemic, WWI, WWII, Vietnam War, Korean War, Bangladesh famine, Great Depression, U.S. Civil War, and times of slavery. So, this is one of the <u>best times to be alive</u>!

History lessons

There has been much hypocrisy and misinformation propagated to Americans by the mainstream media regarding U.S. history, world history, slavery, Democrats, Republicans, and the 45th U.S. President. Sadly, identity politics is the current answer to winning elections for the progressive movement of the Democratic Party. So, they aim to bury much of the past in the shadows and use racist baiting rhetoric to incite anger. This is evident when they use slavery, <u>an abhorrent concept</u>, as an issue. But, fortunately, some have become wise to their very divisive tactics. They comprehend that some of our African-American brothers and sisters are being duped, so that they will vote for Democrats.

In 2018, rapper Kanye West and conservative Candace Owens bravely spoke out to agree that blacks should not be placed in a box and forced to vote for Democrats. West believes in "independent thought" and tweeted out the Republican President is his "brother". Both West, Owens, and other African-Americans understand that the Democrats suppress real data about history and give false narratives because they seek to control the minority vote. And, the biased media assists liberal agendas by lobbying for government programs instead of pushing the notion of striving for the 'American Dream'. But it's just a matter of time before others jump out of the box Democrats believe they should be in.

Regardless, a few short history lessons will be revealed that will refute the alternate realities Democrats are pitching. Some think being liberal means *they have the freedom to change facts*. But real history can be researched in libraries and on the Internet. Examples can be seen at PragerU.com (*The Inconvenient Truth about the Democratic Party*).

Lesson 1 – Records show in 1643, Anthony Pearse, blackamore, a black man, lived in the first colony of Plymouth. He was <u>not</u> a slave, voted, and had land.

Lesson 2 – In the 17th century, African *and* European <u>*indentured servants*</u> arrived and labored in Virginia. Anthony Johnson arrived from Africa (Angola) as an indentured servant but worked his way to freedom. He <u>became one of the first land owners and</u> had five indentured servants. Then, through a civil suit Johnson became master to John Casor - *the first colonial African slave.*

Lesson 3 – In 1830, the census concluded that about 12,700 black slaves were <u>owned</u> by 3,775 free black people - as reported by historian R. Halliburton Jr. Many black slaves owned businesses and had jobs. By 1860, William Ellison, a black plantation owner, became <u>the largest slave owner</u> in North Carolina.

Lesson 4 – In the 19th century, five Native American Indian tribes owned thousands of black slaves (Chickasaw, Choctaw, Cherokee, Creek, & Seminole).

Lesson 5 – Slavery has been going on since the beginning of civilization in Mesopotamia, Assyria, Babylonia, Ancient Egypt, Ancient China, Ancient Greece, the Roman Empire, as well as in South and Central America. But the majority of these slaves, many acquired from war conquests, were <u>not</u> black.

Lesson 6 – In America, slaves were involved with building the U.S. Capitol, the White House, much of New York City and Wall Street, the University of North Carolina-Chapel Hill, Washington & Lee University, the University of Virginia, an old masonry fort Castillo de San Marcos, railroads, and more. So, like some of our statues, are we going to tear down these structures to appease the few who wish to remove and cover-up history?

Lesson 7 – Many Democratic Presidents owned slaves: Andrew Jackson, Andrew Johnson, James K. Polk, James Madison, Martin Van Buren, etc.

Lesson 8 – Lincoln was a Republican against slavery and freed the slaves with the Emancipation Proclamation.

Lesson 9 – Democratic President Woodrow Wilson (1913 – 1921) praised the Klu Klux Klan and had replaced black Republicans with white Democrats.

Lesson 10 – David Duke and KKK were Democratic Party supporters originally.

Lesson 11 - The Nazis (National Socialist German Workers' Party) were a left-wing ideology. Adolf Hitler said, "We are socialists, we are enemies of today's capitalistic economic system. We will finish properly what Karl Marx began."

Lesson 12 – In 1956, after the ruling of the Supreme Court (*Brown v. Board of Education*) the <u>southern Democrats</u> countered it with the *Southern Manifesto*. This defied the justice system and allowed racial segregation to continue.

Lesson 13 – In 1964, most Democrats voted against the *Civil Rights Act*. The NO Votes were 112 Democrat and 41 Republicans. In 1965, most Democrats voted against the *Voting Rights Act* – prohibiting racial discrimination. There were 78 Democrats and only 25 Republicans who voted NO.

Lesson 14 – In 2007, during an interview with the *New York Observer*, then-Senator Joe Biden made a quasi-racial remark about then-Senator Barrack Obama's potential to gain the Democratic Presidential bid. He said,

"I mean you've got the first sort of mainstream African-American who is articulate and bright and clean and nice-looking guy."

Lesson 15 - A Former Democratic politician, Andrew Stein of New York, knows first-hand the President is not a racist. Three small examples are 1) when the businessman, and President-to-be originally moved to Mar-a-Lago he thought it was crazy that blacks were not let into fancy clubs. He wanted to change that, and sued Palm Beach; 2) in 1980, during the Haiti Crisis he gave donations and a plane to Haiti; 3) in New York, he gave donations to Reverend Flake, whose church was in trouble and consisted mostly of black parishioners.

Lesson 16 – Need more proof the President isn't a racist? He campaigned in black neighborhoods in Detroit and Flint, Michigan, met with Historical Black College and Universities, had meetings with black business leaders, attended a black mass during the 2016 election, and played with black children after Hurricane Harvey in Houston. He also famously said during the 2016 election, "What the hell do you have to lose?" by voting for him when speaking about African-Americans. The President gained 8% of the black vote - 1/3 better than Mitt Romney. Also, he received 28% of the Hispanic vote. Cuban Americans love him. African-American and Latino unemployment reached an all-time historic low in 2018. He kissed a gay African-American when presenting her with a commendation medal for saving Republican Steve Scalise's life. He has met with Hispanic business leaders. So, would a bigot do all this and more?

Lesson 17 – How can the President be a bigot? This is a list of significant non-whites who work for or support the 45th President of the United States.

- Raj Shah (Principal Deputy Press Secretary; Deputy Assistant to President)
- Ben Carson (Housing and Development Secretary - HUD)

- Alexander Acosta (Secretary of Labor)
- Dr. Alveda King (Niece of Martin Luther King, author, activist, and former congresswomen)
- Herman Cain (Author, business executive, radio host, columnist, and Tea Party activist)
- David A. Clarke Jr. (Former Milwaukee Sheriff, spokesman for American First Action)
- Allen Bernard West (Former Army Lt. Colonel, former member of House of Representatives)
- Larry Elder (Radio show host, attorney, author)
- Reverend Darrell Scott (American pastor and part of President's transition team)
- Mike Tyson (Boxer legend and actor)
- Kanye West (Singer, fashion designer, entrepreneur)
- Candace Owens (writer, producer, and conservative commentator)
- Don King (Boxing legend promoter)
- Dennis Rodman (Former NBA basketball legend)
- Niger Innis (Congress of Racial Equality spokesman)
- Dr. Walid Phares (Lebanese-born American and conservative pundit)
- Raheem Jamaludin Kassam (British political activist/editor of Breitbart News London)
- Michelle Malkin (Conservative commentator, talk show host)
- Deroy Murock (Political commentator and National Review writer)
- Reverend D.L. Bryant (Former radio and talk show host)
- Deneen Borelli (Conservative author, columnist, TV personality)
- Dennis Onyango (National Super Alliance (Nasa) leader Raila Odinga's spokesman)
- Patrice Lee Onwuka (Senior analyst of Independent Women's Forum)
- Diamond and Silk (Internet, radio, and television personalities)
- James T. Harris (Internet, radio, and television personality)
- Harris Faulker (Television newscaster and host)
- Charles Payne (Television host)
- Stacey Dash (Television host)
- Azelia Banks (Singer and actress)
- Joy Villa (Singer)
- Titi Ortiz (Former mixed martial artist and champion)
- Terrell Owens (Football legend and sportscaster)

- Hershel Walker (Former AFL football star, sprinter, bobsledder
- Shawne Merriman (Former NFL star)
- Tila Tequila (Television and social media personality)
- Latinos for Trump (Facebook)
- Blacks for Trump (Website)
- Asians for Trump (Facebook)
- Korean Americans for Trump (Website)

Lesson 18 – The President is <u>not</u> sexist. Here's a list of women in top administration positions for the 45th President of the United States.

- Kirstjen Nielsen (Secretary of Homeland Security)
- Nikki Haley (Ambassador to the United Nations)
- Sarah Sanders (White House Press Secretary)
- Mercedes Schlapp (White House Director of Strategic Communications)
- Gina Haspel (CIA Director)
- Elaine Chao (Secretary of Transportation)
- Betsy Devos (Secretary of Education)
- Linda McMahon (Administrator of Small Business Administration)
- Kellyanne Conway (Counselor to the President)
- Ivanka Trump (Advisor to the President)
- Hope Hicks (Former White House Communications Director)

Lesson 19 – The President is <u>not</u> a homophobe. In 2016, on the campaign trail, Matt Lauer on *NBC's Today* show asked him "So, if Caitlyn Jenner were to walk into Trump Tower and want to use the bathroom, you would be fine with her using any bathroom she chooses?" The then-Presidential candidate said, "That is correct." He also stated transgender people should use "whatever bathroom they feel appropriate" in.

Lesson 20 – There are many well-known entertainers and sports icons who registered Republican during their lifetime. They have since died. So, we don't know whether or not many of these celebrities were really independent voters.

These are the deceased registered Republicans:
Bob Hope (actor, movie/TV star), John Wayne (actor), Cary Grant (actor), Charlton Heston (actor, author), Frank Sinatra (singer, actor), Jimmy

Stewart (actor), Elvis Presley (singer/musician), Cecil B. DeMille (film director and producer), Merv Griffin (TV host, actor), Hank Williams Sr. (singer/ musician), Dennis Hopper (actor), Sonny Bono (singer), Johnny Ramone (guitarist), Bob Feller (baseball star), Jack Kemp (football star), and many more...

Lesson 21 - Lastly, there is a difference between Republicans and Democrats. But it may not be what one thinks. Each political party's characterizations have been misconstrued for many years. Here is more clarity.

The Republican Party

The Republican's color is red. Initially, the symbolic elephant meant that it scared the other animals. But this means strong and dignified. The party was created in 1854 by anti-slavery activists and modernizers. They are called the Grand Old Party (GOP), and is the second oldest party in the U.S., after the Democratic Party. It gained political power for the first time in 1860, when Abraham Lincoln won the presidency. Members are considered conservatives, which believe in continuing America's traditional values, including upholding the constitution, laws, giving privilege and authority back to the citizens and the states. They believe in free enterprise, wanting the people to establish their own ways to improve their lives with limited government interference. Republicans like to reduce taxes and social programs like welfare and healthcare so all people of every race, color, and creed can make their own choices to thrive. Usually, they adhere to having a strong military and defense for the country. Most are for modifying immigration laws, desire a secure border for our country from criminals and terrorists, defend the first amendment (i.e. freedom of speech, religion, etc.), allow for second amendment rights (i.e. guns laws), and have a pro-life ideology. Republicans are <u>not</u> the party of just white people and the rich. This is a huge misnomer propagated as fact to the public for years.

The Democratic Party

Founded in 1792, the Democrat's color is blue. The Democratic Party first gained true political power in the 1830's when Andrew Jackson became the seventh President of the United States. Their symbol is a jackass because Jackson's opponents called him that. But members claim it means smart and brave. The founders include James Madison, Thomas Jefferson, and others who were against the Federalist Party. Democrats are in favor of having control over a large federal government. Therefore, they desire the power to limit some rights of citizens. They believe the government should take care of its people; and, they, as elected officials, know best what the people should need or want. They fervently urge supporters to enroll in governmental social programs, such as welfare and healthcare. They think raising taxes is good because it gives the government funds for these social programs. But Democrats believe the rich were always rich, and they should be taxed to give back to the poor. They don't consider that most individuals who become successful started at the bottom in society. Democrats *don't believe* in spending for a strong military, 2nd Amendment (gun laws) rights, strongly securing our borders, reforming immigration (so they can obtain lawless votes), pro-life ideologies, job programs instead of gov't. subsidies, or a *choice* to buy better healthcare and education. Moreover, they are <u>not</u> the only political party desiring to aid the poor and minorities. However, very sadly, Democrats do utilize the weapons of identity politics and political correctness whenever necessary.

In this world we live in, the people must not give in to rhetoric and untruth. We must draw conclusions from facts. One can't color a picture without first sketching the muse. Therefore, the present should be created from recognizing the characteristics and realities of our past, regardless of the ugly undertones, dark images, or mistakes made. We must take our memories, knowledge, and wisdom to lend a coat of credibility to the portraits we paint in our lives. When we do this, while mixing the shades of black, white, red, brown, yellow, and blue, then often vibrant beauty can be depicted. So, don't separate the colors on your canvas because those seeking self-aggrandizements insist you do so. Artists like Picasso rejected being *told how* to imagine. We must too!

Chapter 8

ACHIEVEMENTS
BY THE PRESIDENT

The wealthy septuagenarian from Queens, New York had never held a government office before being elected as the 45th U.S. President. But as a much younger man, for many years, he had hobnobbed with many politicians as a citizen - including his opponent in the 2016 Presidential election. Obviously, the engagements he did partake in with political elites was to help him advance his business projects or to aid them gain funds from him for upcoming elections. Back then, he had no intention of becoming embedded in the world of politics. It was because there were too many ambitious endeavors he wanted to pursue.

Before being elected into the Oval Office, the would-be-President's goals were focused upon having a successful business. He wanted to create a world-renowned corporation. By midlife, he fulfilled his dream. He became a marketing genius and a billionaire through his many business ventures and real-estate projects. He gave back to the community through charitable donations - to organizations such as: Citymeals-on-Wheels, National Network to End Domestic Violence, Joe Torre Safe at Home Foundation, NYC Police Foundation, Marine Corps-Law Enforcement Foundation, Navy Seal Foundation, Veterans Airlift Command, American Hero Adventures, American Cancer Society, American Diabetes Association, Alliance for Lupus Research, Autism Speaks, Crohn's & Colitis Foundation of America, The Institute for Implant Analysis at the Hospital for Special Surgery, Gay Men's Health Crisis, United Way, Ronald McDonalds House of New York, Billy Graham Evangelistic Association, and so on. But, unquestionably, the President will tell anyone who asks that his crowning achievement was and continues to be the love and life he has established with his family. But, now, as President, he has a new extended family – the American people. Millions feel the passion he exudes for them. And, with their help he will keep his promise to "Make America Great Again."

Summary of President's family and business history

In 1885, the President's paternal grandfather, Fredrich, emigrated to the U.S. from Germany. Within seven years he became an American citizen. After making a large fortune from restaurants and boarding houses in the U.S. and Canada, his grandfather married Elisabeth Christ in 1902. They moved to New York in 1905; and, the President's father, Fred, was born in the Bronx. After his grandfather died in 1918, Fred helped his mother with the real estate business. Together they sold and built many houses and apartments in Queens and Brooklyn.

In 1936, the President's father Fred married Mary Anne, who had come to America from Scotland. They were wed in Jamaica, N.Y. (Queens). Then, the future U.S. President was born on June 14, 1946. He lived with three elder siblings - Fred Jr., Elizabeth, and Mary Anne – as well as one younger brother Robert. But in 1981 his oldest brother Fred Jr. died of alcoholism. This had a profound impact on the President-to-be, as he would never smoke, take drugs, or drink liquor.

This young boy attended elementary school (kindergarten to seventh grade) at Kew-Forest School. He was then enrolled in the New York Military Academy at 13 years old. After his training, high school, and reaching the age of 18, he went to Fordham University in N.Y. But he transferred to the Wharton School in Pennsylvania because it offered real-estate courses. In 1968, graduating with a Bachelor of Science degree in economics, he jumped into the family real-estate business.

In Brooklyn, after receiving a million-dollar loan from his dad, which he would have to repay with interest, he thought it best to start moving the business into Manhattan. While his business and career were on the rise, he began acquiring and building skyscrapers, hotels, casinos, and golf courses outside of New York City. He ventured into branding and licensing his name on real estate and luxury products. By the late 1980's, he became a billionaire and continued to expand his career. He wrote several books, including *Art of the Deal*, owned the Miss Universe and Miss USA beauty pageants (1996 – 2015), and had a hit reality television show called *The Apprentice* (2003 – 2015).

In 1977, he married his first wife Czech model Ivana Zelnickova. Subsequently, they had three children: Donald Jr. in 1977, Ivanka in

1984, and Eric in 1981. By 1992 the couple divorced. But the business tycoon would marry his second wife, actress Marla Maples in 1993 after she had given birth to their daughter Tiffany. The couple grew apart, however; and, in 1999, they too divorced. Tiffany would grow up with her mother in California. In 2005, he married his third wife, a Slovenian model, Melania Knauss at Palm Beach in Florida, with a wedding reception at Mar-a-Lago estate. They had a son, Barron, in 2006, the same year Melania became an American citizen.

When the billionaire wed his third wife, his children had been ready for families of their own. Three marriages occurred - Donald Jr. & Vanessa (2005); Ivanka & Jared Kushner (2009); Eric & Lara (2014). As of 2018, the President has five children and nine grandchildren.

In 2016, the man from Queens, N.Y. became the 45th U.S. President. Although he had to give up his company to his sons, Eric and Donald Jr., his net worth was still $3.1 billion. But knowing he doesn't need the money, and his future objective is to make a better and safer America, each year he will donate his Presidential salary - except for $1.

Fighting criticism to "Make America Great Again"

It was apparent from the very beginning that the mainstream media, activists, establishment politicians, and deep state officials within the government opposed the election of this 45th American President.

On inauguration day, January 20, 2017, his message was extremely hopeful and inspirational. Some of the excerpts from his speech stated,

"...Today's ceremony, however, has a very special meaning. Because today we are not merely transferring power from one administration to another, or from one party to another – but we are transferring power from Washington, DC, and giving it back to you, the American people.

For too long, a small group in our nation's capital has reaped the rewards of government while the people have borne the cost. Washington flourished – but the people did not share in its wealth.

Politicians prospered - but the jobs left, and the factories closed. The establishment protected itself, but not the citizens of our country. Their

victories have not been your victories; their triumphs have not been your triumphs; and while they celebrated in our nation's capital, there was little to celebrate for struggling families all across the land. That all changes-starting right here, and right now, because this moment is your moment: it belongs to you..."

"...The forgotten men and women of our country will be forgotten no longer. Everyone is listening to you now..."

"...It is time to remember that old wisdom our soldiers will never forget: that whether we are black or brown or white, we all bleed the same red blood of patriots, we all enjoy the same glorious freedoms, and we all salute the same great American flag..."

"...And whether a child is born in the urban sprawl of Detroit or the windswept plains of Nebraska, they look up at the same night sky, they fill their heart with the same dreams, and they are infused with the same breath of life by the same almighty Creator..."

These excerpts from his inaugural address were uplifting to many. But to the mainstream media and pundits around the nation, it was "dark". Yet his speech was in the *ears of the beholders*; and, those who gave negative feedback heard but never listened to him.

His inauguration speech was positive and gave a promise for 'real hope and change' in America. He adapted the phrase "peace through strength", spoken by many, including President Reagan, to signify his central theme of America's foreign policy. It was a good start.

But the President's detractors only saw him as someone who wanted to start a war, as a totalitarian or akin to "Hitler", and as a racist. None of these depictions are accurate. They see what they want to see. These resentful people haven't stopped bashing him for his personality, way of achieving goals for America, or the manner in which he speaks. He doesn't act like a stuffy politician but more like an average citizen. The elites detest that the President doesn't subjugate to them. Those in Washington, D.C., New York, and California now realize their gig is up. Finally, there is a leader in the White House who desires to curb their unethical shenanigans and shady dealings. And, so they are very scared.

Therefore, his critics are embedded in their trenches to win the battles against this President. And, yet, although they attack from every direction, he may win the overall war. He is fighting back and rallying the public through social media. Through sheer will, character, and words, his strategy has spawned success, even with small misfires.

Regardless, being a brilliant businessman, he knows how to market, negotiate, and sidetrack those who oppose him. He befuddles them, and they are made to look like idiots chasing their own tails, as they continually chant "the sky is falling". For example, as the first semblances of the tax plan was being unveiled by Republicans, the Democratic leader Nancy Pelosi responded with hyperbole, such as,

"The debate on health care is life and death. "

"This is Armageddon."

When the Obamacare mandate, which had forced the American people to buy expensive health insurance and pay high premiums, was overturned through the new tax bill, Democrats were so upset that Nancy Pelosi exclaimed,

"In terms of the bonus that corporate America received versus the CRUMBS that they are giving to workers to kind of put the schmooze on — it's so pathetic."

Ironically Pelosi once praised a measly $40 Obama-era tax cut for workers. Employees of hundreds of companies have been getting bonuses, wage raises, and contributions to retirement funds – some up to $2,000. Since she is a multi-millionaire, the money an average family and individuals are receiving because of the tax plan may seem like *crumbs* to her. But to hard working Americans they are tasty *morsels*!

It's the same old tired cliché rhetoric Democrats, and the biased mainstream media have been stating to the American people about Republican politicians for years. They always insist that Republicans only hurt the people because they aren't in favor of big government programs. So, they use outlandish examples to prove their point.

For instance, during the 2012 Presidential election, the Democrats put an extremely deceptive and immoral video together to insinuate that if one voted for the Republican Candidate for President then *granny would be thrown off the cliff.* The reason for the unjust video was because Republicans wanted to alleviate the burdens of Obamacare (a government program) on the American people.

Of course, other harsh examples have been continuously echoed by Democrats. There are the smears alleging that all Republicans: 1) are racist, 2) hate immigrants, 3) are anti-feminists, 4) don't support gay rights, 5) care only about the rich, 6) don't believe in climate change, 7) only like country music, 8) are the only gun owners, 9) are Christian fanatics, 10) are war mongers, and much more. These statements are totally untrue. The reason Democratic politicians and the mainstream media have been using these identity politics phrases to the fullest is because they want to muster up votes from uninformed independent voters; and, undeniably, to incite their core supporters. It's their crude tactics when running against Republicans, or any other party that stands in their way, to gain any governmental office.

The mainstream media elites, their pundits, and like-minded politicians, who dwell mostly on the American coasts (i.e. New York, New Jersey, Connecticut, Massachusetts, California, Washington, Oregon) and "Inside the Beltway" (i.e. Washington, D.C., Maryland, and Virginia), are relentless in their constant drumbeat of negativity toward the 45th U.S. President. Whenever this President has achieved something of major importance, there is either silence or very little told in a positive manner. The reason why the mainstream media does this is obvious to the fair-minded observer. They are an extension of the Democratic Party and support their progressively liberal ideologies, which in some cases are lawless in nature. One can even say that they have become a fourth branch of our U.S. government (i.e. Legislative, Executive, Judicial, and *Mainstream Media*) who benefit Democrats.

Yet despite all the negative press, constant daily resistance of discontent, and unabashed hateful rhetoric being spread, this 45th American President remains undeterred and resilient. While all these people want the President to fail, and don't care if America fails in the process, he stills goes forward with his agendas. This U.S. President continuously moves in a positive direction to protect and build-up America. He desires that all Americans prosper, be happier, and gain more health. And, regardless of what the mainstream media and their cohorts tell us, this President has accomplished much. Therefore, what will be revealed are the facts regarding the President's achievements. They prove he is keeping his promise to "Make America Great Again."

The first year (January 2017 – May 2018)

THE ECONOMY

1. Tax Cut/Reform Bill: Biggest tax cut in 30 years and simplification of code. About 80% of Americans, including lower and middle-class individuals, saw tax cuts in their pay starting February 2018. This tax bill gets rid of the Obamacare individual mandate too, which forced everyone who didn't have insurance through an employer to pay for health insurance. This caused massive increases in health insurance prices and deductibles. The bill also opens energy exploration and creation of oil reserves in Alaska (ANWR). After forty years of others trying to pass the ANWR bill, the President did it. This provides energy independence, non-reliance on other countries for oil and natural gas, an ability to create more jobs, and a possibility to lower gas prices.

2. Hundreds of companies have given pay raises, more benefits, or up to $2,000 bonuses to employees. These companies have also been able to contribute hundreds of millions of dollars in donations to charitable organizations because of this robust new tax plan.

3. The President convinced Ford, Chrysler and Carrier Air Conditioners to manufacture and build plants in America. In addition, Corning stated it would invest $500 million in new U.S. production while aiming to create 1,000 new jobs. Foxconn, the manufacturer which makes the iPhone, indicated it would invest $10 billion in Wisconsin to build a factory which would employ about 3,000 workers directly, and up to 22,000 workers indirectly.

4. The tax plan pushed Apple to take $250 billion from overseas to add 20,000 jobs in the U.S. within five years. Also, Apple will pay $38 billion in taxes, and give employees 2,500 worth of stock as bonuses.

5. Chrysler has plans to move plants from Mexico back to Michigan.

6. Broadcom Limited (CEO Hock E. Tan) committed to $20 billion in spending on employees that will be hired in the U.S. after moving its headquarters from Singapore.

7. The Gross National Product (GDP), which was stagnant under the Obama economy, never reaching a full year of 3% growth, is rising.

8. Stock Market at All-Time Highs: The day of the Presidential election (Nov. 8, 2016) the Dow Jones Industrial Average (DJIA) ended at 18,259.60. Since the election of our current President the Dow Jones continues to rise. The Dow's rise from 19,000 to above 21,000 in just 66 days in 2017 was the fastest 2,000-point rise ever recorded.

9. The S&P 500 and NASDAQ have also reached all-time highs.

10. Consumer confidence reached a 17-year high from 2017 to 2018

11. Almost 2.2 million jobs were created in first year - and counting.

12. The unemployment rate hit an 18-year low (4.1 % - Dec. 31, 2017)

13. The female unemployment rate hit a 17-year low.

14. Black unemployment hit 16.8% under Obama; Under OUR President it dipped to 6.8% (lowest on record).

15. Black family income fell by more than $900 under Obama; Under OUR President black family income has increased more than $1000.

16. Hispanic unemployment is at an all-time historic low.

17. Food stamp use is at a 7-year low. Within a year, more than a million less people got off the dependency of food stamps.

18. Home prices up 6% starting 2018. U.S. homebuilder confidence is at its strongest marks in 12 years.

19. Housing sales recently have doubled compared to the same period under President Obama in 2018, according to the U.S. Census Bureau.

20. Manufacturing is at its best level since 2004.

21. An executive order was signed to enable businesses to start and expand apprenticeship programs.

22. Wages have begun to increase beginning in 2018.

23. The President signed an executive order allowing oil and gas drilling and development on federal lands.

24. The Dakota Access Pipeline project and the construction of the Keystone XL oil pipeline from Canada, expecting to create more than 42,000 jobs and $2 billion in earnings, was approved by the President. The Dakota Access Pipeline, which transports 500,000 barrels of oil a day, has given more energy to the North Dakota economy. He also approved production of the New Burgos Pipeline to Mexico.

25. An executive order was signed to extend offshore oil drilling to the

Arctic and on the Atlantic Ocean to improve energy independence.

26. The President kept his promise to coal miners by ending the "Stream Protection Rule", while inducing the mining industry to reopen businesses and hire again to produce "clean" coal.

27. He signed the "Buy American and Hire American" executive order to provide clarity and prioritize the rights of American businesses and workers. The "Buy American" portion of the bill reduces unfair competition from an offensive law binding waivers and exceptions. "Hire American" enforces laws to reform visa programs and entry of foreign workers so that American workers are not displaced from unemployment opportunities.

28. Women-owned businesses were allotted $500 million in SBA loans.

REFORMS AND REGULATIONS TO IMPROVE GROWTH

1. Many Obama's 855 job killing regulations are in the process of being rebutted or have been rebutted by the new President.

2. There was a weakening of Dodd-Frank regulations on the banking institutions by removing Consumer Financial Protection Bureau's power over banks and financial companies. This gave control back to federal and state regulators.

3. He eliminated a Dodd-Frank regulation requiring oil companies like Exxon Mobile to publicly disclose taxes and fees they pay to foreign governments, saving about $385 million annually.

4. An executive order was signed to direct the Department of Agriculture to find and purge unnecessary NAFTA regulations harming farmers.

5. A task force was established in all agencies to remove all job killing regulations and increase economic opportunity.

HOMELAND SECURITY/LAW ENFORCEMENT/DOJ

1. Temporary travel ban executive order was upheld by the Supreme Court. It reassesses the entry of potentially harmful persons into the U.S. This helps protect our homeland from terrorist threats.

2. The Department of Justice is fighting back against the unlawful "sanctuary cities" which harbor illegal immigrants, set free criminal illegal immigrants, and 'catch-and-release' illegals. In 2018, Orange, San Diego, and other counties in California have joined the fight against these unlawful acts. Hopefully, more U.S. districts will follow.

3. An executive order was signed to protect police officers and gave back control to the police departments which was curbed under Obama.
4. The Immigration Crime Engagement Office was created for victims.
5. The Department of Justice is targeting dangerous gangs in the U.S., especially one like MS-13 who commit felonious crimes. Thousands of MS-13 gang members have been arrested.
6. The law enforcement agencies are combating unlawful and inhumane human trafficking of illegal immigrants over border.
7. An executive order was signed to target drug cartels.
8. The new administration implemented a new method of tracking persons who come and go from the U.S. because many overstay their visas. The last three administrations (Bush, Clinton, Obama) never took action to install an entry-exit tracking system.
9. To fight the horrible opioid prescription abuse problems in America, the Department of Justice (DOJ) launched an opioid fraud and abuse unit. The DOJ charged hundreds of doctors, medical facilities, and other prescribing opioids that led to addiction and current drug crisis.
10. Legitimate federal gun-crime DOJ prosecutions increased in 2017.
11. There were so many illegal leaks of crucial information to the press in the infancy of this presidency that the DOJ continues to do its best to crack down on them. A counterintelligence unit was created for this.
12. The President signed three executive orders, to enhance our law enforcement. The first order reinforced the law against international crime organizations. The second order fights anti-law-enforcement crimes. And, the third order asks to reduce all crime in general, especially illegal immigration, drug trafficking and violent crimes.

IMMIGRATION

1. In the first 100 days, illegal immigration border crossing was down over 70 percent. But border security and "the wall" need more funding.
2. Border Patrol arrests dropped to a 45-year low in the fiscal year (Sept. 30, 2017), which was down 25 percent from previous year because of a secure ICE agency (Immigration and Customs Enforcement).
3. ICE arrests on average are up. This indicates illegal immigration into the U.S., especially on the southern border, is being deterred. An executive order was signed reiterating those who cross the border illegally are punishable with a criminal offense.

4. The Secretary of State office is withdrawing from the Global Compact on Migration. It would "undermine the sovereign right of the United States to enforce our immigration laws and secure our borders."

5. A 70-point proposal was provided to include increased border security, merit-based immigration, protection people against "sanctuary cities", ending chain migration, constructing a southern border wall, and expediting the removal of illegal aliens.

6. The President rescinded the illegal executive order imposed by President Obama that granted children of those who came to America illegal temporary protection status. This DACA order (Deferred Action for Childhood Arrivals) affects 800,000 to 3.6 million people.

7. The Central American Minors Parole Program allowing certain minors from El Salvador, Guatemala, and Honduras to enter the U.S. was stopped by the Department of Homeland Security.

8. In August 2017, after reforms and the additional hiring of immigration judges, deportations increased 28 % from the same time in 2016.

9. Many illegal immigrants in federal prisons are either being deported or serving their time until deported.

10. Denial requests were delivered by U.S. Citizenship and Immigration Services to those employers not able to explain why they wanted to import foreign labor and pay lower wages for high-skilled jobs.

11. The DACA program was re-evaluated and cancelled to force Congress to write a legal bill that would lead to Immigration Reform which has not been solved by past administrations for decades.

12. Despite opposition, the President signed an executive over that would cut funding for "sanctuary cities", which aids and abets illegal and criminal immigrants to roam free from prosecution.

13. The Attorney General and others are attempting to end the illegal "sanctuary cities" in America.

SUPREME COURT/JUSTICE SYSTEM

1. Neil Gorsuch, a Conservative Supreme Court Judge (life-time), was appointed. This was done to protect the U.S. constitution and laws.

2. The President had also chosen 27 federal lower-court judges as of mid-July 2017, but only 12 have been confirmed in his first year. Still, it's the most by any President in history. (President Obama had 3; Bush had 6; Nixon and Kennedy had 11 each). More are to follow in 2018.

3. The Supreme Court upheld the President's Travel Ban, which was challenged by liberal lower courts. Now, the administration can review people coming into the U.S. from eight dangerous countries (Chad, Iran, Libya, North Korea, Somalia, Syria, Venezuela, and Yemen).

4. The Justice Department eliminated Operation Choke Point, an Obama program encouraging banks not to do business with "high risk" businesses utilized to target gun dealers.

5. The President signed a bill repealing an Obama-era Social Security Administration rule which added mental disability determinations to background check registries, which potentially denied many competent and mentally healthy citizens Second Amendment rights.

6. The administration added 100 new immigration judges.

NATIONAL SECURITY/VETERANS

1. The President signed a memorandum to begin the expansion and rebuilding of the U.S. military in January 2017.

2. He signed the National Defense Authorization Act in December 2017.

3. The President changed the Rules of Engagement against ISIS and decimated them on the battlefield. They lost most of their territory in Syria and Iraq not allowing caliphate to grow and take hold.

4. Approximately $400 million for U.S. missile defense systems was given to the U.S. Department of Defense.

5. The President increased the status of the Department of Defense's Cyber Command to the status of Unified Combatant Command in August, which increased focus on cyber security.

6. A deal was reached with Lockheed Martin to purchase 90 F-35 jets at the lowest price in history. The first 90 planes would cost $725 million below budget, with billions of dollars in additional savings expected. This deal saved at least one U.S. ally, Japan, $100 million.

7. When the Syrian regime used chemical weapons against civilians, the President authorized strikes against the airbase that launched those chemical attacks, destroying 20% of Syria's operational aircraft. In April 2018, another offensive bombing of Syria, joined by Britain and France, occurred in response to another chemical attack on civilians.

8. Defense Secretary James Mattis was given autonomous control to set troop levels in Iraq and Syria to combat ISIS. In addition, military commanders were given authority to act out military operations without approval from Washington. This would result in a successful

campaign against defeating ISIS on the battlefield.

9.   A speech addressing the nation stated the new military strategy was to put Pakistan on notice for supporting jihadists. Also, he warned Afghani leaders in Kabul that they would no longer get a "blank check." This ensured the U.S. was focused on killing terrorists and will not impose itself on other countries – better known as "nation-building."

10. The U.S. delivered a very heavy blow to ISIS in Afghanistan by dropping a GBU-43B, better known as MOAB (Mother of All bombs) on a complex of ISIS tunnels. This is the largest non-nuclear bomb in existence. Over 90 ISIS fighters and four commanders were killed. Their tunnels and weapon stockpiles were destroyed too.

11. The Defense Department was authorized by the President to set troop levels in Afghanistan. This expanded authority given to the military may also be seen by U.S. operations in Somalia.

12. The President's administration halted a CIA program to arm "moderate" Syrian rebels because these efforts seemed to have helped Islamic jihadists - including those terrorists who carried out the disastrous Benghazi attack in which four Americans were killed, including a U.S. Ambassador to Libya.

13. The Iraqi coalition forces finally pushed out ISIS fighters from Mosul, after many months of fighting. The U.S. is supporting efforts to help the Philippines alleviate themselves of ISIS cells.

14. The President directed the military not to move forward with an Obama-era mandate that allowed transgender individuals to be recruited into the armed forces. The reason for the change is that individuals were using the military to perform sex change operations, reducing their costs and increasing the cost of American tax payers.

15. The President signed a Veterans Administration Choice and Quality Employment Act of 2017. It authorized $2.1 billion in additional funds for veterans 1) living more than 40 miles from the closest eligible VA medical facility, 2) experiencing wait times of more than 30 days to schedule an appointment, or 3) meeting other special criteria to be treated outside the VA system.

16. The Veterans Accountability and Whistleblower Protection Act was signed by the President to allow senior officials in the VA to fire failing employees and establish safeguards to protect whistleblowers. The department reported it fired hundreds of employees since January 2017. The VA also suspended many others as part of the President's efforts to restore integrity and accountability.

17. The Veteran Administration adopted a medical records system successfully used by the Defense Department, ending a decades-old problem of sharing information between the two agencies.
18. A White House Veterans Administration Hotline, fully staffed by veterans, went live to help veterans.
19. The Veterans Appeals Improvement and Modernization Act were signed to streamline the long process involved when veterans undergo the appeal for disability benefit claims with the VA. The Veterans Affairs administration is the first agency to post data on employee disciplinary action online.
20. The Harry W. Colmery Veterans Educational Assistance Act was signed to provide educational benefits to veterans, service members and their family, including tuition, fees, books, and housing costs.
21. Although not the best, the President was forced to sign an OMNIBUS bill, including giving our military/ national defense about $600 billion
22. In 2018, the National Guard was deployed to secure southern border.

FOREIGN POLICY/TRADE

1. North Korea was sanctioned over their on-going nuclear missile program; the U.N. Ambassador got a unanimous vote for sanctions against N. Korea; they have been designated as a terrorist state; the President may meet the North Korean leader in 2018. If this occurs, it will be the first time in history for a *sitting President* to do so.
2. There were sanctions over the Iran missile program.
3. The President took historic trips to Europe (NATO, G8 Summit/Paris Accord, visit Pope), Middle East (Saudi Arabia speech to Arab Nations, visit Israel–Wailing Wall, via Delarosa, & Dome of the Rock Mosque), and Asia (Japan, Philippines, Vietnam, South Korea, and China).
4. The President said he was moving the U.S. Embassy to Jerusalem in 2017, and recognized Jerusalem as Israel's capital. Many Presidents said they would do this, but he is the first to keep his promise.
5. There are still on-going peace talks between Israel and Palestine, even after announcing move of U.S. embassy.
6. The U.S. denied Pakistan military aid amounting to $255 million. They made it clear that the U.S. expects Pakistan to take decisive action against terrorists in its country. Islamabad was urged to support U.S. security strategy because South Asia "will ultimately determine the trajectory of our relationship, including future security assistance."

7. He signed Trade and Investment deal with China worth more than $250 billion, which should create jobs by increasing exports to China.

8. Presidential memorandum issued determined U.S. has enough petroleum coming from other countries instead of Iran. Therefore, it significantly reduced purchases from this terrorist sponsoring regime.

9. The Iran nuclear agreement was an ill-advised move by the Obama administration. The President certified it initially but monitored it carefully. He knew the rogue Iranian mullah-led regime had defied the deal by engaging in suspicious activities leading to the development of nuclear weapons. So, he sanctioned 25 entities that dealt with Iran. (With evidence from the Israeli Prime Minister, in May 2018, the Iran deal was ended).

10. He is renegotiating the U.S. South Korea Free Trade Agreement.

11. After the President's warning and deployment of the THAAD missile defense system to South Korea, the North Korean dictator backed off his threat to attack the U.S. territory of Guam.

12. An executive order was signed to provide U.S. oversight that will target persons, companies and financial institutions willing to trade with North Korea. China followed suit limiting banking with North Korea.

13. President signed executive order to investigate Chinese theft of U.S. intellectual property. The IP Commission Report indicates that annual cost to the U.S. economy from intellectual property theft may be up to $600 billion. Of course, China is the major perpetrator of this.

14. For the first time since 1992, the U.S. made a deal with Argentina to allow U.S. pork to enter the Argentine market, which could be worth $10 million a year to the U.S.

15. American beef imports have now returned to China. This is the first time since 2003 and breaks open a market potentially worth $2.5 billion for U.S. ranchers and producers.

16. The administration will roll back the Obama administration's agreement with Cuba, which the President contends benefited the Cuban regime at the expense of the Cuban people.

17. The President urged NATO members to pay fair share of financial support for a military alliance. Some have complied with his request.

18. The administration implemented the Global Magnitsky Human Rights Accountability Act, which blacklisted certain Russian citizens for human rights violations.

19. The U.S. Treasury Department imposed sanctions on 38 Russian individuals and entities involved in the conflict with Ukraine.

20. In his first foreign trip as President, he announced signing some $110 billion arms deal with Saudi Arabia, and another $350 billion arms deal for the following 10 years. During his speech to fifty Islamic nations he urged them to fight Islamic terrorism.
21. To benefit the American economy, Mexico agreed curbing its exports of raw/refined sugar to the U.S.
22. New sanctions were ordered on the dictatorship in Venezuela.
23. The President intends to still revisit and renegotiate NAFTA (North American Free Trade). He will pull out of this pact if it remains to be non-beneficial to the U.S.
24. An investigation began to discover whether Chinese and other foreign-made steel and aluminum threaten U.S. national security.
25. The administration refused to sign the G-7 joint statement because other nations could not agree to support nuclear and fossil fuels while supporting the Paris climate agreement.
26. The administration refused to issue waivers to companies wanting to do business with Russia, which was under economic sanctions.
27. An executive order was signed to review and report on major U.S. trade deficits around the world.
28. The President's administration forced the G-20 to remove its opposition to protectionism and temper its support for free trade. Climate change was eliminated from its joint statement.
29. The President rescinded the Trans Pacific Partnership (TPP) act through an executive order, which will hopefully initiate fairer and reciprocal deals with countries in Asia.
30. China and Canada were fined $2 billion for illegal trade practices.

UNITED NATIONS

1. In his speech to the U.N. General Assembly, the President said to world members he would "put America first and you should do the same with your nations." He denounced socialism and communism, while pointing to Venezuela as an example of what happens when socialism is successfully implemented. And, he acknowledged North Korea, Iran, and ISIS must be dealt with through global cooperation.
2. Since the United Nations voted against U.S. moving embassy to Jerusalem, recognizing the city as Israel's capital, U.S. ambassador to the U.N. Nikki Haley negotiated a $285 million cut in the global body's "bloated" budget for 2018. After the U.N. vote, she also announced the

U.S. would "remember this day", since the U.S. makes the largest contribution to the United Nations of about 25%.

3. U.N. Ambassador Nikki Haley condemned a report against Israel by the U.N. Economic and Social Commission for Western Asia which was deemed anti-Semitic. It prompted the immediate resignation of the commission's executive director.

HEALTHCARE

1. Opioid Addiction Commission created to deal with opioid epidemic.
2. An additional $500 million was added to the budget to fight this crisis.
3. The President named opioids a National Public Health Emergency.
4. There is a new five-point strategy to combat the opioid crisis.
5. There were 400 arrests in related to opioid fraud.
6. The administration stated that overdoses were underreported by 24%.
7. The DEA (Drug Enforcement Agency) collected 456 tons of drugs on National Drug Take Back Day.
8. Removed Obamacare mandate with Tax Bill, which forced people to buy health insurance (i.e. expensive premiums and deductibles).
9. Signed order reinstating the Mexico City Policy, which defunded the International Planned Parenthood Federation and others promoting foreign abortions.
10. President signed an executive order directing agencies to rewrite regulations to encourage the purchase of health insurance over state-lines, which could lead to competition/cheaper prices on the market.

WOMEN'S ISSUES/HUMAN RIGHTS/RELIGION

1. The first sitting President to speak at March for Life (pro-life group) did so at the White House Rose Garden in January 2018. This was done after establishing a "Conscious a Religious Liberty Protection Unit". It will allow healthcare professionals to opt out of unwise abortions and perform gender reassignment surgeries.
2. The Women in Entrepreneurship Act was signed and promoted.
3. The President signed an executive order halting and citing individuals and groups the administration deems to be perpetrators or enablers of human rights abuses and corruption. The order declared a national emergency related to "serious human rights abuse and corruption

around the world" and imposed sanctions on 13 individuals. He also exercised authority under the 2016 Global Magnitsky Act.

4. The President signed an executive order for Religious Freedom. The Attorney General reiterated this when providing 20 high-level principles that can be implemented through the government for the lawful protection of these religious liberties.

5. The Department of Agriculture provided issue of guidance for the non-discrimination of Christians who adhere to their beliefs and are opposed to same-sex marriages.

6. Issued in a needed Statement of Administration Policy, the Office of Management supported the Budget for the Pain-Capable Unborn Child Protection Act. It's unlawful for people to attempt to or actually perform an abortion of an unborn after 20 weeks post-fertilization

7. The President acknowledged his support for those with Down syndrome, saying, "there remain too many people – both in the United States and throughout the world – that still see Down syndrome as an excuse to ignore or discard human life." He said Americans and their government "must always be vigilant in defending and promoting the unique and special gifts of all citizens in need" and "should not tolerate any discrimination against them, as all people have inherent dignity."

8. The President's administration provided needed religious and moral freedom from Obamacare that forced most insurance plans to cover abortion-inducing drugs and contraception or be fined. This was supported by a ruling made by the U.S. Supreme to protect the rights of the Little Sisters of the Poor, which objected to the Obamacare mandate opposing their faith and religious beliefs.

9. A new executive order overturned an Obama executive order requiring public schools to allow students the use of bathrooms and locker rooms according to their preferred gender.

10. An executive order was signed to provide religious liberty from the Johnson Amendment, without the threat of a fine from the IRS due to political activities or speeches by tax-exempt religious groups. The order made it easier for employers not to provide contraceptives.

11. The administration expanded the scope of the Mexico City Policy to restrict funding to any international health organization that performs or gives information about abortions.

12. He signed a pro-life bill which removed an Obama administration regulation that would have prohibited states from discriminating in

awarding Title X family planning funds, which is based upon whether a local clinic also performs abortions.

13. The U.S. cut off funding to the United Nations Population Fund, which has links to inhumane abortion programs such as China's one-child policy (which became a two-child policy in 2015). Over $32 million was shifted to the U.S. Agency for International Development.

14. The President appointed pro-life advocate Dr. Charmaine Yoest, the former President of Americans United for Life, as assistant secretary of public affairs for the Department of Health and Human Services. He would replace a strong Planned Parenthood supporter. Two pro-life advocates who had worked for the Family Research Council were subsequently appointed to key positions.

15. The United States-Canada Council for Advancement of Women Entrepreneurs and Business Leaders with Canadian Prime Minister Justin Trudeau was implemented for women in business.

16. The President pledged that Christian refugees suffering persecution in Muslim countries would be given priority over other refugees seeking to enter the United States.

ENERGY PROTECTION/ENVIRONMENT/CLIMATE CHANGE

1. An executive order to promote energy independence and economic growth was signed by the President.

2. The President ended the war on clean coal (opening mines up again).

3. The President authorized the construction of the Keystone Pipeline.

4. There has been a move toward drilling in Alaska and offshore in the U.S. (Gulf of Mexico and off the east and west coasts), which is vital for American energy independence.

5. Mining increased 28.6 percent in the second quarter of 2017.

6. Two executive orders gave back about 2 million acres of land to Utah by modifying Obama executive orders. The new President said the Antiquities Act "requires that any reservation of land as part of a monument be confined to the smallest area compatible with the proper care and management of the objects of historic or scientific interest to be protected." First, there was a reduction of the federal government's control of Bear's Ear National Monument to just 201,876 acres, while pointing out that the important objects of scientific or historic interest described in Obama's proclamation are already protected under existing laws. Second, he reduced the land

protected by government around the Grand Staircase National Monument (Utah) from nearly 1.9 million acres to about 1 million.

7. He removed the USA from Paris Accord (saving trillions of dollars). According to a study by NERA Consulting, the agreement could have cost $3 trillion, and by the year 2040 up to 6.5 million industrial sector jobs would be lost (including 3.1 million manufacturing sector jobs).

8. Climate change was removed from the global threats list in the U.S. National Security Strategy, reversing an Obama admin. decision.

9. Director of the EPA put new experts (66) with conservative views on three different EPA scientific committees. A directive was signed banning those working on the EPA independent advisory boards from receiving grants to avoid conflict of interest.

10. The Environmental Protection Agency implemented a new set of rules to supersede the Clean Power Plan (implemented by President Obama for climate change). It shall rollback more than 30 environmental, which would be the largest regulatory cut in the EPA agency's history.

11. A climate change advisory panel under the direction of NOAA, the National Oceanic and Atmospheric Administration, was shut down because all it did was promote President Obama's climate policies.

INFRASTRUCTURE

1. A new Integration Pilot Program was introduced to aid the Department of Transportation establish innovation zones for tests that integrate drones into local and national airspace system. This will also create more new jobs with this technology.

2. The administration seeks to reduce the amount of time needed to get a permit from 10 to 2 years, hopefully 1 year, for entities needing to develop infrastructure. This will invigorate investments and jobs.

FRAUD/WASTE IN GOVERNMENT

1. An executive order was signed to perform an audit on every executive branch to cut down on the number of employees, reduce spending and waste, while improving services.

2. He created a Commission on Election Board (voter fraud - dead people voting, illegal immigrants voting, and people voting in two states). This program stopped because not all states cooperated and gave administration data. The administration will pursue Voter ID laws.

3. The Environmental Protection Agency has been cut by more than 700 people since Trump took office. This was almost a quarter of the personnel projected to be eliminated from this bloated agency.
4. An executive order was signed for a hiring freeze on federal employees.
5. Cutting back the operations of the East Wing, Melania Trump, the First Lady, reduced the number of aides needed in the Administration. Only four people, as of June 2017, were working for the First Lady with a total payroll of $486,700 per year. That is opposed to Michelle Obama's staff which earned about $1.24 million per year.
6. Office of American Innovation will improve government for the future.
7. An executive order was implemented to strengthen new lobbying standards for political appointees. This includes a five-year lobbying ban and lifetime ban on lobbying for foreign countries.
8. To expedite environmental reviews of infrastructure projects and to incite industry spending/investment, an executive order was signed.

NATIONAL SPACE PROGRAM

1. National Space Council was revived after 25 years to develop long-term goals for America's space policies. It involved national security, human exploration, discoveries in the universe, a renewed focus to have a presence on the moon and need to send humans to Mars.

EDUCATION

1. Education Secretary, Betsy DeVos, seeks to revoke the Obama administration's implementation of Title IX – the much-abused 1972 federal law which bars discrimination in education "on the basis of sex". Therefore, she hired Adam Kissel as deputy assistant secretary for higher education programs. The staff of the Title IX enforcement office was reduced in the 2018 budget.
2. The administration announced it will create a school choice plan so that states have an option of implementing it, rather than forcing the state to use a federal program.
3. An executive order was signed that giving Secretary of Education Betsy DeVos the ability to review department regulations with the purpose of returning power to the states and local governments.
4. The Education Department aims to boost computer science programs.

MISCELLANEOUS

1. The President signed at least 96 bills into law in first year (more now).
2. He made at 119 Presidential Proclamations in first year (more now).
3. The President signed a minimum of 55 new Executive Orders. Many of President Obama's executive orders were rescinded.
4. His administration has exceeded its promise to eliminate regulations at a 2:1 ratio and impose no lifetime net regulatory costs. In practice, the administration has exceeded this by rescinding or delaying more than 860 regulations (16 regulations for every new one implemented).
5. Federal agencies also achieved $8.1 billion in lifetime net regulatory cost savings - the equivalent of $570 million per year.
6. The President donated one million of his money to hurricane victims.
7. He reduced White House payroll, starting with his annual salary of $1.
8. Providing government transparency, over 13,000 documents about President John F. Kennedy's assassination were released to America.
9. November 7th, 2017 was proclaimed as National Day for the Victims of Communism on the 100th anniversary of the Bolshevik Revolution.
10. He rescinded Waters of the United States rule (2015 executive order), which controlled expansion of government control over private land. This Obama regulation pertained to navigable waters, ridiculously including man-made ditches and waters created by heavy rains.
11. Negotiated release of several prisoners: C. Coleman, J. Boyle, and 3 children (Afghanistan); A. Hijazi (Egypt); ex-CIA agent S. De Sousa (Italy); college basketball students L. Ball, C. Riley, and J. Hill (China); O. Warmbier, K. Dong-Chul, T. Kim, and K. Hak-Song (North Korea).

In just over a year, this President and his administration has completed "nearly two-thirds of the 334 agenda items" called for by the conservative group called the Heritage Foundation". He even surpassed the 49 percent mark President Reagan achieved at this time in his presidency. So, this 45th U.S. President is definitely on the right path to accomplishing his goals; and, there should be many more achievements completed by him in the future.

Therefore, do not listen to the mainstream media or Democratic pundits who have constantly told the pubic that the 45th President of the United States didn't have many successes in the first year or so of his presidency. As was mentioned previously, they are practicing "yellow journalism" and identity politics, respectively. This corrupt bunch of mainstream media and political elites only want to besmirch and demonize the President with tales of Russian collusion, obstruction of justice charges, smut, or anything they can spin into a negative connotation regarding his character or policies. They are relentless in their pursuit of seeking his political demise through impeachment. This motley crew just will not give credit when credit is due him - even as he continues to show everyone that a businessman can fix the problems of a nation (and world) better than most politicians.

As the 45th U.S. President moves forward each day, committed to undertake difficult tasks, he also fulfills the pledges he had made on the 2016 campaign trail. His word is his bond, as many PROMISES MADE have been many PROMISES KEPT. So, the mainstream media, and those against him, are only fooling themselves if they want to see this man fail. In their utter delusion, they may have to contemplate the possibility of seeing two Presidential terms worth of his achievements. This will blow their minds. Then, some may finally have to give up living in their fantasy worlds and accept the inspiring and profound realities this President has accomplished for America, and the world.

When speaking about the President one must point to a perfect quote from the renowned English novelist, short story writer, poet, screenwriter, and fighter pilot.

"And above all, watch with glittering eyes the whole world around you because the greatest secrets are always hidden in the most unlikely places. Those who don't believe in magic will never find it." – Roald Dahl

Chapter 9

INSPIRATIONAL SPEECHES

Since the 45th American President's inauguration day, the amount of speeches made when he addressed the nation, at rallies, or in other countries are numerous. Of course, to fully comprehend the breath and scope of his spoken words during any speech one must go on the Internet to find the full-transcript or *YouTube* to view a video of it. Also, to select his best speeches would be very difficult because they are diverse. There are three major speeches, however, which are very well-rounded and inspirational in tone and content. They are the speeches in Saudi Arabia, Poland, and the U.S. Capitol (State of the Union). But for brevity's sake, only a summary and excerpts shall be shared.

Saudi Arabia speech (Riyadh: May 21, 2017)

After the President thanked King Salman of Saudi Arabia, he reminded the leaders of the Muslim world who were in attendance that the King's father, King Adulaziz began a partnership with President Franklin Roosevelt which has endured. Then, the 45th U.S. President stated,

"I stand before you as a representative of the American People, to deliver a message of friendship and hope. That is why I chose to make my first foreign visit a trip to the heart of the Muslim world, to the nation that serves as custodian of the two holiest sites in the Islamic Faith.

In my inaugural address to the American People, I pledged to strengthen America's oldest friendships, and to build new partnerships in pursuit of peace. I also promised that America will not seek to impose our way of life on others, but to outstretch our hands in the spirit of cooperation and trust.

Our vision is one of peace, security, and prosperity—in this region, and in the world. Our goal is a coalition of nations who share the aim of stamping out extremism and providing our children a hopeful future that

does honor to God. And so, this historic and unprecedented gathering of leaders—unique in the history of nations—is a symbol to the world of our shared resolve and our mutual respect. To the leaders and citizens of every country assembled here today, I want you to know that the United States is eager to form closer bonds of friendship, security, culture and commerce."

The President spoke about the many successes of the American economy. He mentioned how King Salam, the Crown Price, and the Deputy Crown Prince had "signed historic agreements" worth $400 billion which will benefit both Saudi Arabia and the U.S the future. This included the Saudi's buying $110 billion of goods for their defense.

He observed how America, Europe, Australia South America, India, Africa, and China have suffered at the hands of extremist attacks.

"...The goal is meet history's great test – to conquer extremism and vanquish the forces of terrorism. Young Muslim boys and girls should be able to grow up free from fear, safe from violence, and innocent of hatred. And young Muslim men and women should have the chance to build a new era of prosperity for themselves and their peoples..."

"...in sheer numbers, the deadliest toll has been exacted on the innocent people of Arab, Muslim and Middle Eastern nations. They have borne the brunt of the killings and the worst of the destruction in this wave of fanatical violence. Some estimates hold that more than 95 percent of the victims of terrorism are themselves Muslim..."

"...The Middle East is rich with natural beauty, vibrant cultures, and massive amounts of historic treasures. It should increasingly become one of the great global centers of commerce and opportunity. This region should not be a place from which refugees flee, but to which new-comers flock.

Saudi Arabia is home to the holiest sites in one of the world's great faiths. Each year millions of Muslims come from around the world to Saudi Arabia to take part in the Hajj. In addition to ancient wonders, this country is also home to modern ones—including soaring achievements in architecture.

Egypt was a thriving center of learning and achievement thousands of years before other parts of the world. The wonders of Giza, Luxor and Alexandria are proud monuments to that ancient heritage.

All over the world, people dream of walking through the ruins of Petra in Jordan. Iraq was the cradle of civilization and is a land of natural beauty. And the United Arab Emirates has reached incredible heights with glass and steel, and turned earth and water into spectacular works of art.

The entire region is at the center of the key shipping lanes of the Suez Canal, the Red Sea, and the Straits of Hormuz. The potential of this region has never been greater. 65 percent of its population is under the age of 30. Like all young men and women, they seek great futures to build, great national projects to join, and a place for their families to call home.

But this untapped potential, this tremendous cause for optimism, is held at bay by bloodshed and terror. There can be no coexistence with this violence. There can be no tolerating it, no accepting it, no excusing it, and no ignoring it. Every time a terrorist murders an innocent person, and falsely invokes the name of God, it should be an insult to every person of faith. Terrorists do not worship God, they worship death..."

"...This is not a battle between different faiths, different sects, or different civilizations. This is a battle between barbaric criminals who seek to obliterate human life, and decent people of all religions who seek to protect it. This is a battle between Good and Evil.

When we see the scenes of destruction in the wake of terror, we see no signs that those murdered were Jewish or Christian, Shia or Sunni. When we look upon the streams of innocent blood soaked into the ancient ground, we cannot see the faith or sect or tribe of the victims—we see only that they were Children of God whose deaths are an insult to all that is holy..."

The President continued, saying we must drive out terrorists.

"DRIVE THEM OUT of your places of worship.
DRIVE THEM OUT of your communities.
DRIVE THEM OUT of your holy land, and
DRIVE THEM OUT OF THIS EARTH."

The President insisted that all Muslim nations must work together, and America would support them in their efforts to send all "wicked ideology into oblivion". He urged all nations to deny funding extremists and terrorists - like ISIS, Hezbollah, and others. And, he added,

"...Many are already making significant contributions to regional security: Jordanian pilots are crucial partners against ISIS in Syria and Iraq. Saudi Arabia and a regional coalition have taken strong action against Houthi militants in Yemen. The Lebanese Army is hunting ISIS operatives who try to infiltrate their territory. Emirati troops are supporting our Afghan partners. In Mosul, American troops are supporting Kurds, Sunnis and Shias fighting together for their homeland. Qatar, which hosts the U.S. Central Command, is a crucial strategic partner. Our longstanding partnership with Kuwait and Bahrain continued to enhance security in the region. And courageous Afghan soldiers are making tremendous sacrifices in the fight against the Taliban, and others, in the fight for their country..."

"...The United Arab Emirates has also engaged in the battle for hearts and souls—and with the U.S., launched a center to counter the online spread of hate. Bahrain too is working to undermine recruitment and radicalism. I also applaud Jordan, Turkey and Lebanon for their role in hosting refugees. The surge of migrants and refugees leaving the Middle East depletes the human capital needed to build stable societies and economies. Instead of depriving this region of so much human potential, Middle Eastern countries can give young people hope for a brighter future in their home nations and regions. That means promoting the aspirations and dreams of all citizens who seek a better life—including women, children, and followers of all faiths. Numerous Arab and Islamic scholars have eloquently argued that protecting equality strengthens Arab and Muslim communities.

For many centuries the Middle East has been home to Christians, Muslims and Jews living side-by-side. We must practice tolerance and respect for each other once again—and make this region a place where every man and woman, no matter their faith or ethnicity, can enjoy a life of dignity and hope.

In that spirit, after concluding my visit in Riyadh, I will travel to Jerusalem and Bethlehem, and then to the Vatican—visiting many of the holiest places in the three Abrahamic Faiths. If these three faiths can join together in cooperation, then peace in this world is possible – including peace between Israelis and Palestinians. I will be meeting with both Israeli Prime Minister Benjamin Netanyahu and Palestinian President Mahmoud Abbas..."

"...The birthplace of civilization is waiting to begin a new renaissance. Just imagine what tomorrow could bring. Glorious wonders of science, art, medicine and commerce to inspire humankind. Great cities built on the ruins

of shattered towns. New jobs and industries that will lift up millions of people. Parents who no longer worry for their children, families who no longer mourn for their loved ones, and the faithful who finally worship without fear.

These are the blessings of prosperity and peace. These are the desires that burn with a righteous flame in every human heart. And these are the just demands of our beloved peoples.

I ask you to join me, to join together, to work together, and to FIGHT together—BECAUSE UNITED, WE WILL NOT FAIL.

Thank you. God Bless You. God Bless Your Countries. And God Bless the United States of America."

The Poland speech (Krasiński Square, Warsaw: July 6, 2017)

The U.S. President and First Lady thanked President Duda, the First Lady, Agata, Prime Minister Syzdlo, and recognized former President Lech Walesa, who had led the Polish Solidarity Movement. Through the speech there was much applause and chants of the President's name.

The President spoke of "stronger ties of trade and commerce" and committed gaining energy for Poland. Then, he moved people with,

"...Poland is the geographic heart of Europe, but more importantly, in the Polish people, we see the soul of Europe. Your nation is great because your spirit is great, and your spirit is strong..." (Applause)

The President praised Poland for withstanding much abuse and prevailing after many "constant and brutal attacks" over two centuries.

"...Despite every effort to transform you, oppress you, or destroy you, you endured and overcame. You are the proud nation of Copernicus — think of that — (applause) — Chopin, Saint John Paul II. Poland is a land of great heroes...." (Applause)

The President spoke about the bonds Poland and America had over the years. He stated Poles had fought side-by-side and died for freedom together in America's war for independence, Afghanistan, and Iraq. Examples of links between the two countries were given by mentioning the statues of "Pułaski and Kościuszko" which stand near the White

House; and, that Warsaw streets and monuments are named after George Washington and Ronald Reagan, respectively.

Then, the U.S. President spoke of the Polish people's spirit through the many brutal occupations, invasions, and destructions of cities. The subjects included the 1) Miracle of Vistula (1920), the way Poland stopped the Soviets, 2) double occupation of Nazis and the Soviet Union in (1939), 3) Katyn forest massacre, 4) Holocaust victims and Warsaw Ghetto, 5) destruction of Warsaw, and 6) monument dedicated to 150,000 who died during the Warsaw Uprising.

The President acknowledged the visit of the Polish Pope John Paul II on June 2, 1979 in Victory Square had a profound impact on the Polish people. During his sermon millions chanted "We want God". This led to "solidarity against oppression", and the achievement of freedom from four decades of communist rule. The President said that like Poland had overcome oppression, America and Europe must stand united with Muslim nations to fight the new oppressive ideologies of terrorism and extremism. And, he stated, Russia must cease "its destabilizing activities in Ukraine and elsewhere." There was applause.

The President continued with inspirational words for all to hear.

"...We write symphonies. We pursue innovation. We celebrate our ancient heroes, embrace our timeless traditions and customs, and always seek to explore and discover brand-new frontiers.

We reward brilliance. We strive for excellence and cherish inspiring works of art that honor God. We treasure the rule of law and protect the right to free speech and free expression. (Applause)

We empower women as pillars of our society and of our success. We put faith and family, not government and bureaucracy, at the center of our lives. And we debate everything. We challenge everything. We seek to know everything so that we can better know ourselves. (Applause)

And above all, we value the dignity of every human life, protect the rights of every person, and share the hope of every soul to live in freedom. That is who we are. Those are the priceless ties that bind us together as nations, as allies, and as a civilization..."

"...Our citizens did not win freedom together, did not survive horrors together, did not face down evil together, only to lose our freedom to a lack of pride and confidence in our values. We did not and we will not. We will never back down..." (Applause)

The President acknowledged that America supports Article 5 of NATO, "the mutual defense commitment"; and, Poland has met its monetary defense investments in NATO. Then, he asked,

"...Do we have the confidence in our values to defend them at any cost? Do we have enough respect for our citizens to protect our borders? Do we have the desire and the courage to preserve our civilization in the face of those who would subvert and destroy it?" (Applause)

The President then spoke of the Warsaw Uprising again. He recognized that "Jerusalem Avenue" in August 1944 was one of the main roads running east to west in Warsaw which the Nazis used to transport their troops. The Polish Army would hold the passage on the north and south side of the street, piling up sandbags, digging trenches, and building barricades to reinforce the Warsaw Uprising. The Nazis would burn buildings and use Poles as human shields during the fighting. Then, finally people flowed back and forth across Jerusalem Avenue through Nazi snipers and machine gunfire. One story tells,

"...The far side was several yards away," recalled one young Polish woman named Greta. That mortality and that life was so important to her. In fact, she said, 'The mortally dangerous sector of the street was soaked in the blood. It was the blood of messengers, liaison girls, and couriers...'"

The U.S. President ended his speech to the Polish people with,

"...The memories of those who perished in the Warsaw Uprising cry out across the decades, and few are clearer than the memories of those who died to build and defend the Jerusalem Avenue crossing. Those heroes remind us that the West was saved with the blood of patriots; that each generation must rise up and play their part in its defense — (applause) —

and that every foot of ground, and every last inch of civilization, is worth defending with your life.

Our own fight for the West does not begin on the battlefield — it begins with our minds, our wills, and our souls. Today, the ties that unite our civilization are no less vital, and demand no less defense, than that bare shred of land on which the hope of Poland once totally rested. Our freedom, our civilization, and our survival depend on these bonds of history, culture, and memory.

And today as ever, Poland is in our heart, and its people are in that fight. (Applause) Just as Poland could not be broken, I declare today for the world to hear that the West will never, ever be broken. Our values will prevail. Our people will thrive. And our civilization will triumph. (Applause)

Thank you. So, together, let us all fight like the Poles — for family, for freedom, for country, and for God. Thank you. God Bless You. God bless the Polish people. God bless our allies. And God bless the United States of America.”

The President's speech in Poland recognized the patriotism and pride the Polish people had gained over many years of struggles and wars. In addition, it strengthened the unity Poland has with America.

The State of the Union (Washington, D.C.: Jan. 31, 2018)

After the President greeted the Speaker of the House, Vice President and Congress, he addressed the nation. He spoke about the fire, floods, and storms the nation had gone through 2017 and into 2018. He said everyone was still behind those suffering in Texas, Florida, Louisiana, Puerto Rico, Virgin Islands, and California. He acknowledged the heroes who helped people during these times of need. And, he thanked Coast Guard Petty Officer Ashlee Leppert, who rescued 40 lives from the aftermath of Hurricane Harvey, and David Dahlberg, who saved 60 children trapped by California wildfires, which were in attendance.

He gave thanks to the Capitol Police Officers, the Alexandria Police, doctors, nurses, and paramedics who saved Congressman Steve Scalise's life, and others. Then, he asked Republicans and Democrats to put their differences aside for the betterment of the country, and added,

"Over the last year, the world has seen what we always knew: that no people on Earth are so fearless, or daring, or determined as Americans. If there is a mountain, we climb it. If there is a frontier, we cross it. If there is a challenge, we tame it. If there is an opportunity, we seize it. So, let us begin tonight by recognizing that the state of our Union is strong because our people are strong. And together, we are building a safe, strong, and proud America."

Then, the President went on to declare that 1) more than 2.4 million new jobs were created, including 200,000 in manufacturing, 2) wages were on the rise, 3) unemployment claims hit a 45-year low, 4) African-American and Hispanic unemployment was the lowest ever, 5) small business confidence was at an all-time high, 6) the stock market has gained $8 trillion in value and 7) a tax cut bill was passed.

He continued observing the benefits of the new tax cut bill. It resulted in 3 million workers getting bonuses. Apple planned to invest $350 billion in America and hire more workers. And, this new bill gave Steve Staub and Sandy Kepinger, who were in attendance, a chance to grow their small business, hire 14 people, and hand-out raises.

The President celebrated the fact that we all are "one American family", and share "the same home, the same heart, the same destiny, and the same great American flag." Then, he stated our police, military, and veterans deserve our unwavering support. As an example of this, he pointed to 12-year old Preston Sharp sitting in the stands - a young patriot who started a movement of placing flags on veteran's graves.

He discussed 1) his appointment of the most circuit court judges in the American history, 2) the new Supreme Court Justice, Neil Gorsuch, 3) signing the Veterans Administration Accountability Act, 4) removing 1,500 VA employees who failed at their job, 5) eliminating the most regulations by any President in his first year, 6) ending the war on coal, 7) Chrysler, Toyota, and Mazda opening new plants in America, 8) giving the terminally ill the "right to try", 9) reducing the price of prescription drugs, 10) unfair trade deals to begin being "reciprocal", 11) proposing a $1.5 trillion new infrastructure investment, 12) moving people off welfare to find work through job training programs and schools, 13) reforming prison inmates to get a second chance, and 14) ending and creating immigration policies that helps immigrants and doesn't harm Americans citizens.

The President acknowledged and sent prayers to the parents of two teenage daughters, Kayla Cuevas and Nisa Mickens, in the audience who had been "brutally murdered" by six members of the MS-13 gangs. Then, he asked Congress to address the loopholes allowing gangs and criminals such as MS-13 into the U.S., and to support our Immigration and Customs Enforcement and Border Patrol Agents. He added,

"My duty, and the sacred duty of every elected official in this chamber, is to defend Americans -- to protect their safety, their families, their communities, and their right to the American Dream. Because Americans are dreamers too."

Homeland Security Investigations Special Agent Celestino Martine was recognized and thanked for his 15-years in the Air Force and 15-years fighting against dangerous criminals as an ICE agent. The President said Martine was brave. Although MS-13 ordered his murder, "he did not cave to threats or fear" and arrested 220 gang members.

The President's four pillars of an immigration plan include 1) a path to citizenship for 1.8 illegal immigrants - three times more than the previous administration, 2) securing the border, which includes the building of a wall, 3) ending the visa lottery program, which randomly hands out green cards, and 4) protecting the nuclear family but ending illegal chain migration. He said chain migration and the visa lottery system permitted two terrorist attacks in New York a few weeks ago; and, that after 30 years, Congress now can solve the immigration issue.

The President remarked that immigration reforms will support opioid and drug addiction problems. In 2016, there were 64,000 lost to drug overdoses. That was 174 per day. And, so, he called for Congress to be much tougher on drug dealers and pushers - pronouncing he was committed to fighting the drug epidemic and providing treatments.

The President acknowledged Officer Ryan Holets from the Albuquerque Police Department, and his wife Rebecca. Ryan had stopped a pregnant homeless woman from injecting heroin. And, then, the couple adopted the woman's baby after she gave birth. The President said these selfless acts "embody the goodness of our Nation."

He mentioned the obvious facts that we must face rogue regimes, nuclear weapons, challenges from Russia and China, and terrorist threats. The President reported a global coalition had defeated ISIS and "liberated almost 100 percent of the territory once held by killers in Iraq and Syria. But there is much more work to be done."

The President recognized Army Staff Sergeant Justin Peck for saving the life of Chief Petty Officer Kenton Stacy, who was severely wounded and needed CPR from an ISIS explosive in Raqqa, Syria. Peck was given a Bronze Star medal with a "V" for valor on it. He went on to say that "terrorists are not merely criminals. They are unlawful enemy combatants." Therefore, the President wants Secretary of Defense Mattis to re-examine the detention facilities in Guantánamo Bay, Cuba. And, he stated no longer would the enemy know our plans.

The President accepted Jerusalem to be the capital of Israel. But he said those who opposed the decision in the U.N. should think twice because the billions of dollars of foreign assistance coming from American taxpayers should only go to America's friends. He stated America stands with the people of Iran against their corrupt dictator, and the terrible Iran deal must be readdressed by Congress. Also, tough sanctions must be continued on Cuba, Venezuela, and North Korea.

The President highlighted Otto Warmbier, a student from the University of Virginia who was studying abroad, arrested, and tortured to the brink of death by a N. Korean dictatorship. He died in America after being released from the horrible regime. His parents, Fred and Cindy, were in attendance and praised for what they had endured.

Finally, Mr. Ji Seong-ho was commended and acknowledged by the President, as the remainder of the speech was spoken.

"In 1996, Seong-ho was a starving boy in North Korea. One day, he tried to steal coal from a railroad car to barter for a few scraps of food. In the process, he passed out on the train tracks, exhausted from hunger. He woke up as a train ran over his limbs. He then endured multiple amputations without anything to dull the pain. His brother and sister gave what little food they had to help him recover and ate dirt themselves -- permanently stunting their own growth. Later, he was tortured by North Korean authorities after returning from a brief visit to China. His tormentors wanted to know if he had met any Christians. He had -- and he resolved to be free. Seong-ho traveled thousands of miles on crutches across China and Southeast Asia to freedom. Most of his family followed. His father was caught trying to escape and was tortured to death. Today he lives in Seoul, where he rescues other defectors, and broadcasts into North Korea what the regime fears the most -- the truth. Today he has a new leg, but Seong-ho, I understand you still keep those crutches as a reminder of how far you have come. Your great sacrifice is an inspiration to us all. Seong-ho's story is a testament to the yearning of every human soul to live in freedom. It was that same yearning for freedom that nearly 250 years ago gave birth to a special place called America. It was a small cluster of colonies caught between a great ocean and a vast wilderness. But it was home to an incredible people with a revolutionary idea: that they could rule themselves. That they could chart their own destiny; And, that, together, they could light up the world. That is what our country has always been about. That is what Americans have always stood for, always strived for, and always done.

Atop the dome of this Capitol stands the Statue of Freedom. She stands tall and dignified among the monuments to our ancestors who fought and lived and died to protect her...Monuments to Washington and Jefferson -- to Lincoln and King...Memorials to the heroes of Yorktown and Saratoga -- to young Americans who shed their blood on the shores of Normandy, and the fields beyond; And, others, who went down in the waters of the Pacific and the skies over Asia. And freedom stands tall over one more monument: this one...this Capitol...this living monument to the American people...A people whose heroes live not only in the past but all around us - defending hope, pride, and the American way. They work in every trade. They sacrifice to raise a family. They care for our children at home. They defend our flag abroad. They are strong moms and brave kids. They are firefighters, police officers, border agents, medics, and Marines. But above all else, they are Americans. And this Capitol, this city, and this Nation, belong to them. Our task is to respect them, to listen to them, to serve them, to protect them, and to always be worthy of them.

Americans fill the world with art and music. They push the bounds of science and discovery. And they forever remind us of what we should never forget: The people dreamed this country. The people built this country. And it is the people who are making America great again. As long as we are proud of who we are, and what we are fighting for, there is nothing we cannot achieve. As long as we have confidence in our values, faith in our citizens, and trust in our God, we will not fail. Our families will thrive. Our people will prosper. And our Nation will forever be safe and strong and proud and mighty and free. Thank you...and God bless America."

The State of the Union was one of the most uplifting speeches spoken by any President in modern day history. It 1) showcased some of the accomplishments of the President's first year in office, 2) aimed to fill Americans with a sense of pride about their country, 3) presented some who are heroes in the face of tragedy and disaster, 4) examined what can be achieved if we work together, and 5) sought to reach out to Democrats, bury differences, and unite the two political parties.

Very sadly, most members of the Democrat Party who sat under the Capitol that evening remained in their seats for nearly the entire speech. It was a pitiful display of partisan politics which only sought to resist the policies and presence of the 45th American President.

Why couldn't the Democrats get up for the symbols that bonded our nation, for unemployment rates being at the lowest ever, for greater economic prosperity, for the initial defeat of ISIS, for Steve Scalise, a Republican representative surviving an almost fatal gunshot wound, and more? It was a despicable to see the jealously in the hearts of the people's Democratic representatives. They showed the disgust on their faces, as well as a lack of respect and dignity toward what our nation has accomplished and how it has positively progressed under our new President. Their contempt for the President blinds them from doing what is right for the American people. To them it's a nightmare they are still dreaming, and they refuse to wake up to see the dawn of a new day.

Then, we have the buffoons in the mainstream media and their pundits, who seem mentally distraught, trying to poison the American people with their falsehoods about the State of the Union speech. They should be ashamed for what they have done and are doing. Despite their best efforts, however, most Americans (75%) approved of the speech.

My thoughts for our nation, world, and President

Around the globe, all people seek hope and inspiration. It doesn't matter if we are American, European, Latino, African, Asian, Russian, or Australian. Our goals are the same. These common bonds are the desires to live in a civilized world, free of war, poverty, and disease. We seek to go positively forward into a safer and securer future, while simultaneously attempting to confront and eradicate evil where we find it. Our objectives are simple as a people. That is, we strive for happiness in our souls and love in our hearts. It's our compassion that moves us to provide shelter, food, and security for ourselves and our families, while also wanting to lend a helping hand to our neighbors. And, it's our wisdom, through years of experience and learning, with religion, philosophy, or knowledge, which brings us closer to what is morally good. It's how we achieve higher spiritual objectives on Earth.

But, sometimes, we need to look to leaders to give us motivation to become the better and stronger person than we know ourselves to be. The words and presence this leader projects can infuse us with a sense of pride, dignity, comfort, and patriotism for our nation, and the world. Therefore, we must thank God for the leader we have elected who can be a trailblazer if given a fair and honest chance. We are only beginning to see the potential this person has shown to us. But once that potential is reached, then, with the light of each new day, hope and inspiration may shine harmony upon us; and, it may shine longer than ever before.

Chapter 10

CRIES OF
RUSSIA, RUSSIA, RUSSIA!

After the election of the 45th President of the United States, the term *Russian collusion* was everywhere. It has been used as the foundation to impeach OUR duly elected President. The "glass ceiling" was supposed to be shattered and wasn't. The outrage was palatable when the 2016 Presidential election was lost by *her*. All those supporting, conniving, conspiring, and spreading falsehoods lost their minds - and arguably still have not found them yet. So, there was a carefully laid plan as an "insurance policy" to rebuke, disparage, and delegitimize the person who was overwhelming selected to enter the Oval Office. They aimed to connect him and his campaign to everything Russia – whether that is Russian salad dressing, Russian roulette, or White Russians. But, was the Russian collusion real? Well, the best response is: da nyet, navernoe (Да нет, наверное)! This can be translated as, yes, no, and maybe. Oh, no, I spoke Russian. Am I guilty of collusion too?

Now, let's ask some questions before we delve into the facts. Did Russia hack into the DNC server? Should we be leery of the Special Counsel and his team in the Russia Collusion probe? Did Russia meddle into the 2016 U.S. Elections? Who was behind the Russian dossier story? Did OUR President collude with the Russians? Let's see.

Did Russia hack into the DNC server?

At the onset of this scandal, the media said there were 17 intelligence agencies indicating that Russia had interfered and hacked our election computers. It was a narrative which had been cherry picked from what Hillary Clinton had said on October 9, 2016:

"We have 17 intelligence agencies, civilian and military, who have all concluded that these espionage attacks, these cyberattacks, come from the

highest levels of the Kremlin, and they are designed to influence our election."

That was a false statement then, as it is now. The assertion was drawn from conclusions by three intelligence agencies – the FBI, NSA, and CIA. In addition, only 16 intelligence agencies exist, and a coordinating body who agreed with the alleged information, the ODNI, was not an actual intelligence agency. It oversees the other agencies. This untrue narrative of 17 intelligence agencies having information about Russian hacking was falsely propagated to America and the world for months. Did members mainstream media become accountable for the misinformation they so willingly participated in and disingenuously disseminating? No. They went on as usual inevitably altering their stories to fit their narrative - as if it was a streamlined process of truth.

Regardless, the alleged Russian hacking of the Democratic National Committee (DNC) during our elections would be a serious one if true. But although there have been assessments and judgments made by intelligence and justice department officials, there still is no actual proof given to the public which makes us believe the Russians hacked into the DNC computers during the 2016 election.

It may be that the Russians attempted to hack into the DNC computers. But it may also be likely that another foreign agent hacked into the DNC, or our own intelligence or cyber agencies placed false data pointing to the Russians because of Hillary Clinton's lost bid for the presidency. Maybe, there was no hack at all. With my personal experience in the computer field and with encryption in the military, I know placing false code into computer systems (i.e. Russian hacking code) is quite feasible. So, all these bold suppositions have merit and been raised because some brave former intelligence agency experts have concluded that, "It wasn't Russia. It wasn't even a hack. It was a leak." (August 14, 2017). What these persons had insinuated is false leaked information was dispersed from intelligence agencies, or others in high positions, to make it seem as though there was a Russian hack on the DNC server or computer(s). This is not as far-fetched as it seems.

Going back to the beginning, FBI Director James Comey testified to Congress that the FBI *relied on a technical report* from a private cyber security firm called Crowdstrike, which the DNC hired, about the alleged hacking. Why is this significant? It's because the FBI usually does its *own* check of any cyber security breaches, and then passes the data off to other appropriate agencies, if necessary. So why didn't the FBI pursue this case if national security was at risk?

Although Crowdstrike told the FBI about the alleged DNC hack, they also didn't follow normal protocol. They were supposed to share the so-called cyber intrusion with the National Cyber Communications Integration Center (NCCIC). But, instead, the Democratic National Committee (DNC) told Crowdstrike to share their supposed findings with the press, specifically the *Washington Post*. The newspaper wrote that Russians were behind the cyberattack (June 14, 2016). Then, the DNC and Crowdstrike refused to turn over their allegedly hacked network server (and still hasn't) to the intelligence agencies. Why?

The answer to why the DNC didn't allow anyone to peruse through their network server may be obvious. They undoubtedly may have had information on it which implicated the DNC or the Hillary Clinton campaign with unprincipled or illegal activities. And, the Russian hacking story was a false cover story because they were in the stages of building a case against their opponent in the 2016 election.

Before the alleged Russian hacking in 2016, the FBI and NSA were tracking cyber intrusions into the DNC server going back to July of 2015. Congressional leaders were briefed by the NSA about the *Advanced Persistent Threat* (APT) *29*, also known as "Fancy Bear". Then in 2016, while APT 29 was still under investigation by the FBI and NSA, the DNC was allegedly hacked. The name for this purported cyberattack was APT 28, or "Cozy Bear". Crowdstrike, which worked for the DNC, insisted that APT 28 was accomplished by the Russian military's main intelligence directorate named "GRU". Subsequently, John Podesta's emails were released by *Wikileaks* to the world to show very disparaging information about Hillary Clinton's campaign. He did not refute the authenticity of the emails revealed. Naturally, broad assumptions were made linking the Russians to *Wikileaks,* the DNC server hack, the released Podesta emails, and other messages from Clinton campaign members. And, yet, our top intelligence agencies, although investigating the "Fancy Bear" cyberattack of the DNC server for a year, didn't alert Podesta that his emails were intruded upon? Why? How could the cyber security group Crowdstrike track the new alleged DNC server hack ("Cozy Bear") and the FBI or NSA could not?

The FBI interviewed Podesta several months after the supposed hack of the DNC by *Wikileaks* and the Russians. But why did the FBI wait months before talking to him, especially since the Presidential election was taking place? These facts confirm Crowdstrike, paid by the DNC, was the only entity which professed that the "Cozy Bear" hack into the DNC server occurred. Again, the network server was never turned over to the proper agency, the NCICC, as per proper protocol, nor was the FBI or NSA allowed to check the new alleged server hack. Could this cyber security group have manipulated computer code to make it appear as if there were cyberattacks by Russia? Did they make up the story and give it to the *Washington Post* to reestablish a narrative that Russia was involved with the 2016 election? Nothing has disproved this. And, in 2018, the DNC wants to sue everyone for *their hoax*?

Then, there was the continuous drumbeat of blaming *Wikileaks* and the Russians for hacking into the DNC server to gain access to damaging emails about the Democratic Party and Clinton campaign. But *Wikileaks* has emphatically denied, on numerous occasions, that they had <u>not</u> received those hacked emails from a foreign state. This means their source which had obtained the emails from the Clinton campaign was not a foreign government. Therefore, it was more likely a domestic or foreign person, or group of individuals, not specifically Russia, was responsible for gaining access to the Democratic emails.

With the Russian hacking allegations swirling, subsequent Congressional inquiries and the release of unclassified intelligence reports occurred. The FBI and the DHS (Department of Homeland Security) put out a Joint Activity Report (JAR) which it called "Grizzly Steppe". It stated there had been malevolent cyberattacks by Russia "to compromise and exploit networks and endpoints associated with the U.S. elections." But in JAR it placed a disclaimer reading that the DHS *"does not provide any warranties of any kind regarding any information contained within"*. But why was the JAR information from a top U.S. intelligence community <u>not guaranteed?</u>

There was also another initial report unveiled to the public by the Intelligence Community. Although extensive, it seemed to provide assumptions from partisan examples inferring that the Russians were aiding one Presidential candidate and opposing another. In addition, this declassified ICA or intelligence community analysis explained the language used in the document. It stated there exist *"judgments"* that *"are not intended to imply that we have proof to show that something to be a fact."* And, the report mentions that when the term *high confidence* is utilized, that *"high confidence in a judgment does not imply that the assessment is a fact or certainty."* It also warned *"such judgments might be wrong"*. Again, it's another tactful document.

To the independent observer, there seems as though there may have been much *CYA* (cover your ass) terminology presented within the JAR, ICA, and other related documents involving the alleged hacks. The reports were mixed with facts and examples which assessed and judged that Russian cyber threats existed. But they didn't confirm it. To some degree, Russian threats did exist. As was later discovered, however, it had more to do with the spreading of misinformation through social media and in person than with the hacking of an election or DNC server.

There are several articles that question the Russian DNC hack story:

WASHINGTONTIMES (July 5, 2017) by Dan Boylan - *"Hacked computer server that handled DNC email remains out of reach of Russia investigators"*
https://www.washingtontimes.com/news/2017/jul/5/dnc-email-server-most-wanted-evidence-for-russia-i/

The NATION (August 9, 2017) by Patrick Lawrence – *"A New Report Raises Big Questions About Last Year's DNC Hack"*
https://www.thenation.com/article/a-new-report-raises-big-questions-about-last-years-dnc-hack/

BUSINESS INSIDER (November 7, 2017) by Michal Krantz – *"Trump reportedly told the director of the CIA to meet with a former intelligence official who claims Russia never hacked the DNC"* http://www.businessinsider.com/cia-pompeo-former-official-dnc-hack-trump-russia-intelligence-2017-11

NEW YORK POST (January 24, 2018) by Michael Goodwin - *"Evidence suggests a massive scandal is brewing at the FBI"* https://nypost.com/2018/01/23/evidence-suggests-a-massive-scandal-is-brewing-at-the-fbi/

Should we be leery of the Special Counsel and his team in the "Russian collusion" probe?

When the 45th President of the United States took office, the national security threats from Russia became a rallying cry to try and overturn the results of a Presidential election. It became magnified a hundred-fold with hysterical news media coverage, and by pundits, Democrats, and all those with allegiance to Clinton who couldn't accept that the candidate they had supported lost. Because Hillary Clinton couldn't forward Obama's liberal agendas, the Russians were to be blamed.

What came next were the accusations that anyone who had visited or had business ties with Russia, including the newly elected President, was culpable of colluding, as grand conspirators, with Russia and their operatives to win an election. Some individuals associated with the President were either assumed guilty of collusion, mocked, considered traitors, or labeled Russian spies. To emphasize this belief, Obama expelled 35 Russian diplomats from U.S. soil. Then, Russian collusion was advanced by a fake Russian dossier (more later). But FBI Director James Comey who had been investigating the Russia collusion issue was fired. So, all the sore losers shouted for a Special Counsel. These haters got their wish - and hoped for an early impeachment of the newly and duly elected 45th President of the United States.

A Special Counsel, appointed by the U.S. Justice Department, is supposed to be impartial. But it seems this type of investigator seeks to indict not to acquit the person being investigated. Also, usually large amounts of human and monetary resources are given to him, along with a wide range of latitude to scrutinize other related matters. Moreover, he is not supposed to have any conflicts of interest involving him or members of his team which would skew the case. Yet conflicts of interest and unethical members *are present* with this Special Counsel.

The conflicts of interest affiliated with the Special Counsel, Robert Mueller, are many. First, after FBI Director James Comey was fired by the President in early 2017, there were several persons interviewing for the position with the President. One of them was Robert Mueller himself. He wasn't selected for the Director of the FBI position. But after his interview, the next day, acting U.S. Attorney General of the DOJ, Rod Rosenstein appointed him as Special Counsel to investigate the President about Russian collusion. Doesn't that seem a bit fishy? Second, Mueller worked with former FBI Director James Comey, who he had been friends with for years. Third, *Wikileaks* exposed that in 2009 Secretary of State Hillary Clinton ordered Mueller to deliver a sample of stolen highly enriched uranium (HEU) to Russia. This led to the Uranium One Deal, in which 20 percent of U.S. uranium was ultimately sold to a Russian firm. In addition, the FBI and DOJ under the Obama Administration knew there were kickbacks and money laundering going on with Russia. And, still, they approved this ill-advised deal. Why? (more later). Lastly, Special Counsel Mueller appointed seemingly unscrupulous and biased persons on his team.

The second in command on Mueller's Special Counsel Team is an attorney whose name is Andrew Weissman. He has been deemed the special counsel's "pit bull." This person not only has conflict of interests but, in the past, he didn't follow the law. For example, 1) Weissman donated thousands of dollars to the Clinton campaign, and other Democrats. He was actually seen under her glass ceiling in New York City where she was supposed to have her Presidential victory party. 2) He had worked under the Department of Justice Fraud section under the Obama Administration. 3) It has been discovered Weissman was investigating Paul Manafort, an early member of President's 2016 campaign, for money laundering crimes before he became part of the Russia collusion investigation. 4) Weissman met with reporters of the Associated Press in which Weissman received information about Paul Manafort before and after the 2016 Presidential election. 5) In 1997, he was reprimanded by a judge in the eastern district of New York for withholding evidence. 6) Well before the 2016 Presidential election, Weissman was reported to the Justice Department's Inspector General by a whistleblower because of his "corrupt legal practices". 7) His conviction of Arthur Andersen employees shredding Enron accounting documents when the company was collapsing was overturned by the Supreme Court because he gave less than credible information to a jury. This cost thousands their jobs. And, he named 114 individuals as "unindicted co-conspirators", which blocked them from testifying in the defense of those who would be convicted of crimes. 8) Weissman aided in criminalizing four Merrill Lynch employees who were sent to jail because of the Enron scandal. His colleagues in the case were said to have not turned over critical evidence that could have cleared the accused. Then, after jail-time was served by these persons, the fraud convictions were overturned by a higher court. Why would the Special Counsel hire someone with this track record to be part of his team?

In addition to Andrew Weissman, eight of the other attorneys involved in the Special Counsel Russia investigation gave contributions to Barack Obama, Hillary Clinton, or the Democratic Party elections. They are Jeannie Rhee, Andrew Goldstein, Greg Andres, James Quarles, Elizabeth Preloger, Branon Van Grack, Rush Atkinson, and Kyle Freeny. Moreover, it was discovered that Jeannie Rhee worked for the Clinton Foundation. And, the disconcerting irony is this Special Counsel team is conducting business in a Washington, D.C. district which has impaneled a grand jury from people who had overwhelming voted for Hillary Clinton (96%)? It's just one of many reasons the investigation seems to be politicized and a "witch hunt".

But one of the biggest names to come out of the Mueller team was Peter Strzok, a FBI Deputy Director of Counterintelligence. After the Special Counsel team had been in place for months, Strzok's blatant bias against the 45th U.S. President, along with his colleague and lover, Lisa Page, would be discovered through thousands of text messages. Also, Strzok's text exchanges with Lisa Page may have unwittingly revealed a high-level cover-up which may implicate many in the Obama Administration (more later). Yet, these revelations of bias and conflict of interest were only discovered many months after Special Counsel Mueller had fired Strzok from the Russia collusion investigation.

If that wasn't enough, reports flowed out that Strzok had been involved with the fake Russian dossier in its initial stages, and had investigated General Michael Flynn, a former National Security Advisor to the President. Also, Strzok was found to have been involved in drafting and re-writing the exoneration letter for Hillary Clinton in her email server case. He allegedly knew Clinton's server had been hacked and said nothing. Strzok may have even given easy interviews to Cheryl Mills and Huma Abedin, Hillary Clinton's top aids, during her criminal email investigation. He remains at the center of much scandal.

But still more was reported regarding the many text message exchanges between Strzok and Page. After the famous *tarmac meeting* between former Attorney General Loretta Lynch and Bill Clinton, it was suggested (July 1, 2016) that Lynch knew Hillary was to be exonerated.

Peter Strzok: "Timing looks like hell"
Lisa Page: "Yeah, that is awful thing"
Lisa Page: "It's a real profile in courage (sic), since she knows no charges will be brought."

This was mere days before partisan FBI Director James Comey had exonerated Clinton in a press conference after the July 4th weekend of 2016. Comey's action was unprecedented because he usurped his boss', Loretta Lynch, authority by revealing the results of an investigation in public. But what he told the public may have been far from the truth.

Comey would later testify at a Congressional hearing under oath that he made the decision on his own to exonerate Hillary Clinton in the email server case. He said this was done without consulting with the former Attorney General Loretta Lynch. But as was just shown through text messages, Lynch, already knew of the exoneration. So, how did Lynch know about the exoneration and Comey didn't know that she knew? Naturally, to any rational person, this doesn't make sense.

In addition, former FBI Director James Comey testified under oath, while being grilled by Congress, that he made the results of the investigation public because AG Lynch wanted to call the investigation into Hillary Clinton's emails a "matter" <u>not</u> an "investigation". This was the same type of term Clinton used when referring to her email scandal on the campaign trail. In addition, Peter Strzok, James Comey, and others were involved with changing the language of the exoneration letter that had read "gross negligence" to "extremely careless". This was regarding how Clinton had handled her classified emails. Gross negligence is a criminal offense, and extreme carelessness is not. But they weren't finished. The wording of the exoneration letter had also been softened from "reasonably likely" to "possible" with regard to the foreign hostile actors and adversaries hacking into Clinton's server. These changes in this crucial letter were just one of the many reasons Hillary Clinton was not charged with any crimes and could continue running for President of the United States. The fix was in - definitely!

That's not all though. It had been discovered that in addition to the initial text messages disclosed, there were actually a total of 50,000 text messages between Peter Strzok's and lover Lisa Page in a two-year period. But, a very key five-month period of text messages (December 2016 – May 2017) were found to have disappeared from the FBI records by January 22nd, 2018 because of a so-called "technical glitch" with the FBI. Current representatives in Congress and Attorney General Jeff Sessions were furious about the developments. Then, after *Judicial Watch* (a conservative foundation, who fights for accountability and integrity in law, politics and government) subpoenaed for the missing text messages, within 48 hours they magically reappeared from the FBI. It was another sign of a cover-up. Some in the FBI wanted to save face.

After these additional texts were found, more incriminating messages surfaced. Strzok had not only been involved with the Clinton email scandal but the *Russia dossier too*. Two days after the Special Counsel, Robert Muller was appointed, Strzok implied he would be part of the Special Counsel investigation against the President, whom he hated. He was glad but was worried there was no investigation to indict the President. On May 19th, 2017, Peter Stzrok said to Lisa Page.

"An investigation leading to impeachment?...You and I both know the odds are nothing. If I thought it was likely, I'd be there no question. I hesitate in part because of my gut sense and concern there's no big there there."

Then, there was another text message exchange between the two secret lovers (since they were both married) from late 2016. It seems to incriminate the former President of the United States (POTUS), Barack Obama, as being complicit in an investigation. It couldn't have been referring to the Hillary email investigation because that had been closed earlier in the year. Therefore, logically, it was likely regarding the Russia collusion which was being *hatched.* The two lovebirds texted about giving talking points (TP) to FBI Director James Comey because the POTUS wanted to be kept informed.

Peter Strzok: "TPs for D?"
Lisa Page: "Yes, bc potus wants to know everything we are doing"

Therefore, it may be that President Obama had given an untrue statement to Chris Wallace on *FOX News* (April 2016) because Obama refuted, he was involved in Justice Department or FBI investigations.

"I can guarantee that. And I can guarantee that not because I give Attorney General Lynch a directive, that is institutionally how we have always operated. I do not talk to the attorney general about pending investigations. I do not talk to FBI directors about pending investigations. We have a strict line, and always have maintained it....I guarantee it. I guarantee that there is no political influence in any investigation conducted by the Justice Department or the FBI, not just in this case, but in any case. Full stop. Period."

After over a year of investigation, Special Counsel Mueller interviewed well over a hundred witnesses. He has also indicted former members of the President's 2016 campaign team on charges *not related to Russia collusion* – his original mandate. There are Paul Manafort who pled not guilty to money laundering and other crimes; Rick Gates pleading guilty to perjury (in plea bargain); General Michael Flynn, Ukrainian lawyer, Van der Zwaan, and George Papadopoulos who were indicted for perjury. Yet, in 2018, evidence keeps surfacing which could allow some of the accused (i.e. Flynn and Manafort) to alter some of their indictments or sentences, or in the future sue. Time will tell!

Did Russia meddle in the 2016 U.S. Elections?

Apparently, the President Obama didn't heed the warnings of many Republicans on Washington's Capitol Hill years ago. In the 2012 Presidential campaign year during a debate with Republican Mitt Romney, President Obama famously mocked his opponent by saying,

"Gov. Romney, I'm glad that you recognize that al-Qaida is a threat, because a few months ago when you were asked what's the biggest geopolitical threat facing America, you said Russia, not al-Qaida. You said Russia ... the 1980s, they're now calling to ask for their foreign policy back because, you know, the Cold War's been over for 20 years."

Obama was wrong about Russian meddling then, and as years passed, he would come to regret his failure to address the issue. After a year and a half of the Russia, Russia, Russia chants there finally came to light some evidence that Russians meddled in our 2016 Presidential election. But they had been involved in this meddling since 2014.

Fast forward to February 16, 2018, Deputy Attorney General Rod Rosenstein announced that a federal grand jury working with Special Counsel Robert Mueller indicted three Russian companies and 13 Russians who allegedly conspired in the 2016 Elections. The first company involved was Internet Research Agency LLC - a Russian company based in St. Petersburg. They employed more than 80 people on data analysis, finance and information technology, graphics, and search engine manipulations. Their budget was in excess of $1.25 million a month by September 2016. The other two firms, Management and Consulting LLC and Concord Catering, were funded and controlled by Evgeny Victorovich Posogon through something called Project Latka. Hundreds of accounts were created on *YouTube, Facebook,* and *Twitter* to draw users to fake accounts. *United Muslims of America* and *Tennessee GOP* were just two of the accounts created for the ruse.

Both Presidential candidate's 2016 campaigns <u>combined</u> spent a total of $2.4 billion. This included $81 million on *Facebook* and *Instagram* advertisements during the election. But the Russians only spent $100,000 worth of ads on *Facebook* and *Instagram,* while buying 3,000 ads from *Facebook* alone. Of the ads posted, *Facebook* indicated that 44% came *before* the election and 56% *after* the election. About 25 percent of the ads were never viewed, according to *Facebook*.

Examining the key swing states, or purple states, in the election, the monetary amounts spent by Russians to meddle in the election were <u>not</u> vast, but instead minuscule. They had bought ads on *Facebook* which were worth $300 in Pennsylvania, $1,979 in Wisconsin, and $823 in Michigan. So, given the data found and released to the public, how much of any impact did Russian meddling have on social media?

Ron Goldman, the Vice President of *Facebook* tweeted,

"The majority of the Russian ads spent happened AFTER the election. We [Facebook] shared that fact, but very few outlets have covered it because it doesn't align with the main media narrative of Trump and the election."

He added it was <u>not</u> the main goal of the Russians to promote the President-to-be. But Goldman mentioned it *was*

"...the main goal of the Russian propaganda and misinformation effort...to divide America using our institutions, like free speech and social media, against us...It has stoked fear and hatred amongst Americans. It is working incredibly well. We are quite divided as a nation."

In tandem with social media accounts, false identities and fraudulent bank accounts were utilized too. Although there were ads and rallies opposing Hillary Clinton, the Russians also staged rallies in favor of her during and after the elections to sow discord in America.

Besides these facts, the result was basically good news for the 45th President of the United States. Deputy Attorney General stated,

"The defendants established social media pages and groups to communicate with 'unwitting' Americans."

In the indictment letter, it reads,

"...some defendants, and without revealing their Russian association, communicated with unwitting individuals associated with the Trump Campaign and other political activists to seek to coordinate political activities."

The word *unwitting* vindicates those engaged with meddling Russians who had been impersonating American citizens. Also, Deputy Attorney General Rosenstein mentioned there was "no allegation" that the Russians' activities "changed the outcome of the election."

From the letter, below are the companies and many individuals indicted in the Russian meddling. But most, if not all, will not face charges unless they are extradited from Russia. That is highly unlikely.

<u>Russian Companies:</u>
*1)   Internet Research Agency LLC a/k/a Mediaintez LLC a/k/a Glavset LLC a/k/a Mixinfo LLC a/k/a Azimut LLC a/k/a Novinfo LLC,
*2)   Concord Management and Consulting LLC
*3)   Concord Catering

<u>Russians Individuals:</u>
*1)   Yevgeniy Viktorovich Prigozhin
*2)   Mikhail Ivanovich Bystrov
*3)   Mikhail Leonidovich Burchik a/k/a Mikhail Abramov
*4)   Aleksandra Yuryevna Krylova
*5)   Anna Vlaislavovna Bogacheva
*6)   Sergey Pavlovich Polozov
*7)   Maria Anatolyevna Bovada a/k/a Maria Anatolyevna Belyaeva
*8)   Robert Sergeyevich Bovda
*9)   Dzheykhun Nasimi Ogly Aslanov a/k/a Jayhoon Aslanov a/k/a Jay Aslanov
*10) Vadim Vladimirovich Podkopaev
*11) Gleb Igorevich Vasilchenko
*12) Irina Viktorovna Kaverzina
*13) Vladimir Venkov

Even though these Russian entities may not be indicted in the U.S., there are several persons who still might be. And, this has nothing to do with the President or people affiliated with him. It has to do with others that were pointing the finger. And, turn around being fair play, the accusers of guilt inevitably may become the guilty. Although it's true that Russian meddling occurred, the *real* Russian collusion may have occurred with Clinton's team, Obama Administration, DOJ, and FBI.

But to be clear and quite honest, Russians are not the only country who meddles in elections. Many other nations get involved in the elections of countries, including the United States of America. The U.S. has attempted to disrupt the process of elections for many decades for the purposes of desiring democracy to take hold there or to halt the rise of a tyrannical regime. In *American Spectator,* reports show:

- In 2006, a U.S. Senator backed a far-left candidate for the Presidency of Kenya. His name was Raila Odinga.

- In 2009, the U.S. supported leftist President, Manuel Zelaya, in Honduras, trying to gain re-election, even though Zelaya tried to change the election process. The Supreme Court of Honduras removed him from office. Then, Zelaya went into exile.

- In 2011, the U.S. aided with the removal of Muammar Gaddafi, the Libyan dictator, from power. After this, Libya became a breeding ground for terrorists like ISIS and al-Qaeda.

- In 2012, the U.S. intervened to help get Mohammed Morsi, a member of the Muslim brotherhood, who supports Sharia law, elected to the presidency in Egypt. Upset by the rise of Morsi, the Egyptian people removed, and then arrested him for treason. The people placed a more pro-America moderate named Abdel Fattah al-Sisi as President.

- In 2015, monies were funneled to Israel to oppose Prime Minister Benjamin Netanyahu

- Millions of dollars had been funneled through the U.S. State Department and USAID, and by the liberal activist billionaire George Soros, to subvert the center-right party in Macedonia. Also, there was U.S. involvements with the elections in other Balkan nations, including Greece, Albania, Bosnia, and Kosovo.

What do all actions of U.S. election meddling have in common? They were under the reign of President Barack Obama. But to be fair, there have been other Presidents that have undoubtedly meddled with other countries' elections. Since the 1940's it has been reported that the U.S. interfered with elections in Italy (1948), Japan (1950's) Iran (1953), Guatemala (1954), Lebanon (1957), Congo (1961), and Chile (1964), and many other unreported places elsewhere around the globe.

In addition, and related to Russian meddling, in recent times, an organization called *Hamilton 68* had been searching for propaganda and disinformation on Twitter about Russia. They are attempting to provide evidence that Russia is our enemy. Although there are many other countries, like China, who are our adversaries, this group seemly only wants to expose Russian internet bots. But could their real goal be politically motivated? Even *Wikileaks* founder Julian Assange tweeted:

"Hamilton 68' doesn't track propaganda. It is propaganda. Its "Council"? Stuffed with Bill Kristol, Michael Chertoff, Mike Morell, etc. Its funding? Opaque (see its 990s). Its methodology? Unfalsifiable--Twitter users put on ad-hoc secret lists based on political view. Appalling."

All this proves is many people have Russia on their brain. They are using this as a ruse. Instead of looking for real Russian influence and collusion, the mainstream media, political operatives, and pundits are doing their best to redirect the American people's attention. They want to keep everyone's eyes and ears upon their shining object - the Russian collusion with the 45th American President. And, they don't speak about the obvious links and dealings of the Hillary Clinton campaign, Obama Administration, and Democratic Party with the phony Russian dossier.

Who was behind the Russian dossier story?

In January 2017, the newly-elected President was visited by then-FBI Director James Comey. He showed the 45th U.S. President the phony Russian dossier, flaunting it in his face. But the FBI Director told the

President three times he was not under investigation. Comey said only the President's campaign team was being examined for possible crimes. So, the President was only a subject <u>not</u> a target of the probe. But Comey took notes of the meeting with the President that day and other times.

Weeks later, Comey was fired by the President because of his mishandling of the Clinton case. This set off a firestorm. Although the President was only the subject of the Russian dossier probe, the biased media and politicians maligned him and ranted "obstruction of justice".

Of course, the mainstream media insinuated that this firing impeded the investigation; and it proved the President colluded with Russia. The media wanted nothing more than to willingly be complicit in promoting a false narrative to the public. Their needs to delegitimize the President was not only out of hatred for him, but to save themselves from possibly being exposed as knowing participants in this scandal.

After the firing of James Comey, under oath he testified to Congress that he leaked notes he had taken from the FBI regarding the President to a friend to give to *The New York Times*. (But in April 2018, these notes and others may have been deemed classified, and Comey may face charges in the future). Since he was very upset about his firing, the ex-FBI Director told Congress he desired a special counsel to investigate Russian collusion and possible obstruction of justice against the President. He also said to Congress that the dossier was "salacious" and "unverified", and the President was <u>not</u> under investigation.

Inevitably, although the dossier was unsubstantiated, it still had been used as a pretense to spur a Special Counsel, headed by Robert Mueller. Why? Since Attorney General Jeff Sessions recused himself from any investigation involving the President (Sessions was part of the 2016 campaign) Deputy Attorney General Rod Rosenstein appointed a Special Counsel to find alleged collusion between Russia and the President. Yet there were conflicts of interest. Rosenstein was one of the persons who signed off on a FISA application to obtain a FISA warrant (more later), and wrote the letter recommending Comey be fired. Also, Special Counsel Mueller had worked for years with James Comey in the Obama Administration, who may be a witness in the case.

In addition, it seems Rod Rosenstein has intentionally given Special Counsel Robert Muller much latitude in this Russia probe. That means Mueller can look at other crimes other than the Russia collusion assertion. The reasoning behind this is simple. There are many who seek to impeach the 45th U.S. President. Those involved with the dossier know it will carry no weight in a case against the President, so they need other options. Anyway, it's important to understand how the Russia dossier became available and is being used against the President. But the story is long and complex. So, it will be explained as best as possible.

The Story:

In the spring of 2017, what was exposed, because of the excellent reporting by a journalist Sara A. Carter, John Solomon, an executive VP and journalist of *The Hill,* and *Hannity* on *FOX News,* was stunning. This Russian dossier was concocted by a British spy Christopher Steele, given to a firm called *Fusion GPS,* and revealed to the Hillary Clinton campaign. This Russian (or Steele) dossier was then utilized by the United States intelligence agencies (FBI, DOJ, and so forth) to obtain a Foreign Intelligence Surveillance Authorization (FISA) warrant to spy on Carter Page. And, yet, apparently, the only minor truths within the pages of the dossier is Page, a member of Trump's early campaign team, went to Russia on business and the Russians didn't like Hillary Clinton.

Carter Page previously worked under-cover for the FBI to capture a Russian Operative Evgeny Buryakov in 2013. So, why, now, would Carter Page's phones, emails, and more come to be under surveillance? The Obama Administration and others needed a *patsy spy* to frame the Russia story. But Page must have been a double-agent if that was true.

The real truth is Page briefly worked in some low capacity role in 2016 campaign at the beginning of the President's election bid. Those looking to delegitimize and criminalize the President wanted a way to provide more evidence there was collusion with the Russians to win the presidency. So, they dishonestly used Page as a pretext to try and obtain a FISA warrant. But a FISA warrant was <u>not</u> granted by the secret FISA court <u>until</u> the Russian (or Steele) dossier and other hearsay data regarding George Papadopoulos became available.

Although this Russian dossier was full of salacious lies, those in the Obama Administration who asked a FISA court to attain a FISA warrant (702) to spy on foreign entities in essence used it to spy on Carter Page, *and* the President-to-be, *and* others in his campaign.

The actual purpose of obtaining a FISA warrant is to allow U.S. intelligence agencies to spy on *foreign adversaries*. But what happens in these instances is there is something called "incidental contact". This means that though intelligence agencies are spying on foreign entities, they may also pick up the conversations or video of American citizens as they watch and listen. Let's be clear. U.S. law permits some to spy on foreign threats. But, it's <u>not</u> legal to use a FISA warrant as a pretense to wiretap an American citizen. This is called unlawful *unmasking*.

In late 2016-early 2017, the 45th U.S. President was tipped off he and others were being unmasked by the Obama administration. After months of confirming this, in March 2017, the President sent out a tweet indicating he had been "wire-tapped". Of course, the Obama Administration denied it and the mainstream media mocked him. But although the President used old terminology, he was right.

Truth be told; however, this type of spying first began during the Bush Administration after '911', under something called the Patriot Act. If you know about Edward Snowden, then you know what has been going on in America. The U.S. was unlawfully spying on its citizens.

Of course, there were doubters and those attempting to cover-up the evidence that the Obama Administration used FISA warrants as a political tool to spy on the President-to-be, his campaign members, and others. As alluded to, this is highly unethical and illegal to use a court issued FISA warrant to purposefully spy on citizens. But it seems this had been done. And, as was touched upon, it may have been part of an "insurance policy" in the event Hillary Clinton lost the Presidential election - which she did. The question was who authorized all this?

Let's get back to discussing the Steele Dossier. This document was obtained by Christopher Steele, a former British secret agent, who received unsubstantiated information from Russian informants. Then,

Perkins Coie, a law firm used by the Clinton campaign and DNC, paid a company *Fusion GPS* for the Russian dossier. But allegedly, Steele knew the Clinton campaign paid for the dossier. And, he was glad because, as was found, he "hated" the President-to-be. So, ironically, the only Russian collusion that has been discovered took place between the Hillary Clinton campaign, the Democratic Party, and the Russians.

Next, it has been reported that when Steele first obtained the dossier, he pitched it to news agencies, such as *The New York Times, New Yorker, CNN, Washington Post, Yahoo News, Mother Jones,* and *Buzzfeed* so they could spread this filth. But other than *Yahoo News,* the other media outlets initially didn't report the findings in the dossier because they may have known about its salacious lies and phony nature.

During this time the FBI was working with Christopher Steele in conjunction with finding out more about the dossier implicating the President-to-be. But when the FBI discovered Steele was fishing this document to media agencies, the FBI stopped working with him.

Nevertheless, even though the FBI ended contact with Steele and knew his information was probably less than credible, the FBI *still* approached a FISA court judge to get a warrant to spy on Carter Page, the President, and others in his campaign anyway. They utilized this dossier and a *Yahoo news* report which came out about the dossier as being *legitimate* and *verified* evidence to obtain FISA warrants from FISA courts. Yet they failed to identify to the court in their FISA application that the Clinton campaign and DNC paid for the Steele dossier. They only put a footnote in it indicating a political party was involved. Why did the FISA court judge not question this? (more later)

Through more digging by reporters John Solomon and Sara A. Cater, other information started being revealed about those who in the intelligence agencies of the Obama Administration. To start with, there was Peter Strzok, FBI Deputy Director of Counterintelligence, Lisa Page, FBI legal counsel to Andrew McCabe, FBI Deputy Director, and Bruce Ohr, DOJ Deputy Attorney General. As was mentioned, Strzok and Page were found to have sent many text messages disparaging the 45th President of the United States. But one of the most damaging texts is one which indicated that while these two FBI members were in FBI

Deputy Director Andrew McCabe's office, an "insurance policy" was to be worked out in case he won the election. This insurance policy may have been *the use of a phony dossier* to delegitimize, appoint a Special Counsel, and begin an impeachment trial against the U.S. President.

During the 2016 elections, FBI Deputy Director Andrew McCabe's wife would also receive campaign finance donations of about $675,000 from two entities associated with long-term Clinton friend, Terry McAuliffe, the governor of Virginia. But this was when Andrew McCabe and James Comey were supposedly investigating the Hillary Clinton email scandal. It was a blatant conflict of interest. And, McCabe should have recused himself from the investigation.

So, in 2017 – 2018, Andrew McCabe drew much scrutiny, and was forced to retire from the FBI in January 2018. Then, in March 2018, the Inspector General Office, who was conducting a huge investigation consisting of examining 1.2 million documents, gave a report to the FBI's own Office of Professional Responsibility. This office in turn told the Department of Justice Attorney General Jeff Sessions why McCabe should be terminated. And so, FBI Deputy Director Andrew McCabe was fired two days before he was about to get his pension.

Although McCabe wouldn't get his pension immediately, he would be eligible to receive it in seven years. But the hysterical media didn't care about his criminality and spun the story to make it seem like he was the victim. They blamed the President for his firing, when it was the Inspector General and FBI who had actually recommended his firing. In the end, this will be the least of McCabe's concerns since he may be in line for criminal charges including obstruction and perjury.

Regarding *Fusion GPS*, this company was the one who obtained the phony Steele dossier and then sold it to the Clinton campaign and DNC. As per Alek Boyd, London-based Venezuelan journalist, this firm was "good at spreading misinformation, disinformation and smears." Boyd said the company was responsible for putting out false reports, labeling him a pedophile and worse, after he had criticized one their clients, Derwick Associates. Bill Broward, an American financier, also said he and his lawyer, Sergey Manitsky, were smeared by Fusion GPS. Manitsky was then discredited, tortured, and killed in a Russian jail.

Also, Thor Halvorssen, CEO of Human Rights Foundation, was probing purported Venezuelan government corruption with firms like Derwick Associates. And, he stated in a congressional hearing that,

"Fusion GPS devised smear campaigns, prepared dossiers containing false information, carefully placed slanderous news items, and possibly even staged a break-in at the home of one of the key whistleblowers."

After Congressional testimony by Glenn Simpson, founder of *Fusion GPS*, bank records revealed and confirmed who had actually paid for the unverified and slanderous Steele dossier. It was the lawyer of the Hillary Clinton campaign and Democratic National Committee (DNC) who did their bidding for them. Apparently, there was a payment of about $12 million for the dossier. And, that was not all that was revealed. Glenn Simpson stated someone had been killed because of this dossier. Could it have been DNC staffer, Seth Rich, which was mysteriously shot one evening for no apparent reason? We don't know. But when his murder was examined nothing was taken from his person, as he trod upon the dirty streets of Washington, D.C. Why? Sadly, there has been no definitive evidence to prove or disprove why he was killed.

Anyway, why would anyone, especially someone running for U.S. President, like Hillary Clinton, use a firm like *Fusion GPS,* which had an apparent record of smearing people? It's obvious why. The Clinton campaign and DNC wanted to delegitimize the newly elected U.S. President. She and others envied and hated his appeal to the American people; and, they are worried because there is much more to the story.

In a significant related matter, it was discovered via more excellent reporting by Carter and Solomon that the fourth highest DOJ official named Bruce Ohr met with British spy Christopher Steele and *Fusion GPS*. Ohr would testify that Steele was "desperate that Donald Trump not get elected and was passionate about him not being President." But, also, in another conflict of interest, Ohr's wife Nellie had worked for *Fusion GPS* - which, as previously noted, gave the Russian (or Steele) dossier to the Clinton campaign. So, after all this came to light, Ohr was demoted twice. Yet, still remained employed at the DOJ.

Additionally, more information was found confirming that the dodgy Christopher Steele had fished the phony dossier to some news organizations. But only *Yahoo News* and *Buzzfeed* reported on it. And, yet, the false dossier and one report from *Yahoo News* were used as two separate sources in part to obtain a FISA warrant. The Steele dossier, however, was the only real source. *Yahoo News* had not done its own independent investigation on the dossier. So, this wasn't a legitimate source. There was only *one source*. This is called circular reporting.

By early 2018, and after many months of interviews by The House Oversight Committee in Congress, a Republican *Surveillance Memo* was drafted and voted upon. It was reviewed and declassified by the President. Then, the committee, led by Republican Chairman Devin Nunes (California) released it to the public (2/3/18). The purpose of the memo was to provide updates of an on-going investigation by the Congressional House Oversight Committee about concerns of unlawful and legitimate actions taken by previous and current DOJ and FBI members - who had possibly participated in FISA warrant abuses.

The memo stated on October 2016, the DOJ and FBI "sought and received a FISA (Foreign Intelligence Surveillance Act) probable cause order authorizing electronic surveillance on Carter Page" – a U.S. citizen and volunteer for the would-be President. The FISA application needed to be certified by FBI Director James Comey, and approved by Attorney General Loretta Lynch, as well as Deputy Attorney General (DAG) Dana Boente or "a Senate confirmed Assistant Attorney General working for the National Security Division". Again, this initial FISA warrant was obtained from the FISA court to spy on Carter Page. Then, every 90 days a new FISA application was needed for a new warrant to continue surveillance. In total, there was one initial FISA warrant, and three renewed ones. FBI Director James Comey signed three FISA applications and FBI Deputy Director Andrew McCabe signed one. In addition, Deputy Attorney General (DAG) Rod Rosenstein, acting-DAG's Sally Yates, and Dana Boente each signed one FISA application to obtain the FISA warrants presented to a FISA court judge.

The relevant and disturbing facts about this investigation were found through the below excerpts of the memo from the Committee.

1) The "dossier" compiled by Christopher Steele (Steele dossier) on behalf of the Democratic National Committee (DNC) and the Hillary Clinton campaign formed an essential part of the Carter Page FISA application. Steele was a longtime FBI source who was paid over $160,000 by the DNC and Clinton campaign, via the law firm Perkins Coie and research firm Fusion GPS, to obtain derogatory information on Donald Trump's ties to Russia.

a) Neither the initial application in October 2016, nor any of the renewals, disclose or reference the role of the DNC, Clinton campaign, or any party/campaign in funding Steele's efforts, even though the political origins of the Steele dossier were then known to senior DOJ and FBI officials.

b) The initial FISA application notes Steele was working for a named U.S. person, but does not name Fusion GPS and principal Glenn Simpson, who was paid by a U.S. law firm (Perkins Coie) representing the DNC (even though it was known by DOJ at the time that political actors were involved with the Steele dossier). The application does not mention Steele was ultimately working on behalf of—and paid by—the DNC and Clinton campaign, or that the FBI had separately authorized payment to Steele for the same information.

2) The Carter Page FISA application also cited extensively a September 23, 2016, Yahoo News article by Michael Isikoff, which focuses on Page's July 2016 trip to Moscow. This article does not corroborate the Steele dossier because it is derived from information leaked by Steele himself to Yahoo News. The Page FISA application incorrectly assesses that Steele did not directly provide information to Yahoo News. Steele has admitted in British court filings that he met with Yahoo News—and several other outlets—in September 2016 at the direction of Fusion GPS. Perkins Coie was aware of Steele's initial media contacts because they hosted at least one meeting in Washington DC in 2016 with Steele and Fusion GPS where this matter was discussed.

a) Steele was suspended and then terminated as an FBI source for what the FBI defines as the most serious of violations—an unauthorized disclosure to the media of his relationship with the FBI in an October 30, 2016, Mother Jones article by David Corn Steele should have been terminated for his previous undisclosed contacts with Yahoo and other outlets in September—before the Page application was submitted to the FISC in October—but Steele improperly concealed from and lied to the FBI about those contacts.

b) Steele's numerous encounters with the media violated the cardinal rule of source handling- maintaining confidentiality - demonstrating Steele had become a less than reliable source for the FBI.

3) Before and after Steele was terminated as a source, he maintained contact with DOJ via then-Associate Deputy Attorney General Bruce Ohr, a senior DOJ official who worked closely with Deputy Attorneys General Yates and later Rosenstein. Shortly after the election, the FBI began interviewing Ohr, documenting his communications with Steele. For example, in September 2016, Steele admitted to Ohr his feelings against then-candidate Trump when Steele said he "was desperate that Donald Trump not get elected and was passionate about him not, being President." This clear evidence of Steele's bias was recorded by Ohr at the time and subsequently in official FBI files— but not reflected in any of the Page FISA applications.

a) During this same time period, Ohr's wife was employed by Fusion GPS to assist in the cultivation of opposition research on Trump. Ohr later provided the FBI with all of his wife's opposition research, paid for by the DNC and Clinton campaign via Fusion GPS. The Ohrs' relationship with Steele and Fusion GPS was inexplicably concealed from the FISC.

4) According to the head of the counterintelligence division, Assistant Director Bill Priestap, corroboration of the Steele dossier was in its "infancy" at the time of the initial Page FISA application. After Steele was terminated, a source validation report conducted by an independent unit within FBI assessed Steele's reporting as only minimally corroborated. Yet, in early January 2017, Director Comey briefed President-elect Trump on a summary of the Steele dossier, even though it was—according to his June 2017 testimony - "salacious and unverified." While the FISA application relied on Steele's past record of credible reporting on other unrelated matters, it ignored or concealed his anti-Trump financial and ideological motivations. Furthermore, Deputy Director McCabe testified before the Committee in December 2017 that "no surveillance warrant would have been sought from the FISC without the Steele dossier information."

5) The Page FISA application also mentions information regarding fellow Trump campaign advisor George Papadopoulos, but there is no evidence of any cooperation or conspiracy between Papadopoulos and Page. The Papadopoulos information triggered the opening of an FBI counterintelligence investigation in late July 2016 by FBI agent Pete Strzok. Strzok was reassigned by the Special Counsel's Office to FBI Human Resources for improper text messages with his mistress, FBI Attorney Lisa Page (no known relation to Carter Page), where they both demonstrated a clear bias against Trump and in favor of Clinton, whom Strzok had also investigated. The Strzok/Lisa Page texts also reflect extensive discussions about the investigation, orchestrating leaks to the media, and include a meeting with Deputy Director McCabe to discuss an "insurance" policy against the Trump election.

This memorandum confirmed some of what has already been uncovered by journalists Sara A. Carter and John Solomon (*The Hill*) on *Hannity (Fox News)* over months of investigations. Then, a second memo was released to the public. This redacted Republican led Senate Judiciary Committee memo came out within a week of the House Oversight Committee memo. This second memo from the Senate corroborated the first Republican led House Committee memo. And, it provided a little more information than the first. It stated:

- The Russian dossier made up the bulk of the FISA warrant.
- Steele was accused of misleading the FBI by telling them he wasn't working with the mainstream media.
- According to British court records, Steele spoke to *The New York Times, Washington Post, Yahoo News, The New Yorker*, and *CNN*, among others.
- Steele may or may not have used Russian sources for the dossier.
- Former FBI Director James Comey relied on the Steel dossier's credibility to get the FISA warrant although the FBI knew Steele was NOT credible.

- *Fusion GPS*, who Steele worked for, was coordinating efforts to send the dossier to media outlets.
- The FBI vaguely referenced the dossier's political origins to the FISA court judge, hiding the fact it was bought by the DNC and Hillary Clinton campaign.
- The U.S. State department fed information to Steele (i.e. Sidney Blumenthal and Corey Shears)

This last note is very relevant. It implicates the U.S. State Department under President Obama. This second memo clearly shows the State Department knew about the Steele dossier. Then, days after the memo's release, an article came out from Jonathan Winer - a former State Department official who worked under the Obama administration (2009 – 2017). He confirmed Christopher Steele and allies of Hillary Clinton gave him intelligence reports indicating the 45th U.S. President was compromised by Russians. Winer said in 2016 Steele gave him a dossier claiming improprieties between the President and Russia. He shared this with former Assistant Secretary of State Victoria Nuland, who then informed former Secretary of State John Kerry.

Later, Winer met with Sidney Blumenthal, the long-time friend, journalist, activist, and political smear artist of the Clinton's, and showed him the dossier from Steele. He said Blumenthal showed him some notes by another Clinton ally, journalist Cody Shearer, who had been compiling a *second dossier* which corroborated the same story Winer had originally received from Steele. Winer mentioned he didn't let anyone know about the meeting between him and Blumenthal at the State Department. And, it was his belief that Steele was not going to distribute this information with anyone else in the government. But Steele did give his unsubstantiated data to others – namely, the FBI, *Fusion GPS*, *Yahoo News*, Clinton campaign, and Democratic National Committee (DNC). So, the Republican Oversight Committee memos uncovered some very interesting facts pointing to the Obama State Department being involved with the Steele dossier.

Then in 2018, there was an email found by the elder statesman of the Senate Judiciary Committee Republican Chuck Grassley that raised eyebrows. He indicated former National Security Advisor (NSA), Susan

Rice, wrote an email just minutes after the 45th President of the United States was sworn into office on January 20[th]2017. The email suggested that Rice, President Obama, former FBI Director James Comey, and former Deputy Attorney General Sally Yates had a meeting in the Oval Office about Russian interference in the 2016 Presidential election two weeks ago. The head of the NSA Susan Rice wrote:

"President Obama began the conversation by stressing his continued commitment to ensuring that every aspect of this issue is handled by the Intelligence and law enforcement communities 'by the book'. The President stressed that he is not asking about, initiating or instructing anything from a law enforcement perspective. He reiterated that our law enforcement team needs to proceed as it normally would by the book."

Senators Chuck Grassley and Lindsey Graham sent a letter to Rice's lawyer to inquire about this peculiar email stating in part:

"It strikes us as odd that, among your activities in the final moments on the final day of the Obama administration, you would feel the need to send yourself such an unusual email purporting to document a conversation involving President Obama and his interactions with the FBI regarding the Trump/Russia investigation. In addition, despite your claim that President Obama repeatedly told Mr. Comey to proceed 'by the book,' substantial questions have arisen about whether officials at the FBI, as well as at the Justice Department and the State Department, actually did proceed 'by the book.'"

It's been speculated that this email from Susan Rice to herself was an obvious way to cover for President Obama. She wanted to stress that as intelligence agencies and law enforcement were investigating Russia, Obama wasn't "initiating or instructing anything". That was false because we know through the text messages of FBI agents Peter Stzrok and Lisa Page that Obama *did* know what was going on. It seems Rice tried to cover-up Obama's knowledge of the Russia probe.

But with regards to the first Republican memo from the House Intelligence Agency, Californian Democrat Adam Schiff rebutted it. Schiff claimed the data disclosed in the memo was illegitimate and contained *sources and methods* endangering national security. That was false! Schiff was worried about the public discovering more truthful facts about the Russian investigation. He wanted the false narratives being pitched by the mainstream and Democrats to continue. But the second Republican memo confirmed the veracity of the first memo.

The reason Schiff attempted to discredit the memo was because he has an extreme partisan bias and disdain for the President. He wants to believe the President colluded with Russia so badly that in April 2017 he accepted a phone call from someone professing to be Adriy Parubiy, the chairman of the Ukrainian Parliament. During an 8-minute phone call, the man told Schiff they had information that Russian President Vladimir Putin had photographs and recordings from 2013 during the Miss Universe pageant in Russia. They said it would give proof showing the President-to-be was with two women, one of them being a model named Olga Buzova, in a compromising position. Schiff asked,

"And what's the nature of the kompromat?"

The reply from the Russian informant said there were,

"...naked photos taken during an affair between the President and a Russian glamour model."

Schiff seemingly excited, ended with,

"I'll be in touch with the FBI about this. And we'll make arrangements with your staff. I think it probably would be best to provide these materials both to our committee and to the FBI."

Then staff member, Rheanne Wirkkala, of Mr. Schiff wrote,

"I understand Mr. Schiff had a productive call with Mr. Parubiy, and that Mr. Parubiy would like to make some material available to Mr. Schiff through your embassy....Please let me know how best to arrange pick-up of those materials from your Embassy in Washington, D.C......do you know when we might be able to meet your colleagues at the Ukrainian embassy here in Washington, D.C. to pick up materials?"

But Schiff had been played! The phone call was just a ruse by a Russian comedian team known as *Vocan and Lexus.* They taped the conversation and sent it to the *The Daily Mail* news outlet.

Then, ironically, in 2018, it was discovered that in the same year, 2013, Schiff was being interviewed on Russian Television channel (RT). He stated on the show that the FISA court should be "more transparent" with their documents. But this is something he is against now because it would disclose the unethical way the FBI, DOJ, and others authorized and obtained FISA warrants to spy on the President and his campaign team. So, does he want less or more transparency?

Adam Schiff desperately desired to disparage the two reliable Republican memos. So, a Democratic House Intelligence Committee memo, composed primarily by Democrat Adam Schiff, was voted on to be delivered to the President for his review and approval. This memo from the Democrats would then be released to the public as were the Republican memos. But Schiff knew that this Democratic memo purposefully contained many classified sources and methods in them.

If the President redacted (blocked out) anything from the memo and released the memo to the public, the Democrats would insist that he blocked important parts of the memo to hide something. But the President saw through the scheme. He reviewed the Democrats memo with the FBI, lawyers, and others to see if it could be released like the other memos. Instead of releasing the memo, however, it was suggested to him by his advisers that the Democratic memo should be redone because it contained classified material. Then, once corrected, it could be released to the public. Of course, the media and Democrats criticized the President for sending back the memo. But they didn't tell the public the memo needed to be redrafted because it had sensitive data in it.

When the Democratic memo was released, it didn't refute any key points and backed up others made by the Republican memos.

- Hillary Clinton's campaign and DNC paid for the phony Steele dossier.
- The FBI relied on the Steele dossier to get the FISA warrants.
- Christopher Steele obtained unsubstantiated anonymous hearsay information from Russian sources in the dossier.
- And, lastly, but most importantly the memo states "The FBI speculates

that the identified U.S. Person was likely looking for information that could be used to discredit Candidate #1's campaign."

After examining this, one key question emerged. Why would the FBI, a top U.S. government intelligence agency "speculate" a *U.S. person* was "likely" looking for information, when they knew perfectly well there was a political motive behind discrediting "Candidate #1"? To clarify, Candidate #1 is the President and Christopher Steele, who hated the President, was the U.S. Person. But Steele was not a U.S. Person. He was a British person. So, it's another oddity with this memo.

Did OUR President collude with the Russians?

Before answering this question, let's state the obvious. What is quite apparent is there are slanted sympathies in the mainstream media toward the Democratic Party, Clinton, and Obama, while there exists hatred toward the 45th President of the United States. The Special Counsel was appointed to build a case against the President based on many falsehoods and unlawful behavior. Also, it has been discovered that Obama's FBI, DOJ, and Administration had undeniable deceptive partisanship during the Hillary email investigation and while involved with the Russian dossier. Many were overtly biased against the 45th U.S. President. They did their utmost to reiterate continuous falsehoods that are still being pushed by the mainstream media. Some of this bias has been shown, and other information assuredly will come out.

Now, let's go back to just after the Presidential election in 2016. What was stated earlier is the then-President-elect thought he was wiretapped. Why? It was discovered that Mike Rogers, former Director of the NSA under the Obama Administration, had visited with the President-elect during the transition phase to tell him in a vague manner that he should not conduct business in his Trump Tower in New York. Therefore, the transition team, which had conducted meetings to ready itself for the transfer of power from President Obama to the new U.S. President (from November 8 – January 20), was moved temporarily out of Trump Tower and to a residence in Bedminster, N.J.

After his inauguration, the 45th U.S. President must have found out more information regarding the spying that had been occurring to him and his transition team in Trump Tower. And, so, he sent out a tweet indicating he had been "wire-tapped". The mainstream media and all those opposed to his presidency mocked him. Although wiretapped is an old phrase, the President and others in Trump Tower were indeed under surveillance by the Obama Administration. And, so, the spying, unmasking, and other found illegalities from the past administration may end up being bigger than the Watergate scandal, *if pursued.*

Since the President's election, several individuals were reassigned, resigned, or removed. Some of these persons who worked in the Obama administration, and may still be working in the new administration, may become implicated in this scandal. It may be ricocheting back to possibly incriminate many of them. So, pay close attention to the news about those listed below (especially with an asterisk * by their name).

- John P. Carlin, Assistant Attorney General (resigns Oct 2016)
- Sally Yates, acting Attorney General (fired January 2017)*
- Preet Bharara, US Attorney for the Southern District of N.Y. (fired March 2017)
- Mary McCord, acting Attorney General of National Security Division (resigns April 2017)
- James Comey, FBI Director (fired 5/9/17)*
- Hui Chen, Counsel in Fraud section of Department of Justice (resigns Jun 2017)
- Peter Strzok, Deputy Assistant Director of Counterintelligence in FBI (removed from Mueller probe July 2017; fired in 2018)*
- Lisa Page, Counsel of FBI Andrew McCabe (removed from Mueller probe in June 2017; resigned from FBI in May 2018)*
- Dana Boente, acting Attorney for National Security Division – NSD (resigns 10/26/17)*
- Bruce Ohr, Deputy Attorney General (reassigned and demoted twice by 12/7/17)*
- Nellie Ohr, Fusion GPS Contractor (2016 and beyond)*
- James Baker, FBI General Counsel (reassigned 12/20/17)*
- Andrew McCabe, FBI Deputy Director (removed 1/29/18)*
- Jim Rybicki, chief of staff to FBI Director (replaced Jan. 2018)*

- Rachael Brand, Associate Attorney General - 3rd in command (resigned 2/9/18)
- David Laughman, Deputy Assistant Attorney General for National Security Division – NSD (resigned February 2018)
- Michael P. Kortan, head of the FBI Public Affairs Office (resigned February 2018)
- Bill Priestap, FBI Director of Counterintelligence (retiring 2018)*

So, has Special Counsel Mueller interviewed these persons in the Russian collusion case? How about Susan Rice, James Clapper, John Brennan, Cody Shearer, Samantha Power, Sidney Blumenthal, Victoria Nuland, Shailagh Murray, John Kerry, Loretta Lynch, Barack Obama, or Hillary Clinton? We don't know. But it's highly likely that some were involved with the dirty Russian dossier, obtaining unlawful FISA warrants to spy on the President-to-be and his 2016 campaign, or framing this President for impeachment. They deflect from the truth in the news. And, so, some, if not all, may be the *real* Russia colluders.

The obvious reason why Special Counsel Mueller may <u>not</u> be pursuing these individuals for questioning is this investigation may be less than credible. It appears Mueller is only interested in trying to discover some crime against the President (not exonerate him) or waiting for some misdemeanor to occur. Mueller wants to show he is not wasting the taxpayer's money and time. Meantime, the President's agendas are hindered every day because he has someone scrutinizing his every move. This bogus investigation plotted by haters is not fair to the President or the American people. But if he does overcome this deceitful plan, heads should roll in Washington; and, those involved with this dastardly plot of trying to unseat a U.S. President should be charged with crimes. Then, the "swamp" will need to be fully drained.

More Emerging Information: <u>(But all this is just the tip of the iceberg!)</u>

*1) In February 2018 there is speculation Bill Priestap, head of the FBI Counterintelligence division, may have been engaged in this Russia scandal as well. It makes sense because Priestap was the boss of Peter Strzok (who had incriminating text messages showing bias against the

President). All approvals for a FISA warrants, which were, actually obtained to spy on U.S. persons, would need to go through Priestap. Even former FBI Director James Comey told Congress in a March 20th, 2017 testimony he was directed by "the director of counterintelligence" to not to disclose the fact the FBI was investigating the President-to-be during 2016. Comey didn't mention Priestap by name; but he may have been casting blame on Priestap so he could become the fall guy.

*2) There is also new evidence that former Australian Foreign Minister Alexander Downer was the person who had given hearsay evidence about George Papadopoulos' conversation in a London bar. Allegedly, Papadopoulos, part of the President's 2016 campaign for a short stint, said he had dirt on Hillary Clinton in the overheard conversation. This data was forwarded by Downer to the Australian intelligence agencies, which subsequently contacted the U.S. FBI. But Downer was found to have had ties to the Clinton's. So much so that Downer had Australia donate $25 million taxpayer money to the Clinton Foundation.

*3) In March 2018, the Congressional Intelligence Committee ended its investigation - finding *no collusion* between the President and Russia.

*4) In March 2018, a report came out stating former DNI director James Clapper under President Obama leaked dossier data to *CNN*.

*5) In March 2018, FBI agent Peter Strzok's text messages revealed he was *friendly* with a FISA court judge, Rudolph Contreras. Then, when former General Michael Flynn was coerced into pleading guilty to having perjured himself to the FBI, this judge was present. The judge later recused himself from the case. Also, the FBI told Flynn not to bring a lawyer to an interrogation and they had a taped transcript. But ex-FBI Director James Comey (and others in the FBI) said that Flynn didn't lie to the FBI. So, was there a set-up by Mueller? The backstory is that Flynn was NSA Director in 2017. But he didn't disclose his contact with Turkey before the elections. So, V.P. Pence asked him to resign. But Sally Yates (former A.G.) cunningly tried getting Flynn indicted under the *Logan Act* (created 1799). This has never been used in U.S. history.

*6) In March 2018, reports show Special Counsel Mueller's reputation to be not as grand as the media trumpets. In 2002, the 911 Commission found then-FBI Director Mueller downplayed intelligence findings which warned of upcoming attacks before the September 11th. Working together, Mueller and James Comey were part of the FBI which botched a 2001 anthrax investigation that led to the death of five and affected 17 others. Then, in the 1980's, Acting U.S. Attorney Mueller in Boston had protected FBI informant and mobster James "Whitey" Bulger because he was a stool pigeon against the mafia. It led to four men being wrongly framed and imprisoned in the 1965 murder of Teddy Deegan. Two men died in prison, and the other two were exonerated and awarded $100 million in 2007. It seems Mueller had enabled a corrupt FBI cover-up.

*7) In April 2018, Special Counsel Mueller told the President's lawyers he was not a criminal "target" of an investigation, but the "subject" of an investigation. A "subject" is a "person whose conduct is within the scope of the grand jury's investigation". But James Comey had already told the President when he first took office, he was not the "target" of an investigation. So, what does this mean? It means Mueller wants the President to let down his guard and interview with him. Then, he will try to entrap him in a possible perjury charge. It is a "witch hunt"!

*8) In April 2018, Congressional lawmakers made a criminal referral to the U.S. DOJ about Comey, McCabe, Clinton, Lynch, Strzok, and Page.

*9) A *second* Special Counsel is being sought to examine FISA warrant abuses, the involvement of the Clinton campaign with the dossier, and the lack of an investigation in the Clinton email server, and more. A second Special Counsel is necessary because the FBI and DOJ can't investigate themselves. In 2018, Inspector General Michael Horowitz and his staff are perusing through 1.2 million documents to investigate many cases. Attorney General Jeff Sessions has federal prosecutor John Huber, outside the Justice Department, looking into any cases which might involve criminality. Check for updates at https:/saraacarter.com

*10) In May 2018, the lawyers of Paul Manafort, who was indicted for crimes in 2010–2014, said Special Counsel Muller had gone way beyond his mandate of finding Russian collusion. A judge agreed, but nothing came of it. Manafort's home was raided by Mueller (7/26/17) before authorization from his boss, Rod Rosenstein (8/2/17).

*11) In May 2018, it was reported that an FBI informant, a British Cambridge University professor (S.H.), and possibly others, infiltrated and spied on the would-be-President's 2016 campaign members (i.e. Carter Page, George Papadopoulos, Paul Manafort, Michael Caputo, and Sam Clovis). The operation code name was Operation Crossfire. Is this Cambridge professor connected to ex-Brit spy Christopher Steele? Could this be a contemporary *"Cambridge Five spy ring"* (1930's)?

*12) In May 2018, *the Federalist* reported Andrew McCabe sent an email with a subject line *"Flood is coming"* to J. Comey and J. Rybicki, which partly read, *"CNN is close to going forward with the sensitive story."* This occurred two days before the Russian dossier went public.

*13) In May 2018, *The Hill* reported the appointment of Special Counsel Mueller and everything in his investigation may be unconstitutional. This is regarding the U.S. Constitution's Article III Appointments Clause. A similar case existed in 1988: *Morrison v. Olson,* asking, did this act violate the constitutional principal of separation of powers?

*14) Sadly, from 2017 through 2018, Congress' requests for critical documents have been *stonewalled* by the FBI and DOJ, specifically by Deputy Attorney General Rosenstein, because they would expose much.

So, did this President collude with Russia? No. Not convinced. Why did the he: expel 60 Russian diplomats, sanction seven Russian oligarchs, give Ukraine weapons, attack Syria, and confront Iran? Compare it to Obama who: was caught on an open mic desiring to talk to Putin after the 2012 election, allowed Russia to invade Crimea and Ukraine, appeased Russia's partners (inaction in Syria and Iran deal), and sold Russia 20% of U.S. uranium. Now, *who* colluded with Russia?

Chapter 11

THE REAL OBAMA YEARS:
FAILURES

Obama was a charismatic figure when he rose in politics as a centrist Democratic in 2008. The speech which sparked interest in him as a Presidential candidate was when he addressed the 2004 Democratic National Convention as an Illinois Senator. His smooth talking, magnetic personality, and the possibility he could instill a sense of peace in the racial divide of America were front and center. Even the fact he attended services at Trinity church in Chicago for years, where the fiery Reverend Jeremiah Wright resided, didn't hurt his chances of beating Hillary Clinton for the Democratic Presidential nomination in 2008. This pastor had preached anti-American sentiments and racism to his congregation. For example, in 2003, Reverend Wright stated,

"The government gives them the drugs, builds bigger prisons, passes a three-strike law and then wants us to sing 'God Bless America.' No, no, no, God damn America, that's in the Bible for killing innocent people......God damn America for treating our citizens as less than human. God damn America for as long as she acts like she is God and she is supreme."

Then, after one of the greatest tragedies in our history, Rev. Wright gave a sermon the Sunday after September 11, 2001 saying,

"We bombed Hiroshima, we bombed Nagasaki, and we nuked far more than the thousands in New York and the Pentagon, and we never batted an eye...We have supported state terrorism against the Palestinians and black South Africans, and now we are indignant because the stuff we have done overseas is now brought right back to our own front yards. America's chickens are coming home to roost."

So, why was Barack Obama attending Rev. Wright's church in the first place? Smartly, Obama did distance himself from Rev. Wright;

but that was when he began campaigning for President. In addition, Obama had affiliations with people such as Reverend Al Sharpton and Louis Farrakhan Sr. who are well-known for embracing and instigating racist rhetoric in our communities. There was even a photo of Obama with Farrakhan in 2005. It had lain hidden from the public for years, until recently. Actually, anti-Semitic and racist Rev. Farrakhan has made several reprehensible remarks in the past.

March 1984: "Here, the Jews don't like Farrakhan, so they call me Hitler. So, that's a good name. Hitler was a very great man."

March 1989: "There is no human being on earth that has murdered more living things than the Caucasian. He's a murderer and a liar."

March 2015: "It is now becoming apparent that there were many Israelis and Zionist Jews in key roles in the 9-11 attacks."

August 2015: "...'cause you see whiter people deserve to die. And, they know, so they think it's us coming to do it.

Feb. 2018: "White folks are going down. And Satan is going own. And, Farrakhan, by God's grace, has pulled the cover-off of that Satanic Jew."

It's ironic how people like Reverends Wright and Farrakhan, as well as violent groups like *Antifa*, are seen only as so-called "fringe" persons or groups by Democrats? Are they not hateful and racist individuals and groups like David Duke (KKK) and the Neo-Nazis? In fact, the KKK and Neo-Nazis were spawned from left-wing movements, not right-wing. Yet some that know this, dismiss or hide these facts. Regardless, people and organizations like these should be denounced and shunned.

Still, the focus in the mainstream media and with Democrats are with the KKK, Neo-Nazis, and white supremacists. Of course, they are not good people. But some liberal elites will still defend evil groups like *Antifa* or personalities such as Rev. Farrakhan. Actually, there are many in Congress who have associated or still keep in contact with this madman. They are Maxine Waters (CA), Keith Ellison (MN), Barbara Lee (CA), Rodney Davis (IL), Andre Carson (IN), and Gregory Meeks

(NY). And, then, in the same breath, they and many others, like Linda Sarsour, Tamika Mallory, and Carmen Perez, heads of the so-called 'Women's March', support the anti-Semitic Farrakhan and call the 45th President of the United States a racist? It's the epitome of hypocrisy.

Anyway, let's get back to Barack Obama. Regardless of his past affiliations with racists, like Wright and Farrakhan, he would beat the Republican candidate Mitt Romney and vice-Presidential nominee Paul Ryan in a historic victory to become the 44th U.S. President.

At first there was excitement in the air that the first black President had been elected. The people anticipated "hope and change" as promised. But that change didn't come in the form which many expected of him. As years passed, *hope* became just an empty word. Very sadly, he fooled many of us. It was a grand disappointment.

As his policies and decisions emerged, it was apparent he was more aligned with domestic and global elites in governments, non-profit organizations, businesses, activist groups, and, of course, media news outlets which had very progressively liberal ideologies. There seemed to be more division and less unity. The cry of "Yes, we can" became the *action* of no we can't. But what had been most disconcerting were the several decisions he made or failed to make during his 8-year reign as President affected many Americans and people around the world. Yet in typical fashion the mainstream media, pundits, and democratic supporters of Obama protected him, and the many missteps of his administration. The major failures that had occurred under President Obama, however, are well-documented - and undeniable.

Obamacare

Four states dominate the utilization of this Obama mandated health care system: California, New York, Massachusetts, and Maryland. These states receive ninety percent of the funds. What do they have in common? They are controlled by the Democratic Party. This political party has convinced the majority of voters in these states that big government is in their best interest, and healthcare should be under their control. But do these people know they are being used to advance policies which will force them into relying on government? Basically, Obamacare began the process of converting our American private healthcare system into socialized medicine. And, the hope of the Democratic Party was it would be continued, and then slightly altered under new President Hillary Clinton. But that didn't happen.

The Affordable Care Act (ACA), or Obamacare, was not only a failure, it was a scam. Before it was passed, Democratic representative Nancy Pelosi said, "we need to pass it to find out what's in it". Then, President Obama said numerous times "you can keep your doctor" and "insurance" under Obamacare. One example of this untruth is when he addressed the American Medical Association in June 2009, stating,

"I know that there are millions of Americans who are content with their health care coverage. They like their plan and, most importantly, they value their relationship with their doctor. They trust you. And that means that no matter how we reform health care, we will keep this promise to the American people: If you like your doctor, you will be able to keep your doctor, period. If you like your health care plan, you'll be able to keep your health care plan, period. No one will take it away, no matter what."

This backroom deal by Democrats was rushed through Congress and made into law in March 2010. It required that every American citizen who didn't have health insurance through their jobs or isn't being subsidized by the government be responsible for signing up for health insurance. It was a mandate imposed by the U.S. government. Insurance companies would get subsidies from the government to cover Obamacare. If an individual or family did not sign up then they would be fined a penalty when they filed their taxes. It was a way for millions of Americans with higher incomes to partly pay for the costs of healthcare for those who had lower incomes. Not only would the people have to pay for Obamacare, but its costs increased our national debt.

So, even with these burdens on America lurking, the Obamacare bill was signed into law. Then, as President Obama was about to announce the health care reform change from a podium in the White House, Vice President Biden excitingly whispered to him,

*"This is a big f*cking deal."*

Obama and Biden both chuckled. But this government-controlled healthcare plan would be no laughing matter for the American people.

In October 2013, that great new billion-dollar government-owned healthcare website crashed. The Obama administration said it was because there were too many people going on to the website to beat the deadline of enrolling in the new healthcare plan. President Obama said,

"The website got overwhelmed by the volume."

It was only partly true. The website "cookie" data had reached its capacity. There were security breaches, syntax mistakes, and duplicate data which all played a role in the website's inefficiency. It cost a billion more dollars of taxpayer money to fix it. But, ultimately the problem with the website was the result of government incompetency.

By 2016, the Affordable Care Act (ACA), or Obamacare, bill was changed about 70 times. But the health insurance companies in many states pulled out from participating in the plan because people were not signing up and premiums had to be increased. That meant people had fewer or no available options for health insurance in some states.

Alaska had yearly insurance premiums go up over 200% from the prior year. Other states, like Arizona, had insurance premiums jump over 100% from the year prior. On top of the initial cost of the premium, to buy into the plan, the out-of-pocket costs were increased as well. For example, if you pay into a health insurance premium, let's say $300 for the year, you also must pay deductible fees for doctor's fees for the year. Once the deductible fees reach a certain threshold for the year, for instance $2000, then the insurance companies will pay for costs after this. But the out-of-pocket costs went up to well over $10,000 for some individuals and families, making it more it more expensive than paying for their mortgages in some cases. To not be able to care for one's family and take advantage of their health insurance plan was awful, especially if someone had a chronic condition. The so-called 'Affordable Care Act' was absolutely <u>not</u> affordable.

But lower income people signing up for Obamacare made out well because the plan was really designed for them. And, the rich who had to get private insurance, although they could afford the premiums and deductibles, were paying the most into this plan. About 11 million people enrolled in the plan. Government funded Medicaid expanded because it was easier to get through Obamacare. In turn, this added to our national debt. And, the people most hurt were the middle-class.

Lastly, and not to be forgotten, is that in some cases Obamacare was deemed *unlawful,* although the mandate portion (forcing people to buy it) of the bill passed the Supreme Court. Religious liberties were being bypassed, and many people of faith were forced to pay for contraception for their employees. For example, the Supreme Court decided in favor of two related cases, *Hobby Lobby v. Burwell* and *Little Sisters of the Poor v. Burwell.* Also, businesses, as well as state and local agencies, sued because employees were gaining tax credits even when they had enrolled in a government program. In wasn't fair because the agencies and businesses would ultimately have to pay for these tax credits. Obamacare had been a disaster from the start. But the 45th American President has begun to dismember it slowly. And, finally, Congress eliminated the Obamacare mandate in the new 2017 Tax Bill.

The stimulus bill (ARRA)

The American Recovery and Reinvestment Act of 2009 was passed because of the financial crash of 2008. Many blamed President George W. Bush for this because of his tax cuts and deregulations. The criticism was unwarranted, because the disaster began a decade earlier.

In 1995, President Bill Clinton had transformed the Community Reinvestment Act (1977) into a program which forced banks to lend money to "underserved" communities. This meant low-income people were being catered to, and they could default on or not pay their loans. Then, Fannie Mae and Freddie Mac, under the Housing and Urban Development (HUD) department of the government, were encouraged to buy subprime loans. And by the year 2000, the then-HUD Secretary, Andrew Cuomo, also pushed these agencies into providing loans for low and moderate-income borrowers - especially minorities.

Banks kept on making quotas to lend unqualified borrowers their loans. Then, Freddie Mac and Fannie Mae bought more loans that comprised subprime loans. Other mortgage and investment companies followed suit. The Federal Exchange began to increase interest rates to slow down inflation and stop soaring prices in housing. But because the process was unchecked and allowed to flourish, low-income people began to default on their loans. Then, the banking and financial systems failed. Wall Street went into a tailspin and a global crisis ensued.

This perspective in history is crucial because although President Bush was in office when the crash happened, it was President Clinton who initiated this. Therefore, since Bush would be leaving office, the next President, whether this was Senator Barack Obama or Senator John McCain would almost immediately have to address this issue. So, some stimulus package was necessary. But the resolution needed wasn't necessarily the 2009 American Recovery and Reinvestment Act.

Nearly a trillion dollars was obtained for stimulus spending. But it created practically no private-sector jobs and it added to the national debt. It was basically a slush fund for Democrats, lobbyists, and more government jobs. It did fund much which was desired. But the economy never had a full year of three percent GDP (Gross National Product), there were no shovel ready jobs as promised, the national debt doubled from about 10 trillion to 19 trillion, and American infrastructure was not tackled. Also, a solar-company, Solyndra, was given over half billion dollars before it went bankrupt. That's called *crony capitalism.* This was both a failure and scandal. Ultimately, American taxpayers footed the bills for the stimulus package and got far less than what we paid for.

In addition to the failure of the stimulus bill, at the end of the Obama-era more glaring facts about the economy became apparent. Firstly, economic growth had been the weakest since the post-recession period of World War II and the worst economic recovery since the 1940's. There were about 855 regulations hindering the economy from growing. When it came to our citizens, almost 95 million were out of the labor force, the country hit the lowest labor participation rate since the 1970's, almost 13 million were on food stamps, 43 million remained in poverty, and home ownership was the lowest in 50 years. Our economy wasn't humming as hoped. It was basically at a standstill.

The rise of ISIS

On May 2, 2011, the leader responsible for knocking down the World Trade Center buildings in downtown Manhattan (NY) and killing thousands was finally dead. After many years of planning between two Presidential administrations, Osama Bin Laden, the founder of al-Qaeda, was killed by Navy Seals inside a private residential compound in Abbottabad, Pakistan. So, Americans praised his death, while also thinking future planned terrorist threats had been thwarted. The Obama Administration, including Secretary of State Hillary Clinton, must have thought so too. So, U.S. troops began being pulled from Iraq. But what the U.S. didn't know is that from the ashes of al-Qaeda a newer and maybe more dangerous terrorist threat would arise.

At about the same time, President Bashar al-Assad was in power as civil war erupted in Syria. Then, Abu Bakr al-Baghdadi, the new leader of al-Qaeda, sent his top deputy, Abu Mohammad al-Joulani, to Syria to setup a new branch of his Sunni extremist group. The goal was to see the Assad regime fall to this extremist group. But although the Syrian President stated he was only fighting extremist groups, Assad would conceal that he was also engaged in a civil war against those opposing his Syrian government - sometimes with chemical warfare.

In 2012, President Obama issued a "red-line" challenge to Assad indicating that further use of chemical weapons would change his "calculus" about using military operations in Syria. Then, later that year, nearly 1,500 were killed in a chemical weapons attack. But since Obama didn't want to upset his dialogs toward an Iran nuclear deal, he *failed* to enforce his own *red-line*. So, many Syrian lives were lost.

In Iraq, also in 2012, with a weak Iraqi government in power and watered-down U.S. forces, Muslim prisoners were freed by the forces of the al-Qaeda leader al-Baghdadi during the Arab Spring uprising. In the aftermath, the number of extremists began growing in Iraq and Syria. The group grew so much by 2013 that al-Baghdadi felt bold enough to claim power in both Syria and Iraq. This was much to the chagrin of al-

Joulani in Syria.

A new group formed under al-Bagdadi's control. It was called "the Islamic State of Iraq and Syria" or ISIS. The al-Qaeda and ISIS factions then split in Syria. Of course, President Assad was glad of this extremist split. Now, he could leave the two groups to fight amongst themselves while he dealt with those who opposed his regime.

In June 2014, hundreds of ISIS fighters defeated thousands of Iraqi government troops to capture Mosul. Much of northern Iraq was overrun with ISIS extremists. A month later, ISIS claimed the land they had conquered was to be their Caliphate (Islamic state). The leader al-Baghdadi said all Muslims were obligated to support the new Muslim state. And, so, from this stronghold, the ideologies of ISIS would begin to expand into terrorist cells around the world. The premature removal of some U.S. troops from Iraq had left a vacuum for ISIS to rise.

Although President Obama had some strategy for fighting ISIS, it failed. He launched thousands of airstrikes against them; but the extremist group kept spreading. His lack of a ground attack, allowing commanders to make their own decisions, and failure to call the enemy by its name ("radical Islamic terrorism") were grave mistakes. As a result, those aligned with ISIS planned their jihad, and became responsible for the deaths of thousands in many cities on six continents.

Creating division

Unfortunately, this was one of the saddest of all his failures. The *hope and change* which was set forth to unite our nation fell well short of the mark. Maybe Obama had begun to willingly align himself with some extreme progressive Democrats. Or, maybe, there was a hidden agenda Obama failed to tell the American people. We will never know for sure.

What we do know is for many long years most members of the Democratic Party, including Obama, have preached they will bridge the divide in our great nations for people of all colors, creeds, and religions if elected. But Democrats have been using identity politics more often to divide us and bring voters to the ballot boxes rather than unify us. They do this while demonizing and falsely accusing conservatives of being racist, homophobic, sexist, xenophobic, Islamophobic, or another derogatory word. Barack Obama was no exception to their rule.

Being the first African-American President, Obama had a great chance to bring social change to America. Quite unfortunately though, the opposite happened. There was resentment among many because he unwittingly or wittingly used his ego and political ideologies to tear people apart instead of utilizing his common sense to bond them. His presence on the 2016 Presidential campaign trail with Democratic nominee Hillary Clinton exacerbated the divide between the American people through identity politics and political correctness. This division reached its zenith when the 45th President of the United States was elected. But Barack Obama had planted the seeds of this division for many years. Some of these examples are known and others may not be.

*1) In 2009, President Obama went on a television show called "*60 Minutes*". He gave an interview prior to meeting the heads of major banks which would address freeing up more credit, boosting job growth, and more. But, on this interview his language and tone about the banks was not the best it could and should have been.

"I did not run for office to be helping out a bunch of fat cat bankers on Wall Street"... they're still puzzled why is it that people are mad at the banks. Well, let's see, you guys are drawing down $10, $20 million bonuses after America went through the worst economic year that it's gone through in -- in decades, and you guys caused the problem..."

Obama may have been right to point out that large incomes go to CEO's of this industry. But those at the top in every business usually get huge paychecks. Regardless, this derogatory term "fat cats" was not appreciated by some bank professionals. This term actually set a precedent, as it was used to insult high-level bankers *and* rich people.

But why place people in one bucket? Some start out poor with hardly any money in the bank. Then, after many years of toiling in their profession, they become wiser and smarter with their money and become more prosperous for themselves and their families. It's called the American dream. But that *fat-cat* term led to painting a bad picture about certain classes of people – further dividing the rich and poor.

*2) In 2010, President Obama spoke to Latinos about the upcoming mid-term elections in the U.S. on Univision radio interview. He said,

"If Latinos sit out the election instead of saying, 'We're gonna punish our enemies, and we're gonna reward our friends who stand with us on issues that are important to us' -- if they don't see that kind of upsurge in voting in this election -- then I think it's going to be harder. And that's why I think it's so important that people focus on voting on November 2nd."

The phrase "punish our enemies" didn't sit well with Republicans. The Speaker of the House, John Boener, responded with,

"Ladies and gentlemen, we have a President in the White House who referred to Americans who disagree with him as 'our enemies.' Think about that. He actually used that word. When Ronald Reagan, George Bush, Bill Clinton, and George W. Bush used the word 'enemy,' they reserved it for global terrorists and foreign dictators -- enemies of the United States...enemies of freedom...enemies of our country. Today, sadly, we have President who uses the word 'enemy' for fellow Americans -- fellow citizens. He uses it for people who disagree with his agenda of bigger government -- people speaking out for a smaller, more accountable government that respects freedom and allows small businesses to create jobs. Mr. President, there's a word for people who have the audacity to speak up in defense of freedom, the Constitution, and the values of limited government that made our country great. We don't call them 'enemies.' We call them 'patriots.'"

For two years, Obama was rewarded with Democratic control of Congress. But even with this political advantage, he would not get much done. The only exception was signing a bill for an inexcusable and unfair healthcare package on Americans. And, still, Obama would attack Republicans during his time in office for his lack of progress.

*3) In 2010, at the Democratic Congressional Campaign Committee (DCCC) in Rhode Island, President Obama made some regrettable remarks. During his speech, he mixed, Republicans, the economy, and the idea of segregation – which had split up our America for decades.

"Republicans had driven the economy into a ditch and then stood by and criticized while Democrats pulled it out. Now that progress has been made......we can't have special interests sitting shotgun. We gotta have middle class families up in front. We don't mind the Republicans joining us. They can come for the ride, but they gotta sit in back.'"

Unfortunately, this was a reference to the way blacks were treated by whites before Rosa Parks changed the course of history. Parks was famous for protesting for the rights of blacks by sitting in the front of the bus, at a time when blacks were belittled and had to sit in the back of the bus. But it was sad Obama chose to characterize Republicans in this way - as *second-class citizens* from the 1950's.

*4) In 2011, President Obama openly supported the *Occupy Wall Street Movement*. This group protested about economic inequalities, with extremely radical views involving the civil rights, anti-nuclear, and global justice movements. The founder and its members were filled with anarchists whose beliefs embraced "horizontalism, autonomy, and defiance". How could any President of the United States support the principles of anarchy? Not only did Obama prop this radical group up, but he compared that ugly movement to the Republican Tea Party.

"In some ways, they're not that different from some of the protests that we saw coming from the Tea Party...Both on the left and the right, I think people feel separated from their government. They feel that their institutions aren't looking out for them."

The Tea Party, however, did not consist of radicals like those in Occupy Wallstreet. They were just conservatives affiliated with the Republican Party who opposed universal healthcare, encouraged lower taxes, and wanted a reduction in government spending. Since Obama was heavily in favor of some form of universal healthcare, raising taxes, and other democratic ideologies, he probably felt as if the Tea Party was a hindrance to him. So, the IRS (Internal Revenue Service) controversy emerged, in which Republican Tea Party members were targeted and wrongly accused of not filing their taxes properly. (more later)

*5) Then, we have the sad shootings deaths of African-American's by police. There were many news stories about these very tragic and terrible incidents. But some of these racially charged cases, and others like it, of so-called *police brutality* were made from false narratives. Unfortunately, President Obama chose to get involved in these high-profile events several times, as polarizing frays erupted on the streets.

On June 22, 2009, Barack Obama jumped the gun without any evidence when Freddie Grey was shot by the Baltimore police, saying,

"The Cambridge police acted stupidly. We have a history in this country of blacks and Latinos being stopped disproportionately by law enforcement."

But even though the judge, mayor, state's attorney, and former police commissioner were African American, the police involved with the shooting of Grey were acquitted from any criminality.

Then, on July 19, 2013, Barack Obama said of the Florida teenager, Trayvon Martin, who was shot and killed by police,

"When Trayvon Martin was shot, I said that this could have been my son."

Why did Obama make this event personal? Even so, the police who had shot Martin in a physical altercation were found not guilty.

And, in September 2014, "hands up don't shoot!" was the cry from activist and the media. People put their hands up in air to protest Michael Brown being shot by the police in Ferguson, Missouri. But it was built on a lie told by one witness. But President Obama had replied,

"We have to close the justice gap — how justice is applied, but also how it is perceived, how it is experienced. That's what we saw in Ferguson this summer when Michael Brown was killed and the community was divided."

Obama also remarked that there were "racial disparities" in our criminal justice system which included "everything from enforcing drug policy to applying the death penalty and to pulling people over." Regardless, several key witnesses testified Brown may have put his hands in the air, but they didn't know what he was doing with his hands. Also, witnesses said that Brown never asked the police officer, "Don't shoot". So, the jury found no probable cause to indict the police officer.

*6) Unfortunately, President Obama ignored or praised many radical leftist groups. In 2008, the *New Black Panther* group was accused of white voter intimidation in Pennsylvania during the election when Barack Obama first ran for the presidency. But, after President Obama took office, nothing was done with this organization - although they openly are anti-white, anti-Semitic, and anti-police. Then, in 2016, during the Presidential election campaigns, Obama was informed by the Federal Bureau of Investigation (FBI) and Department of Justice (DOJ) about a radical extremist and anarchist group causing much domestic violence. This group was called *Antifa*. Since then, the group has grown. Through 2018, they have been involved in many violent protests, including those in Berkeley, California and Charlottesville, Virginia. But, now, they have been declared a domestic terrorist group.

Also, in September 2016, during the heat of the Presidential election, President Obama invited left-wing anti-police and racially motivated activists *Black Lives Matter* to the White House. This was an ill-advised act given their past and recent histories.

Lastly, Obama preached to and pleaded with black voters at Union Temple Baptist Church to vote for Hillary Clinton. This was after the black supremacist Rev. Farrakhan had a few choice words for him.

"... my name may not be on the ballot but our progress is on the ballot. Tolerance is on the ballot ... I will consider it a personal insult. An insult to my legacy if this community lets down its guard and fails to activate itself in this election ...there's your legacy Mr. President. It's in the street, with your suffering people ... And if you can't go and see about them, the white people you've served so well, will preserve your legacy. The hell they will. You didn't earn your legacy with us ... you didn't earn your legacy with black people. You fought for the rights of gay people. You fight for Israel. Your people are

suffering and dying in the streets!"

Rev. Farrakhan's last reference is about the many minorities, especially blacks, which have suffered and are being killed from gang violence on the streets of Chicago during Obama time in office.

*7) From around the mid 1980's to the time he was elected President, Obama had been involved with the community in Chicago. He was *their* State Senator of Illinois. But during his eight years in the White House, many in Chicago were shot. More specifically, there were about 18,000 people shot in that city between 2009 and 2016 - even with the strict gun laws in this city. But as if that wasn't bad enough, nearly 4,000 gun-related deaths occurred in Chicago while Obama was in office. To place this into perspective, there were 4,229 American lives lost during the Iraq war during the President Bush era. But these soldiers died in a *war zone*. Sadly, it's what some parts of Chicago are called today.

*8) Then, during the 2012 Presidential election, in Danville, Virginia, Vice President Joe Biden got involved in race-baiting. With a mostly black audience present, he said the Republican Presidential candidate

"...is going to let the big banks once again write their own rules, <u>unchain</u> Wall Street," Then, he added, "He is going to put <u>y'all back in chains</u>."

He emphasized the words "in chains". The Vice President later backtracked saying he was referring to Republican House Speaker John Boener's remarks. Boener said the last time Democrats had power they "unshackled the economy". But this wasn't a racial slur. He was talking about the middle-class in America. So, Biden's explanation was not valid. He used identity politics to rile up his audience during a rally.

*9) In 2011, an America ally was disparaged by Obama. At a private G20 meeting with French President Nicolas Sarkozy, a microphone was supposed to off but wasn't. It picked up the French President saying,

Sarkozy: "I cannot bear Netanyahu; he's a liar."

Obama: "You're fed up with him, but I have to deal with him even more often than you."

The United Nations, after declaring Israel a Jewish state in 1947, has sided against Israel in recent years. And, before Obama left office in 2016, a UN Security Council resolution was passed betraying one of our closest allies by demanding they end building businesses and homes on Palestinian territory. Though the U.S. Ambassador to the UN, Samantha Powers, had the power to veto the approval by 15 nations, the U.S. abstained from the vote. It was a slap in the face to Israel.

Then, adding insult to injury, the Obama State Department sent thousands of American tax-payer grants to build an unjust campaign against a strong U.S. ally, Israeli Prime Minister Benjamin Netanyahu. *OneVoice*, was funded with $350,000, which was supposed to provide a bridge for Palestinian-Israeli peace talks. But the group also used the money to build a voter database, train activists, and hire a political consulting firm to oppose Netanyahu during elections. Nevertheless, despite Obama's efforts, the Israeli Prime Minister was re-elected.

Pardons, clemencies, and commutations

President Obama's decision to trade five terrorists, who now roan free, with the awful Taliban of Afghanistan for the release of Sergeant Bowe Bergdahl was highly controversial. The Army soldier allegedly deserted his post and was captured by the enemy. But when he made his choice to leave his station of duty, six men were killed searching for him.

Yet, the National Security Advisor (NSA), Susan Rice, in the Obama Administration stated he had served with "honor and distinction." Subsequently, Bergdahl would stand trial for his actions. Thankfully, Obama did not pardon him. But in 2017, he would escape prison time. The presiding judge reduced Bergdahl's rank from sergeant to private, asked him to pay $1,000 a month for ten months, and gave him a dishonorable discharge. Reportedly, he wanted to appeal the decision.

Then, there were the flagrant pardons by President Obama of Chelsea Manning and James E. Cartwright. Chelsea Manning, an ex-Army intelligence analyst and transgender was born Bradley Manning.

She was commuted after being in prison only seven of the 35 years her sentence demanded. She was convicted of 2010 leaks to *Wikileaks* which had showed American classified military and diplomatic activities around the globe. Then, a retired Marine General James E. Cartwright, who pleaded guilty to lying about leaking classified data dealing with cyberattacks on Iran's nuclear program, was also freed.

In addition to the Manning and Cartwright pardons, Obama provided clemency to 330 prisoners convicted of long drug-related offenses. But he did not pardon them. (To be clear, a pardon absolves someone from a crime.) Moreover, Obama granted a total of 1,715 prisoner commutations. It's more than any other U.S. President in history. These commutations and clemencies are the changing of prison sentences to something less severe. In this case, it was the release from prison. But these are somewhat riskier than granting pardons. You have to think twice about releasing from prison members of a radical group who claimed to have been responsible for detonating 100 bombs in the U.S. And, yet, Bill Clinton did so when he commuted 16 members of the Puerto Rican FALN. Then, years later, Obama followed in his footsteps by commuting the sentence of FALN member, Oscar Lopez Rivera.

Reportedly about 98 percent of the Obama era commutations were for convicted drug offenders. Others commuted had committed forgery, counterfeit, and other crimes. But the large number of pardons, clemencies, and commutations by Obama is very debatable.

Bad foreign deals

Besides the Iran Nuclear Deal, which shall be discussed later as a scandal, the other two prominent agreements which were arguably failures by the Obama Administration were the "Cuban-Thaw" and "Trans-Pacific Partnership Deal". The so-called Cuban thaw was aimed to warm the relations between the United States and Cuba in 2014. It would end the 54-year cold war between the two nations. President Obama was the first sitting President to visit Cuba since 1928 when he met with Cuban President Raul Castro (brother to Fidel). And, he wanted to remove Cuba from being on the state sponsor of terror list, lift U.S. travel restrictions, reduce the limits U.S. persons had to send remittances to Cuba, reopen embassies in Havana and Washington, D.C., as well as free up bank and businesses transactions. But those thousands of Cubans who had to flee Cuba under the Communist Fidel Castro knew better than to trust this regime, even in the 21st century. So, many were outraged in the U.S. and around the world with this deal.

In 2017, OUR President began reversing the Cuba deal. He halted the unwise executive order by Obama, and discontinued U.S. business and travel to Cuba. But, then, subsequently, 21 diplomats were attacked with some type of sonic weapon and diagnosed as being in dire mental and physical health. It had been speculated, like everything today, that Russia was behind the despicable act. Regardless, the deal by Obama with Cuba was ill-advised. So, now, the U.S. must re-think foolish deals such as these with other totalitarian nations in the future.

In 2016, the Trans-Pacific Partnership Deal involved 12 countries which had borders on the Pacific Ocean and represented 40% of the world's economic wealth. Members included Japan, Malaysia, Vietnam, Singapore, Brunei, Australia, New Zealand, Canada, Mexico, Chile, Peru, and the U.S. It was designed to be something like the EU.

The 45th U.S. President pulled out of this deal, however, because it was skewed to favor economic prosperity for other nations while leaving the U.S. as the majority economic contributor to the plan. The new President believes in "reciprocal" deals which are fairer and more balanced, and that involve bi-lateral agreements with nations. OUR President may jump back into a new deal which is very similar to this. But he shall be leery and cautious because he realizes the U.S. has been taken advantage of in the past by many countries. Its why tariffs are a major sticking point as well. America pays high tariffs when shipping goods into other countries, but it has allowed low or zero tariffs with the same nations. So, in 2018, this President may introduce tariffs to level the playing field. It's time to rid the U.S. of bad trade deals.

Russian meddling

How much did the Obama Administration know about the threats from

Russia? How much did they care about it? To what extent were these threats by the Russians? We probably shall never find out for sure. But what we do know is that President Obama was warned by Mitt Romney about the Russian threat during a Presidential debate in 2012. Yet, Obama, mocked and didn't take Romney seriously. Then, in the same year, while running for a second-term for President, Obama was caught on an open microphone whispering to former President Dmitry Medvedev about an unsavory deal with his successor, Vladimir Putin.

Obama: "This is my last election. After my election I have more flexibility"

Medvedev: "I understand. I'll transmit this information to Vladimir."

What exactly had they been talking about? Why did Obama not listen to Mitt Romney? If Russia was such a bad country, why didn't the media speak about it while Obama was President? The Russians invaded Crimea and Ukraine. But the media and others waited until OUR President was elected before going bonkers about Russia. Why?

Regardless, there is evidence that since 2014, well before the 2016 Presidential elections, Russia was beginning to meddle in U.S. affairs. The Obama administration was warned on multiple occasions that the Kremlin was building up disinformation networks to disrupt the American political system. One official understood this, saying,

"You have no idea how extensive these networks are in Europe ... and in the U.S., Russia has penetrated media organizations, lobbying firms, political parties, governments and militaries in all of these places."

So, why didn't the Obama administration heed the warnings from many Republicans? Wasn't he concerned about protecting *both* 2016 Presidential candidates from any Russian meddling?

The ironic side to this is President Obama had gone on a rant after hearing one of the Presidential Debates in 2016. The candidate and would-be President responded to a question posed to him pertaining to whether or not he would "accept" the results of the election. He said to let him "think about it", because as Bernie Sanders had stated too, he thought the election process might be "rigged". There was a great uproar in the mainstream media, amongst Democrats, and Clinton campaign which thought it was terrible a Presidential candidate wouldn't accept the results of an election. It was "un-American" to them. So, Obama remarked with vigor and sarcasm,

"I have never seen in my lifetime or modern political history any Presidential candidate trying to discredit the elections...and the election process before votes have even taken place. It's unprecedented. "

Obama continued with declaring, there wasn't a "serious person out there" who believes anyone could "rig America elections." And,

"There is no evidence that that has happened in the past or that there are instances in which that will happen this time."

Therefore, he advised the then-Republican candidate for the presidency "to stop whining and try to make his case to get votes." But Obama was wrong on two fronts. First, he knew Russia was attempting to meddle with our election. Second, the "whining" was not done by the 45th American President after the election. It was by Obama, Clinton, Democrats, and the complicit mainstream media after a demoralizing historic defeat. So, who can't accept the results of the election now?

The media hid Obama's mythical failures in history because...

"Myth is much more important and truer than history. History is just journalism and you know how reliable that is." *- Joseph Campbell*

<u>Chapter 12</u>

THE REAL OBAMA YEARS:
SCANDALS

Many scandals emerged under President Obama which were only briefly mentioned in the mainstream media. Even though they carried much weight, they were mostly ignored. Because many anchors, reporters, and journalists in the mainstream media supported Obama's ideology, they dismissed all the scandals. Some were bigger than others. Nonetheless, they were treated as being illegitimate or not a big deal. With great allegiance, the media spun their web of deception. But the truth can't be erased or altered. So, the focus herein will be to detail those scandals which were not given much credence in the news.

In December of 2017, Vice President Biden praised President Obama on the *CBS "This Morning"* show. He stated,

"I've served with eight Presidents and I've gotten to know four of them very well. I've never met any President that has more character, more integrity, and more backbone than this guy does. And, eight years, not a hint – not a hint – of a scandal."

Biden had told the American people one of the greatest fibs of all-time. And, not to be outdone, President Obama echoed the same sentiments in March 2018 at MIT in Boston, Massachusetts, saying,

"We didn't have a scandal that embarrassed us."

Whether Obama had a scandal that "embarrassed" him may be the truth. Maybe he didn't consider any of the wrongdoings by him or his administration to be scandalous. But, actually, there were more than a dozen scandals during Obama's presidency. Some of them are recognizable, some led to deaths, while others didn't get the news coverage they so richly deserved. And, so, some shall be revealed here.

Operation Fast and Furious cover-up

An undercover sting operation involving the ATF (Bureau of Alcohol, Tobacco, Firearms and Explosive) which "allowed licensed firearms dealers to sell weapons to illegal straw buyers, hoping to track the guns to Mexican drug cartel leaders and arrest them" became known as *Operation Fast and Furious* in 2010. To be clear, a *straw buyer* is someone who buys something on behalf of someone else, often presenting themselves as the actual buyer. It was a "letting guns walk" or "gun-walking" scheme. The ATF watched as roughly 2,000 guns were purposefully sold to these straw buyers and others. The result of this program led to the deaths of many, including Border Patrol Agent Brian Terry, Immigration and Customs Enforcement Agent Jamie Zapata, and Mexican citizens. Still others like Victor Avila were seriously wounded during this very questionable operation.

Instead of being accountable for the fact that this program risked the safety of American people, the Obama Administration put a political spin on this. Of course, the mainstream media followed their lead and was complicit with this cover-up since they favored and would not refute the policies of a Democrat in the Oval Office. But "hell hath no fury" if a Republican President had allowed this to happen. The onslaught of questions, criticisms, and calls for impeachment would have been overblown to the stratospheres.

Plausible deniability, when senior officials deny knowledge or responsibility for any damning actions committed by others under an organization hierarchy because of sufficient evidence that confirms their participation, was the Obama Administration's willfully ignorant stance in this matter. And, at the center of this cover-up was former Attorney General Eric Holder. Through this clear denial of knowledge by Holder's subordinates, he basically escaped perjury charges that could, and probably should have, been brought upon him.

The first whiff of this scandal, which the Brian Terry family called it, occurred when A.G. Holder was on the brink of being held in contempt of Congress. Of course, the mainstream media downplayed the <u>contempt</u> charges that were a result of evasive remarks under oath and failing to turn over appropriate documents to Congress. The plausible deniability and citing of "executive privilege" by A.G. Holder and others would give credence to much speculation about the Obama Administration. It was said that they may have wanted to create gun crimes in Mexico, so they could express outrage about lax regulations involving guns sold in the U.S. It's an interesting theory. But that has not been undeniably proven, as of yet.

But what is assuredly so is that the smoke perpetrated by the Obama Administration working in tandem with the mainstream media was thicker than the smoke that had risen after gunfire had killed these Americans. Attorney General Holder argued the contempt charges were not part of a scandal but just some "political theater" by the opposition party in Washington. Eventually, a U.S. District Court Judge Amy Berman Jackson concluded Holder should not be held in contempt of court or jailed. He was ordered, however, to release all the Department of Justice documents regarding the case to Congress.

Regardless of whether A.G. Holder was held in contempt, the facts from confirmed reports are undeniable. They are as follows:

- Prior to U.S. Federal agents Jaime Zapata being killed and Victor Avila being seriously injured, concerns were expressed to their supervisor over a government document from the U.S. State Department that forbade these U.S. Embassy members from being sent to an area they were not allowed in. This area was controlled by the Zetas cartel. Yet, still, they were ordered to transport surveillance equipment to this dangerous location anyway. This would ultimately lead to more than 90 shots being fired at Zapata and Avila while in their vehicle by brutal cartel members surrounding them.

- By cross-referencing serial numbers from the guns used in Operation Fast and Furious with guns seized in Mexico, almost 100 weapons were used in crimes. Over 50 of them were not spoken about during the many Congressional investigations.

- In 2010, three guns from America were used in the Salvarcar massacre in Mexico. The Juarez cartel mistook 15 people, mostly teenagers, as Sinaloa cartel members, and killed them.

- The Mexican government was aware of the "gun-walking" Fast and Furious operation as well as others taking place in spite of their denial of the program. Andrew Selee, Vice President of programs at Woodrow Wilson Center situated in Washington, D.C., confirmed this. In addition, a special agent in charge of an ATF field office in Phoenix, William Newell, said the Mexican Procuraduria General Del La Republica (PGR) had knowledge about what was happening in their country.
- Only 700 of the 2,000 firearms sold were recovered by 2012.

In 2016, the DOJ documents from the Fast and Furious case were given to Congress. After review, Jason Chaffetz, Chairman of the House Committee on Oversight and Government Reform, released a memo which reads as follows.

More than previously understood, the documents show the lengths to which senior Department officials went to keep information from Congress. Further, the documents reveal how senior Justice Department officials -"including Attorney General Eric Holder" - intensely followed and managed an effort to carefully limit and obstruct the information produced to Congress.

Holder and his subordinates:

1. Presumed that allegations about gunwalking in Arizona were false and refused to adjust when documents and evidence showed otherwise.

2. Politicized decisions about how and whether to comply with the congressional investigation.

3. Devised strategies to redact or otherwise withhold relevant information from Congress and the public.

4. Isolated the fallout from the Fast and Furious scandal to ATF leadership and the U.S. Attorney's Office in Arizona.

5. Created a culture of animosity towards congressional oversight.

Obviously, the memo condemns the actions of the DOJ and former Attorney General Holder. But what can't be lost here is there was a fast and furious effort to cover-up the truths about the operation. It was a scandal which involved the deaths and injuries of many.

Secret death lists of the Veterans Administration (VA)

Being a veteran myself, and having gone to VA hospitals, this scandal is extremely disturbing. Initially, this scandal involved the Veterans Administration hospital in Phoenix, Arizona. It had been discovered that two sets of waiting lists were created by employees of the facility to make it appear as if veteran patients were being serviced for their medical needs in a timely manner. One list showed the actual long wait times of veterans for internal processes, while the phony list created wait times of shorter length for the public and external purposes. The *real* long wait times veterans experienced through the Phoenix VA facility resulted in as much as 40 alleged deaths.

Purportedly, the former Veterans Administration Secretary Eric Shinseki stated he was "mad as hell" and President Obama called it "an outrage", as whistleblowers from around the nation stepped up and further exposed the scandal. In 2013, the VA admitted that only 41 percent of new veterans were seen within their specific guidelines. The percentage of veterans which had actually been seen for medical treatment within the outlined time period was down 90 percent from 2012. These veterans who were making appointments were supposed to be provided medical care within 14 days. But Dr. Sam Foote exposed some wrongdoings at the Phoenix VA facility. Many employees were instructed not to enter the appointment into the system, pretend to do so, copy the screen, print it out, and then delete the information. About 1,500 to 1,600 veterans had no choice but to wait for months before seeing a doctor. Some veterans died waiting because of the malfeasance at this medical facility. It was disgraceful!

Besides Arizona, this 'cooking of the books' also happened within VA facilities in Colorado, South Carolina, Georgia, Pennsylvania, Tennessee, and other elsewhere. As many as 6,300 veterans waited for months to be treated by a physician at the VA in Fort Collins, Colorado. In Columbia, South Carolina, the Williams Jennings Bryan Dorn Veterans Medical Center had patients waiting up to a year, or longer, for routine gastrointestinal procedures. Six patients died as a result of a delay in treatment. Three deaths also occurred because of long wait lists of over 4,500 patients at the Charlie Norwood VA Medical Center in Augusta, Georgia. Of the specific list of 700 newly enrolled veteran appointments in a Pittsburgh, Pennsylvania facility, some waited over a year to see a physician. Also, during a six-month period, from 2013 to 2014, an estimated 29% of the over 4,700 veterans who had made appointments were cared for by a doctor within the 14-day guidelines of the VA hospitals in Nashville and Murfreesboro, Tennessee. In the end, nearly two thirds of the 216 VA facilities in our nation had been instructed to falsify wait times for veterans making appointments.

Some tried to blame the actions of the VA hospitals on the fact there was an increased influx of injured veterans coming back to the states from the Iraq or Afghanistan wars. But the real problems may have been attributable to a shortage of medical professionals, budgets, outdated computer systems, and bonuses which were not sufficiently addressed. For example, at the Phoenix VA facility, administration and operations personnel were paid 59% of all salaries, a higher percentage than those being paid for medical services. In addition, in 2008 a billion dollars was budgeted for an integrated healthcare system. Yet, by 2012, not one line of code was created to rectify the problem. So, it was very plausible there was an incentive to lie about the secret waiting lists because bonuses were based upon performances in these VA facilities.

Senator Richard Blumenthal said there was credible "evidence of wrongdoing within the VA system". Senator Patty Murray exclaimed to VA Secretary Shinseki that the "practice at the VA seems to be to hide the truth". But Attorney General Eric Holder said he didn't "have any announcements at this time with regard to anything the Justice Department was doing" about what was transpiring at the VA. With all the evidence of corruption and whistleblowers coming out of the shadows of the VA facilities, why wasn't a criminal investigation being undertaken? The Obama Administration, again, wanted to save face.

In May 2014, Rep. Steve Stockman released a statement which concluded Obama was aware of problems throughout the VA (Veterans Administration) and "chose not to act for years, even as veterans died." Again, at least 40 veterans died because of this grand scheme to falsify appointment books, and maybe more. The fixed books gave the false impression that those veterans were being given medical care on a timely basis. Although the *Washington Times* reported it had received documents which showed these problems dated back to the Bush Administration, no apparent aggressive actions were taken to defuse the undignified, corrupt, and tragic situation occurring to veterans under the Obama Administrations. Very sadly, this is a scandal which should definitely be placed in the 'record books' (pun intended!)

The IRS targeting conservatives

During the Obama-era, there were unwarranted and deliberate political actions by the Internal Revenue Service (IRS) taken against the Republican Tea Party and some pro-life groups. These targeted persons were conservatives (or registered Republicans) who had their tax exemptions applications grossly delayed and scrutinized. This was done until after Obama's Presidential election in 2012. The IRS, Democrats, and mainstream media brought out their playbooks to obscure the truths by dancing around the facts. But if this had occurred under a Republican administration the uproar and coverage would not have let up until the issue was resolved immediately. These double-standards between conservatives and liberals in America are incredibly apparent.

The IRS deliberately held the processing of applications for 501(c)(4) tax-exemption status, which had been received from organizations with "Tea Party", "Patriots", "9/12" Project, "Israel", or other words in their names. The Internal Revenue Service also targeted applications from businesses that were advocating to make "America a better place to live", criticized how the country was being run, had challenged Obamacare, wanted people to become more aware about the Constitution and Bill of Rights, and so forth. Lois Lerner, the Director of the IRS Exempt Organization division, from 2006 to 2013, was at the center of this scandal.

In March 2017, *The Hill* reported "the IRS revealed that it had found nearly 7,000 documents potentially related to the targeting of tea party groups." This agency basically obstructed Congress from gathering information by stating they had "lost computers and hard drives and tens of thousands of emails". As with almost everything associated with Democrats, Obama, and Clinton, there seemed to be computer related problems and ignorance was professed. But the email exchanges which were eventually recovered, some of which involved the IRS division head Lois Lerner, revealed an anti-conservative bias. Although she was held in contempt by Congress, Lerner escaped charges and jail time. It was another Obama Administration official being let off the hook and freed of wrongdoing. Yet, after being hired in 2014, new IRS John Koskinen would keep the façade going during his tenure. That changed in 2017 when the 45th American President took office. He replaced Koskinen with someone more honorable.

During this time, it should be recalled that President Obama professed he was "outraged" and "angry" when learning the IRS had admitted to targeting conservatives. Then, years after this occurred, Obama falsely stated there was "not even a smidgeon of corruption" with the IRS scandal. So, how could he be outraged about the scandal and then later declare no corruption existed? Obama could deny the IRS scandal wasn't corrupt; however, could he also claim that secret lists causing deaths of veterans, Operation Fast and Furious deaths, or spying on Americans, imprisonment of journalists, and Hillary Clinton cover-ups (discussed later) weren't corrupt? Apparently, he thought so.

Denouncing conservative news and wiretapping journalists

While President Obama was in office, his administration had a history of blaming or denouncing *Fox News,* and still continue to do so even after leaving their lofty positions. Obama's administration would exclude the conservative news group from a round of interviews with Treasury Department official Kenneth Feinberg in 2009. To top it off, Stephanie Cutter, former White House Communications Director, went on *CNN* to declare *Fox News* a "wing of the Republican Party". She also said the administration would stop calling them a "news network". It's because *Fox News* has fair and balanced reporting. They seek and focus on uncovering truth, no matter the consequences. Rather than giving opinionated and fabricated stories, which the mainstream media does, *Fox News* releases trustworthy news. So, some twist facts about them.

Regardless, in 2010, the Obama Justice Department obtained a search warrant to search computer and phone records of conservative *Washington Post* journalist James Rosen. He was charged with being a co-conspirator and violating the *Espionage Act.* Rosen had received and published data about North Korea leaked from a State Department official, Stephen Kim. Yet most reporters frequently receive leaks from government officials. And, usually, the reporters are not charged with a crime, only the leaker of classified information. So, Kim pleaded guilty to one count under the Espionage Act and served jail time. But the unwarranted scrutiny Rosen received from the *unjust* Obama Justice Department was unprecedented. The Obama administration had even called Rosen a flight risk, which the government had never done before to a reporter. And, Rosen continued to be investigated for seven years with the threat of jail time hanging over his head. Not only that, but he was *wiretapped.* It was an egregious abuse of power.

This just verifies the terrible double standards in this country. When Obama goes after *Fox News*, then it's *food for fodder* for the left-leaning news outlets. But when the 45th American President, calls out the mainstream media for their bias, he is denounced as a tyrant. And, yet, despite 90% plus of news coverage being either negative, fake, leaked, anonymous, or misleading, the new President still has not wiretapped anyone or held the *Espionage Act* over a journalist's head.

Illegal spying on Americans

Besides the journalist James Rosen being secretly spied upon, there were undoubtedly many others which were under surveillance by the Obama Administration. To be fair, the spying did not originate while President Obama was in office, it was done decades before him by the government. For example, in the 1970's it was found that the National Security Agency (NSA) spied upon anti-war protestors, civil rights activists, and political opponents. In 1978, the Foreign Intelligence Surveillance Act (FISA) was created in response to this. Then, when the attacks on September 11, 2001 occurred, surveillance techniques were enhanced by the intelligence agencies. Under President Bush, the USA Patriot (Uniting and Strengthening America by Providing Appropriate Tools Required to Intercept and Obstruct Terrorism) act was enacted. An enormous eavesdropping operation was undertaken by the NSA and other agencies for the surveillance of domestic and foreign individuals. Then, some computer and telecommunication companies became involved with the government. There were even court cases filed which were in reference to this spying, such as *Hepting v. AT&T, Jewell v. NSA,* and *First Unitarian Church v. NSA.* During this time Eric Snowden, a highly gifted computer professional, was hired by the U.S. government as a member of the CIA (Central Intelligence Agency), and, subsequently, as an intelligence contractor.

Through the administrations of Presidents Bush and Obama, Eric Snowden didn't agree with what he had discovered about the secret surveillance practices of the American intelligence agencies. But he reluctantly remained employed by the government.

When James Clapper, Director of National Intelligence, had lied under oath to Congress about the NSA's role in the data collection of millions of Americans, it's been documented that Snowden was upset. Then, three days later, President Obama appointed Leon Panetta, a California Democrat, who had served under several titles and was Chief of Staff for President Bill Clinton, to head the CIA (Central Intelligence Agency). Snowden would have enough. He exclaimed,

*"Obama just named a f*cking politician to run the CIA".*

So, Snowden exposed the NSA was spying on many by copying and leaking classified data to the *Guardian, Washington Post, New York Times* and *Der Spiegel* during 2013. Obviously, Obama and many in his administration weren't too happy about the leaking of information. But Snowden, although partly wrong for disseminating foreign intelligence data, was right for unveiling more truth about what was happening to innocent citizens. James Clapper would be replaced with John Brennan to head the CIA. Although Brennan had been in the CIA years before this, Obama had selected someone who voted for a communist in 1976.

Under the Obama Administration reign (2008 – 2016), there were many intelligence tools used for domestic and foreign spying, including a Skype surveillance program called Project Chess. And, the NSA used its intelligence tools in many ways.

- U.N. Security Council members were spied upon, as reported by *EPOCA*.
- Chancellor Angela Merkel was spied upon, as reported by *Der Spiegel*.
- Al Jazeera was hacked, as reported by Eric Snowden and *Der Spiegel*.
- *Yahoo* and *Google* data centers were breached, as reported by Eric Snowden and the *Washington Post*.
- The NSA infiltrated the Tor network to try and change the privacy rights of people on-line, as reported by the *Guardian*.
- Online video game users were spied upon by the NSA, as reported by *Guardian* and *The New York Times*.
- A Chinese company Huawei's server was hacked into, as reported by Eric Snowden and *The New York Times*.
- The NSA spied on love interests of people under the label 'LOVEINT', as reported by the *Wall Street Journal*.

Then, there were the court cases that were filed. There was 1) *Klayman v. Obama*, a case filed over the unjust collection of data the NSA gained from telephone customers of Verizon 2) *Wikimedia v. NSA*, a case filed by the ACLU on behalf of the NSA surveillance of education, legal, human rights, and media organizations, and 3) *Atkisson v. DOJ*, a major case filed in which a former *CBS* news correspondent Sharyl Atkisson's computer was hacked because she had been reporting on the highly amoral Benghazi cover-up, amongst other things. But, most importantly, is the recent scandal of spying which was perpetrated by the Obama Administration. There is credible evidence to support that unmasking and surveillance of the 45th U.S. President and his campaign team occurred during and after his election. Hopefully, more light will be shed on many of these partisan, unethical, and maybe illegal actions.

This can all be best summed up by what Joe Newman of POGO, an independent watchdog group stated in 2014.

"The thing that makes the Obama administration really stand out is the use of the Espionage Act. They've invoked it seven times [against leakers] and that's more than every other administration combined when it comes to going after people who have leaked to the media."

Iran nuclear deal

In 2015, the Iran Nuclear Deal was agreed upon by the United States, the United Kingdom, Russia, France, China, Germany, the European Union, and the Islamic Republic of Iran. The deal was made with the conditions that Iran stopped their nuclear enrichment programs and the reprocessing of heavy waters leading to the creation of nuclear weapons. Iran would also need to be monitored with inspections and transparency. In return, Iran would have economic and financial sanctions lifted by the European Union, the U.S., and the United Nations. The deal was referred to the U.N. Security Council. But several months later, President Obama also was willingly to pay $400 million to Iran. At the same time, there was the release of four American hostages. Then, within three weeks or so of the initial payment, $1.3 billion was sent to Iran. Both transactions involved sending *planeloads of currencies in cash*. Why would the U.S. do this? Whether intentional or not, one can be sure the cash was filtered out to terror organizations which Iran sponsors around the world.

You can be sure Hezbollah and the Islamic Revolutionary Guard Corps (IRGC) were very happy with that Iran deal. In addition, Project Cassandra, the operation by the DEA (Drug Enforcement Agency) to prevent Hezbollah from funding unlawful drug-running, money laundering, and terrorist operations, was undercut by the Iran Nuclear deal. CIA Director John Brennan, Secretary of State John Kerry, and President Obama all had a hand in trying to pacify Iran, while at the same time ignoring Hezbollah. To be clear, Hezbollah is a terrorist group which has far reaching hands around the globe to countries. It even stretches below America's southern border such as to, reportedly, Mexico, Venezuela, Paraguay, Argentina, and Brazil.

There is no doubt the Iran regime's hatred toward the U.S., Israel, and the western world will lead them to covertly building nuclear weapons. But did President Obama have to help them do so, while, in turn, funding the terrorist groups they support? The situation in Iran was monitored from 2017 – 2018 by the U.S. and others. But by May 2018, a decision had to be made about whether pulling out of the Iran deal was a good idea. Backed with clear evidence by Israeli Prime Minister Netanyahu that Iran was not being compliant with the letter of the deal and creating nuclear weapons, the U.S. had only one choice to make after reconfirming intelligence reports. The 45th U.S. President kept another promise he had made to Americans. Regardless of the criticism, he finally ended Obama's disastrous deal with Iran.

What was most laughable then, and now, was President Obama won the Nobel Peace prize within a year of his presidency in October 2009 for doing nothing. The prestigious award was handed to Obama for his supposed "extraordinary efforts to strengthen international diplomacy and cooperation between peoples" and would start "a new beginning between the United States and Muslims around the world." This is a farce because he did nothing during his first year in office to warrant this honor, or in the years that followed. All Obama did was appease some Muslim countries, indirectly funded terrorist groups, and aided with the building of nuclear weapons. The Iranians have been shouting "death to America" since the 1970's. The war in Afghanistan has continued for nearly two decades. Did he change any of that?

In contrast, in just over a year, the 45th U.S. President has eliminated the ISIS Caliphate in Syria / Iraq, made mutually beneficial investments with Arab nations, gave a well-received speech in Saudi Arabia, attempted to address the chemical weapons issue in Syria, and tried to denuclearize North Korea. So, where is his Nobel Peace Prize?

The Hillary Clinton cover-ups

This will be discussed in more detail in the Chapter "What really happened with Hillary?" But below is a summary of the wrongdoings the Obama administration was involved in with Hillary Clinton while she was Secretary of State and as Presidential candidate.

- Benghazi Cover-Up: On September 11, 2012, there was an attack by Islamic extremists on U.S. government agencies in Benghazi, Libya, where four Americans were killed. The U.S. Secretary of State Hillary Clinton and, then, U.S. Ambassador to the UN, defended the actions of the administration with political spin. But the truth was they failed four men that were in harm's way.
- Uranium One Deal: In 2010, a deal was made to sell Uranium One, to a company known as ARMZ, which had ties to Rosatom, a Russian nuclear energy agency. Uranium One was a company based in Canada, which had 20% of U.S. uranium in Wyoming. The Obama Administration approved the sale of our uranium to the Russians through a board known as CFIUS. Why?
- Hillary Clinton email server: During her time as U.S. Secretary of State, Hillary Clinton kept a suspicious secret email server hidden. It has come to light President Obama did know about the server which had classified information on it. But Clinton, during the 2016 Presidential campaign, was not charged with any wrongdoings. The investigation is being re-examined...

In April 2016, President Obama was interviewed by Chris Wallace of *FOX News* to discuss the Clinton email server "matter".

Obama: "I can tell you that this is not a situation in which America's national security was endangered."

Wallace: "Since then, we've learned that over 2,000 of her e-mails contained classified material, 22 of the emails had top secret information.

Can you still say flatly that she did not jeopardize America's secrets?"

Obama: "I've got to be careful because, as you know, there have been investigations, there are hearings, Congress is looking at this. And I haven't been sorting through each and every aspect of this. Here's what I know. Hillary Clinton was an outstanding secretary of state. She would never intentionally put America in any kind of jeopardy. And what I also know, because I handle a lot of classified information, is that there are -- there's classified, and then there's classified. There's stuff that is really top secret, top secret, and there is stuff that is being presented to the President or the secretary of state that you might not want on the transom, or going out over the wire, but is basically stuff that you can get in open source."

Wallace: "But last October, you were prepared to say she hadn't jeopardized. And the question is, can you still say that?"

Obama: "Well, I continue to believe that she has not jeopardized America's national security. Now, what I've also said is that -- and she's acknowledged -- that there's a carelessness in terms of managing emails that she has owned. And she recognizes. But I also think it is important to keep this in perspective. This is somebody who had served has her country for four years as secretary of state, and did an outstanding job, and no one has suggested that in some ways as a consequence of how she's handled emails, that that detracted from her excellent ability to carry out her duties."

Wallace: "Mr. President, when you say what you've just said, when Josh Earnest said as he did, your spokesman, in January, the information from the Justice Department is she's not a target, some people, I think, are worried whether or not the decision, whether or not -- how to handle the case -- will be made on political grounds, not legal grounds. Can you guarantee to the American people, can you direct the Justice Department to say, Hillary Clinton will be treated as the evidence goes, she will not be, in any way, protected?"

Obama: "I can guarantee that. And I can guarantee that not because I give Attorney General Lynch a directive, that is institutionally how we have always operated. I do not talk to the attorney general about pending investigations. I do not talk to FBI directors about pending investigations. We have a strict line, and always have maintained it. Previous Presidents."

Wallace: "So, just to button this up..."

Obama: "I guarantee it. I guarantee that there is no political influence in any investigation conducted by the Justice Department or the FBI, not just in this case, but in any case. Full stop. Period."

Wallace: "And she will be treated no differently?"

Obama: "Guaranteed, full stop. Nobody gets treated differently when it comes to the Justice Department, because nobody is above the law."

Wallace: "Even if she ends up as the Democratic nominee?"

Obama: "How many times do I have to say it, Chris? Guaranteed."

The phony Russian dossier

During the 2016 election, the Clinton campaign and DNC bought a salacious unverified dossier and used it against the President-to-be. The Obama Administration intelligence agencies knew Russia was spreading around misinformation. Even so, this dossier seems to have been 'weaponized' by the FBI and DOJ to obtain FISA warrants and spy on people affiliated with the Republican Party during the 2016 election. This is currently UNDER INVESTIGATION.

The Pigford lawsuit

In 1997, a lawsuit (*Pigford v. Glickman*) was won by 91 black farmers who were unjustly denied loans by the USDA (United States Department of Agriculture). Then, the number of defendants filing claims which cited the original Pigford court ruling jumped to around 90,000. These people seeking funds were not only African Americans, but females, Native Americans, and Hispanics as well. The original payments were reported to have cost about $120 million. But by 2010 when Attorney General Eric Holder took over the case, under the Obama Administration, the number of payments increased to an estimated $1.25 billion. And, yet, that number was incorrect too. More people filed, and the payments would amount to about $4.4 billion with $130 million in legal fees. People declared they were would-be farmers applying for loans and they would receive payouts. But there was much fraud in the claims process. For example, some people living in urban New York City received a $50,000 payment. It was an obvious scam aimed to gain political favor from anyone receiving payouts.

The abusive racial inequality led to the resignation of USDA Director Shirley Sherrod, who was exposed making some very racist remarks. She said,

"The first time I was faced with having to help a white farmer save his farm, he took a long time talking. But he was trying to show me he was superior to me...I know what he was doing. But he had come to me for help. What he didn't know while he was taking all that time trying to show me, he was superior to me, was I was trying to decide just how much help I was going to give him. I was struggling with the fact that so many black people had lost their farm land. And here I was faced with having to help a white person save their land. So, I didn't give him the full force of what I could do...."

In addition, in places such as Alabama, Arkansas, Mississippi, and North Carolina, the number of farms were far fewer than the Pigford claims. But even though the elements involved with the Pigford filings cried out with obvious racism, it received little coverage in the mainstream media. This major scandal was basically ignored.

Sebelius violations

Former U.S. Health and Human Services Secretary Kathleen Sebelius had oversight over Obamacare, the Affordable Care Act. The rollout of President Obama's legacy policy received much tumultuous negative feedback. Then, at a human rights event Sebelius campaigned for Democrat Walter Dalton for North Carolina Governor and Barack Obama in a re-election bid for President. These partisan acts of influence as a Cabinet member in the Obama Administration, along with the taxpayer dollars spent, was a violation of the Hatch Act. But, also, Sebelius would allegedly ask insurance companies, health industries and pharmaceutical firms that would participate in the new

Obama mandated health care system to make donations to Enroll America. In addition, Anne Filipic, the President of Enroll America, a community organizing group, had also worked in Obama's 2008 campaign. Later, she would become Deputy Executive Director to the Democratic National Committee, and Deputy Director of the Office of Public Engagement. Yet the Obama Administration said this was not political. Inevitably, Sebelius was forced to resign under all the scrutiny.

GSA waste

In 2010, the General Services Administration (GSA) held a training conference in Las Vegas, Nevada which amounted to over $800,000. In addition, the Obama Administration led department was accused of other excessive spending for travel and conferences, forcing the administrator, Martha N. Johnson, some top deputies, and senior executives of the agency to resign. One of these executives, Jeffrey E. Neely, who arranged the lavish Las Vegas event, would be sentenced to serve prison time for being convicted of false claims and documents. Johnson would confess "taxpayer dollars were squandered."

Secret service mishaps

There were several secret service mishaps that took place under the Obama Administration. Some of these incidents will be listed below.

*1) November 2009 – Television stars Michaele and Tareq Salahi passed through two secret service security check points to crash the White House dinner between President Obama and Indian Prime Minister Singh. Isn't that trespassing and a security breach?

*2) November 2011 – A gunman, Oscar R. Ortega-Hernandez, parked his car south of the White House and fired at a second-floor window. Luckily, President Obama and Michelle Obama were not in the White House. But their daughter Sasha was there. Even so, one agent told the others to "stand down" in order to hide the incident. Several days later, however, the bullets were found. Then, the story was uncovered.

*3) April 2012 – A few agents were nabbed soliciting prostitutes at the Hotel Caribe in Cartagena, Columbia during a Summit of the Americas.

*4) November 2013 – During an encounter with a woman in a Hays-Adams hotel room in Washington, D.C., Ignacio Zamora, secret service agent, took the bullet out of his gun to show he wasn't a threat. But after leaving the room, Zamora tried getting back in. He had left the bullet.

*5) December 2013 - When President Obama was attending the Nelson Mandela funeral in Pretoria, South Africa, a schizophrenic man who allegedly saw angels, Thamsanqa Jantjie, pretended to be the sign language interpreter. Somehow, he had faked his way into the event.

*6) March 2014 – A hotel member in Amsterdam (Holland) alerted the U.S. that three secret service agents had been drinking. One of them had been found in the hallway passed out. This was prior to going on detail for President Obama for the upcoming European Summit.

*7) September 2014 – A man, Omar Gonzales, who had a folded knife in his pocket jumped over the White House fence. He managed to make it to the Green Room. Gonzales stated,

"...that he was concerned that the atmosphere was collapsing and needed to get the information to the President of the United States so that he could get the word out to the people."

Colorado river pollution

In the summer of 2015, millions of gallons of contaminated toxic waste water rushed from the Gold King Mine in an area north of Silverton, Colorado into Cement Creek and into the Animas River. The release of heavy metals into the water turned the water orange. The discolored and toxic water made its way into Durango, Colorado and into the San Juan River in New Mexico. The accident happened when workers from the climate change conscience Obama administration Environmental Protection Agency (EPA) triggered water to pour out as they were ironically investigating the mine for contamination. Of course, the mainstream media was eagerly complicit in covering up the fact that it was the EPA who were ultimately responsible for the pollution.

Government shutdown fiasco (2013)

Although not a scandal per se, in October 2013, this 16-day government shutdown was implemented because an agreement couldn't be reached by Congress to fund Obamacare, forcing American taxpayers to buy a socialized and unconstitutional healthcare service. As a result, up to 800,000 non-essential employees were furloughed, but would get paid upon return. Also, the National Zoo, National Parks, and NASA were closed and the National World War II Memorial in D.C. was barricaded so veterans and visitors could not access it. The cost of this unnecessary fiasco was estimated to be 24 billion dollars. Of course, there will be new shutdowns for political reasons in the future. But, hopefully, this time there will be an adequate reason – like funding THE WALL to secure our southern border from drugs, crime, terrorists, and illegals.

****

So, given all that was mentioned, if the mainstream media, Democratic Party representatives, or those defending the legacy of Barack Hussein Obama II profess to Americans and the world that *no scandals existed* from 2009 to 2016, and beyond, they are fabricating the past. These persons are just delusional or hiding the truth about what occurred during this 8-year period. It's a time when one can clearly look through the dark dirty stained glassed window of hope and see some of the most dishonorable abuses of power in American political history. Very sad!

A quote from the work of Sir William Shakespeare (from *The Rape of Lucrece*), arguably the greatest writer ever, may best describe those in high places which were involved with these Obama scandals.

"The mightier man, the mightier is the thing
What makes him honour'd, or begets him hate;
For greatest scandal waits on greatest state."

Chapter 13

WHAT REALLY HAPPENED WITH HILLARY?

A year after the 2016 Presidential Election one of the biggest stars in Hollywood gave one of the most honest critiques of Hillary Clinton. In September 2017, actor, political activist, and humanitarian, George Clooney, spoke to the *Daily Beast* saying,

"Hillary, for years and years and years, has been the presumptive nominee, and quite honestly, she was incredibly qualified for the job...But being qualified for the job does not necessarily mean you're the right person to be President. Here's what I mean. She was more qualified than even her husband was when he was elected President, but she's not as good at communicating things. That's simply true. When she got up and gave a speech, it didn't soar." And, he also stated, "It was frustrating because I never saw her elevate her game," Mr. Clooney continued. "I never saw it. And I had a lot of liberal friends who were like, 'She's not good at this.' And I see that, and I understand it."

So, that's it in a nutshell. With the nearly two billion dollars she had invested in her campaign, the speeches of Presidents Bill Clinton, Bernie Sanders, and Barack Obama, other politicians supporting her at events, celebrities advertising and appearing at concerts for her, all the mainstream media bias, and polling numbers having her ahead in the race, she still lost. Personality and authenticity go a long way in an election; and, she had neither.

As bad as her personality and authenticity traits were on the campaign trail, they were overshadowed by the lack of truthfulness she exuded to millions. We must remember she had been an attorney many years before her political life. So, Hillary knew how to mislead others to get an end-result in her favor. For instance, she defended a 41-year old man who raped a 12-year old girl, Kathy Shelton, and said at the trial,

"I have been informed that the complainant is emotionally unstable with a tendency to seek out older men and to engage in fantasizing...I have also been informed that she has in the past made false accusations about persons, claiming they had attacked her body. Also, that she exhibits an unusual stubbornness and temper when she does not get her way."

Shelton said years later, during the 2016 Presidential campaign,

"Hillary then began to attack my character, forcing me to undergo multiple polygraph tests where I was asked explicit sexual questions I didn't even understand. Next, I was sent for a psychiatric examination. It felt like I was the one on trial."

And, Hillary Clinton was the one who was supposed to be a feminist, supported women's rights, and thought that women should be heard when alleging sexual abuse? These character flaws undoubtedly contributed to her downfall. Millions of women would come to discover that Clinton was not who she proclaimed to be on the surface. It wasn't about who she was running against but who she had been in the past. It was her own fault what she said, didn't say, did, and didn't do.

Therefore, understanding a bit about what really happened in the past of Hillary Clinton will give one a better idea about how she reacted and operated to fend off scandals, survive in politics, and run for President of the United States. Although there are many examples of inappropriate behavior, the most prominent newsworthy issues that plagued her will be provided so one can evaluate her history. The topics which shall be covered are the mentors (Saul Alinsky and Robert Byrd), bimbo eruptions, birther movement, Russian reset gaffe, Uranium One deal, four killed in Benghazi, her secret email server, Clinton Foundation, 2016 Presidential campaign, and Russian dossier.

The mentors (Saul Alinsky and Robert Byrd)

First there was Saul Alinsky, a community organizer, who brought and spread his Marxist message through the Catholic Church. His socialist views coupled with the fact that Alinsky recognized Lucifer as "the first radical" in his incendiary book *Rules for Radicals* put a magnifying glass up to the man. When interviewed in *Playboy* magazine, Alinsky would talk about the afterlife, saying,

Alinsky: "... if there is an afterlife, and I have anything to say about it, I will unreservedly choose to go to hell."

Playboy Magazine: "Why?"

Alinsky: "Hell would be heaven for me. All my life I've been with the have-nots. Over here, if you're a have-not, you're short of dough. If you're a have-not in hell, you're short of virtue. Once I get into hell, I'll start organizing the have-nots over there."

To promote his view of a socialist state Alinsky wrote:

1. Healthcare – Control healthcare and you control the people.
2. Poverty – Increase the poverty level as high as possible; poor people are easier to control and will not fight back if you are providing everything for them to live.
3. Debt – Increase the debt to an unsustainable level. That way you're able to increase taxes, and this will produce more poverty.
4. Gun control – Remove people's ability to defend themselves from the government. That way you're able to create a police state.
5. Welfare – Take control of every aspect of people's lives (food, housing and income).
6. Education – Take control of what people read and listen to; take control of what children learn in school.
7. Religion – Remove the belief in God from the government and schools.
8. Class warfare – Divide the people into the wealthy and the poor. This will cause more discontent and it will be easier to take from (tax) the wealthy with the support of the poor.

If one examines these eight rules carefully with an open mind, then it's evident the extremely left-leaning part of Democratic Party in America is using this playbook now. President Obama, who had also been a community organizer, began to adopt these rules. And, Hillary Clinton assuredly wanted to continue this new progressive movement.

Hillary Rodham, before her marriage to Bill Clinton, wrote her senior thesis for Wellesley College about Saul Alinsky entitled, *"There Is Only the Fight...: An Analysis of the Alinsky Model."* She was offered a job by Alinsky but declined since she wanted to go to Yale to study law. But as she made her way into politics, she would distance away from her association with the socialist who showed admiration for Lucifer. Nonetheless, although Clinton did disassociate herself from the man, she didn't do the same for his principles. Actually, they are at the heart of her "Insist, Resist, and Persist" message; and, the basis for the progressively left-wing movement opposing the 45th U.S. President.

Next, there was the association Hillary Clinton had with Robert Byrd. He had been a Democrat and member of the U.S. Senate for years. But although he supposedly overcame his dark past, there was no denying that in his youth Byrd was a staunch supporter and member of the Klu Klux Klan (KKK). He infamously stated,

"I shall never fight in the armed forces with a negro by my side... Rather I should die a thousand times, and see Old Glory trampled in the dirt never to rise again, than to see this beloved land of ours become degraded by race mongrels, a throwback to the blackest specimen from the wilds."

And, years later, after disavowing the KKK, he would say,

*"There are white n*ggers....I've seen a lot of white niggers in my time, if you want to use that word. We just need to work together to make our country a better country, and I'd just as soon quit talking about it so much."*

Hillary called him "friend and mentor" at his memorial service.

Bimbo eruptions

During the 1992 Presidential campaign, Bill Clinton would be accused of an alleged affair with a model and actress, Gennifer Flowers. She indicated they had a 12-year affair. However, when questioned about Flowers, wife of the-then Arkansas Governor, Hillary, said she was a,

"...failed cabaret singer who doesn't even have much of a résumé to fall back on."

Then, later, when asked what she would do if a chance arose to cross-examine Flowers, Clinton replied,

"I mean, I would crucify her."

And, yet, her husband, Bill Clinton, later admitted he indeed did have one sexual encounter with Flowers.

Then, after Bill Clinton became President of the United States, the Whitewater scandal erupted. The President and his wife would be exonerated of any financial fraud or banking crimes to do with their partnership in a real estate firm years ago in Arkansas. But Bill Clinton was accused of sexual harassment and exposing himself to a former Arkansas state clerk, Paula Jones. Yet Hillary would once again defend her husband. Then, Jones had to settle for $850,000 to end the lawsuit.

During the same investigation, the President was caught in a lie about another sexual encounter. This time it was with an intern, Monica Lewinsky. Hillary would call the young girl a "narcissistic loony toon". But Special Prosecutor Ken Starr would present the case to Congress. Subsequently, the President would be impeached for perjury and obstruction of justice charges by the House of Representatives. But the Senate would let him off the hook. Still, this sexual encounter wasn't the first extra-marital affair President Clinton would be accused of during his presidency.

In 1998, a White House aide, Kathleen Willey, said President Clinton had sexually assaulted her in the study of the oval office in 1993. Willey mentioned he "kissed" her, groped her "breast", and forced her to touch his "genitals." Then, in 1999, Juanita Broaddrick came forward to say that then-Arkansas Attorney General, in 1978, had raped her. Of course, Bill Clinton denied these accusations and Hillary followed suit.

But there is another alleged extra-marital affair by Mr. Clinton which has not been well reported. This one involved Connie Hamzy, a groupie who bragged to have sex with rock stars. She accused the then Arkansas Governor Bill Clinton of sexually propositioning her in 1991. George Stephanopoulos, a senior advisor to President Clinton, was reported as stating that Hillary told him that,

"*...we have to destroy her story.*"

And, later, after the ordeal was over, Hillary would exclaim,

"*We'd survived our first bimbo eruption.*"

But in 2015, Hillary Clinton tweeted out,

"*Every survivor of sexual assault deserves to be heard, believed, and supported.*"

Really? What about all those women her husband allegedly sexually abused, and worse? So much for supporting and believing the sexual harassment or abuse allegations of women.

Birther movement

After becoming First Lady, Hillary Clinton had visions of sitting in the Oval Office of the White House as President of the United States. She was elected as a Democrat to be the junior U.S. Senator in New York in 2000. Clinton served in that role for eight years. Then, she took on Barack Obama in the Democratic Primary. That is when one of her closest confidants, Sidney Blumenthal, spoke to a McClatchy DC Bureau chief and allegedly dug up dirt on Obama – including some data about his birth certificate. This exchange and the release of Obama's birth certificate by his brother, Malik, began what has been dubbed the 'birther movement.' Of course, Hillary denies being part of this plan.

Russian reset gaffe

In 2008, after President Obama was elected, he chose Hillary Clinton to be his Secretary of State. They worked in tandem to try and smooth over U.S. and Russia relations. So, on March 6, 2009 in Geneva, Clinton presented former Russian Foreign Minister Sergei Lavrov with a gift. It was a plastic red reset button with the inscription "peregruzka" on it. Secretary of State Hillary Clinton stated and then asked the Russian Foreign Minister,

"We worked hard to get the right Russian word. Do you think we got it?"

Lavrov chuckled and replied,

"You got it wrong...this says 'peregruzka' which means overcharged."

This would not *reset* our relations with Russia then, nor would it reset our relationship with our adversary during the time Clinton or Obama were in office. Russia would annex Crimea and become involved with pro-Russian unrest in Ukraine, as well as back Syria and Iran.

Uranium One deal - UNDER INVESTIGATION

In 2010, the Obama Administration, specifically CFIUS (Committee of Foreign Investments in the United States), approved the sale of Uranium One, a Canadian based company, to ARMZ – owned by the Russian nuclear company Rosatom. This uranium was sold by top members in the Obama Administration who comprise the CFIUS board, one of which was Secretary of State Hillary Clinton. In essence, since the Uranium One firm owned 20% of U.S. uranium, which makes nuclear fuel, weapons, and high-energy x-rays in our country, this vital product was sold to Russia. The CFIUS board consented to this deal even though they knew the FBI, headed by Robert Mueller (the Special Counsel who is searching for the President's Russian collusion), had gathered evidence to prove that Rosatom officials were involved in global bribery, kickbacks, and money laundering. One of the targets of the investigation was a Russian businessman, Vadim Mikerin. He was a very high official with a subsidiary of Rosatom, called Tenex. This company, Tenex, had allegedly been involved in shenanigans of bribery and money laundering. So why would our government give 20% of our uranium to a Russian firm who was affiliated with companies under investigation? The answer was very simple. The U.S., or should we say Hillary Clinton, may have wanted something in return.

In June 2010, former President Bill Clinton went to Moscow to give an approved speech by the State Department, headed by Hillary, worth $500,000. The speaking fee was paid by Renaissance Capital, a Russian bank with ties to the Kremlin. Former President Bill Clinton also was to meet with Arkady Dvorkovich, a government official who served on Rosatom's board of supervisors, and Viktor Vekselberg, a businessman heading the Skolkovo Project which was to fuel the design of Russia's Silicon Valley. Bill also purportedly met with the future President of Russia, Vladimir Putin, at his home. But three months prior to Bill's visit to Moscow, Hillary Clinton, being Secretary of State, had met with Putin and then-President of Russia Dmitri Medvedev.

Years later, on February 7, 2018, an informant testified before Congressional committees to begin exposing what happened with the Uranium One deal. He was a member of the CIA and FBI for over three decades. His lawyer, Victoria Toesing, mentioned the whole thing was hatched by Russia years ago. It occurred in 2005, when Bill Clinton went overseas with his billionaire friend, Frank Giustra, and bestowed praises upon the dictator of Kazakhstan. Clinton and his partner ended up with Uranium mining rights. That's when Russia started to plan to deal with the U.S. to acquire its uranium. The Russians were counting on the CFIUS board under the Obama Administration, in which Hillary Clinton was Secretary of State, to approve this deal. Russia wanted to get control of uranium in the U.S. The top board members which would ultimately approve the deal were the heads of nine agencies. Other members privy to the information looked on as the Uranium One deal threatened our national security. Hillary Clinton was one of those top members, who was looking to accommodate foreign entities so she could fill her coffers in preparation for a run for the White House.

The members of CFIUS at the time of the Uranium One deal are listed below. But as matter of further reference, the Secretary of the Treasury is the Chairperson of CFIUS. Notices to CFIUS are received, processed, and coordinated at the staff level by the Staff Chairperson of CFIUS. This staff chairperson is the Director of the Office of Investment Security in the Department of the Treasury.

The members of CFIUS include the heads of the following departments:

1. Department of the Treasury (chair) - Timothy Geithner
2. Department of Justice - Eric Holder

3.   Department of Homeland Security - Janet Napolitano
4.   Department of Commerce – Gary Locke
5.   Department of Defense - Robert Gates
6.   Department of State - Hillary Clinton
7.   Department of Energy – Steven Chu
8.   Office of the U.S. Trade Representative - Ron Kirk
9.   Office of Science & Technology Policy - John Holdren

The following offices also observe. and if needed. participate in CFIUS's activities:

1.   Office of Management & Budget
2.   Council of Economic Advisors
3.   National Security Council
4.   National Economic Council
5.   Homeland Security Council

Note: The Director of National Intelligence and the Secretary of Labor are non-voting, ex-officio members of CFIUS with roles as defined by statute and regulation.

Regardless of who had been members of the CFIUS board in 2010, a savvy reporter, Sara A. Carter, who had been keenly investigating the Uranium One story, wrote the following years later in 2017/2018:

"An informant who spent years gathering information on the Russian energy and uranium market industry for the FBI, met staff members of the Senate Judiciary Committee, House Oversight, and House Intelligence Committees on Wednesday. He gave explosive testimony on his years as an undercover informant providing information to the FBI on Russian criminal networks operating in the United States. He also contends in his testimony, and written briefs, to the FBI that Russia attempted to hide its ongoing aid to help sustain Iran's nuclear industry, at the time the Obama administration approved the sale of 20 percent of U.S. uranium mining rights to Russia.

William D. Campbell, an American businessman, provided extensive information on other counterintelligence issues to the FBI for decades and he had also provided information to the CIA on various issues during his time overseas."

In addition, Sara A. Carter reported that the counterintelligence informant, Campbell, testified he had warned the FBI in 2010,

"TENEX continues to supply Iran with fuel through their Russian company TVEL."

The informant also stated to Congress that TVEL is a Russian nuclear fuel cycle company headquartered in Moscow, and said,

"They (TVEL) continue to assist with construction consult and fabricated assemblies to supply the reactor. Fabricated assemblies require sophisticated engineering and are arranged inside the reactor with the help and consult of TVEL."

Therefore, TENEX and TVEL were involved with the supply and assembly of nuclear materials. The informant also told Congress,

"I was speechless and angry in October 2010 when CFIUS approved the Uranium One sale to Rosatom. I was deeply worried that TLI continued to transport sensitive uranium despite the fact that it had been compromised by the bribery scheme...I expressed these concerns repeatedly to my FBI handlers. The response I got was that politics was somehow involved. I remember one response I got from an agent when I asked how it was possible CFIUS would approve the Uranium One sale when the FBI could prove Rosatom was engaged in criminal conduct. His answer: 'Ask your politicians.'"

Moreover, the informant, William D. Campbell, stated that APCO Worldwide, an independent global public affairs and strategic communications consultancy firm, was paid $3 million by Russia for lobbying. It also reportedly provided pro-bono work amounting to more than $1 million for the Clinton Global Initiative while she had been Secretary of State. APCO denied any wrongdoings, by saying,

"APCO Worldwide's activities involving client work on behalf of Tenex and The Clinton Global Initiative were totally separate and unconnected in any way...all actions on these two unconnected activities were appropriate,

publicly documented from the outset and consistent with regulations and the law. Any assertion otherwise is false and unfounded."

This reliable informant has been ridiculed and discredited by the mainstream media, former Obama Administration officials, and many pundits. But he has videotapes, documents, and recordings of these many events leading to and during the Uranium One deal. Campbell, the informant, also has over three decades of service in the U.S. intelligence agencies - undercover and otherwise. This should confirm something about his commitment and character.

Although more information will assuredly come out about the Uranium One deal, these points are a matter of record. In 2015, Vadim Mikerin, the Russian official of Tenex, a subsidiary to Rosatom, pled guilty to money laundering and had been previously arrested for racketeering in 2004 (serving 4 years in prison). Boris Rubizhevsky, a consultant to Mikerin, a Russian living in New Jersey and President of NEXGEN Security, pled guilty to conspiracy to commit money laundering. Daren Condrey, businessman for Transportation Logistics International, pled guilty to conspiring to violate the Foreign Corrupt Practices Act (FCPA) and wire fraud. Lastly, Mark Lambert a co-owner of Transportation Logistics International was charged with 1 count of conspiracy to commit wire fraud, 7 counts of violating the Foreign Corrupt Practices Act, 2 counts of wire fraud, and, lastly, 1 count of international promotional money laundering. This information was released by the Department of Justice and reported by Sara A. Carter.

Clinton Foundation - UNDER INVESTIGATION

The Uranium One deal has been tied to the Clinton Foundation. If this is found to be true, as there is a mountain of evidence to support this, Secretary of State Hillary Clinton would have used her office in a pay-for-play scheme which is unlawful. This means Clinton may have received *dirty money* in the Clinton Foundation so some of the funds could eventually be used to run for President of the United States.

But there is more to the story of the Clinton Foundation. In 2007, Frank Giustra, a billionaire, sold his interests in UrAsia Energy Ltd. to the firm Uranium One. He was an associate of President Bill Clinton. The *Washington Post* reported in 2015 that Giustra himself has given more than, a whopping, $30 million directly to the Clinton Foundation, while sitting on the organization's board. He has separately pledged $100 million to the Clinton Giustra Enterprise Partnership, making him one of the foundation's largest donors. But Giustra is not the only donor to ensure the Clinton Foundation had contributions while Hillary was Secretary of State. It has been surmised that her foundation may have received up to $145 million in donations from those linked to the Uranium One deal.

And, yet, there is still more to be told. After President Clinton and Hillary left the White House in 2001, she professed they were "dead broke" because of massive debts. Then, during Hillary Clinton's tenure as Secretary of State (2008 – 2012), they became worth more than $200 million. How? It's called pay-to-play politics.

Since 2001 the Clinton Foundation had raised about $2 billion. The Clinton Foundation was getting donations (or kickbacks) from foreign entities which had been granted favors by Secretary of State Hillary Clinton. It has been alleged that this foundation was really just *a front* so she could receive money for her Presidential campaign in 2016. For example, it has been reported that while Clinton was Secretary of State, Saudi Arabia sent between 10 and 25 million dollars to her foundation. Then, Saudi Arabia got some massive arms deal worth $29 billion. Boeing, which made F-15 jets as part of the Saudi deal, sent $900,000 to the Clinton Foundation. Furthermore, $165 billion in arms deals was allegedly approved by Clinton with about 20 countries, which had also donated to her foundation. And, lastly, in 2009, ConocoPhillips, Exxon Mobile, and Chevron lobbied for a new oil pipeline from Canada to Wisconsin. Her foundation received between 2 and 3 million dollars from these companies.

The countries which gave to the Clinton Foundation included Qatar, Brunei, Kuwait, Saudi Arabia, Oman, and United Arab Emirates, and Yemen. It's known that some of these countries, although presently trying to change their policies, allowed marital rape, required women to ask for decisions from men, required women not be in clothes or make-up to show-off their beauty, didn't allow women to drive, and engaged in killing gays for homosexual intercourse. But why would Hillary Clinton, a so-called feminist and advocate for women, have her foundation accept donations from countries such as these?

And, still, it doesn't end there. In 2010 Haiti needed relief funds for an earthquake. The recovery committee asked an Irish mobile company Digicel to create an effort to transfer relief money by phone to Haiti. In 6 months, $50 million in revenue was made by Digicel, a firm owned by Bill Clinton's billionaire buddy Dennis O'Brien. Of course, Mr. O'Brien contributed some of that to the Clinton Foundation. But did Haiti get the much-needed funds to rebuild their nation? It's likely Haiti didn't see all of what was owed them. Yet Hillary would get what *she* wanted in the Clinton Foundation, so she could become the next President of the United States. But that didn't quite pan out for her.

Four killed in Benghazi

On September 11, 2012, an extremist group called Ansar al-Sharai, who had ties to al-Qaeda, attacked a US diplomatic outpost in Benghazi, Libya. Americans Sean Smith, Ty Woods, Glen Daugherty, and U.S. Ambassador Chris Stevens were all ambushed and killed.

Secretary of State Hillary Clinton spoke out with,

"I condemn in the strongest terms the attack on our mission in Benghazi today...Some have sought to justify this vicious behavior as a response to inflammatory material posted on the Internet."

She blamed and linked an Internet video of protests in Libya to the death of four Americans. The Obama Administration and Clinton would continue the narrative with White House spokesman Jay Carney,

"We have no information to suggest that it was a preplanned attack. The unrest we've seen around the region has been in reaction to a video that Muslims, many Muslims find offensive..."

Susan Rice, then-U.S. Ambassador to the U.N., said on national television the Benghazi attack occurred because of an anti-Islam video called *"Innocence of Muslims"*. But the narrative was getting old and thin. The public wasn't buying what the Obama officials were selling. And so, investigations ensued into what really happened in Benghazi.

What was being uncovered was alarming. First, the White House foreign policy adviser Benjamin Rhodes had sent an email to officials with the subject line of "goals" with text indicating the emphasis of the Benghazi incident should be that,

"...these protests are rooted in an Internet video, and not a broader failure of policy."

Second, after Clinton initially blamed the Internet video, she then emailed her daughter, Chelsea, writing,

"Two of our officers were killed in Benghazi by an al Qaeda like group."

Third, in a private call with the President of Libya Mohammad al Magariaf, Hillary Clinton talked about terrorism <u>not</u> a video. A partial transcript of the call read,

"[O]ur diplomatic mission was attacked[.] ... [T]here is a gun battle ongoing, which I understand Ansar as-Sharia [sic] is claiming responsibility for."

In addition, Clinton told the Egyptian Prime minister,

"We know that the attack in Libya had nothing to do with the film. It was a planned attack — not a protest. ... Based on the information we saw today we believe the group that claimed responsibility for this was affiliated with al Qaeda."

The hearings into Benghazi also unveiled a stunning remark by Hillary Clinton. After being grilled by the U.S. House Oversight Committee in May 2013, Clinton was asked about misleading the public regarding the protests which allegedly caused the Benghazi raid. After referring to the four Americans that had died in Benghazi, Clinton gave an answer with the now infamous statement.

"...what difference at this point does it make?"

It seems she didn't care about how she and others had deceived the American people regarding the Benghazi story. That was because it had been the most expedient move the administration could make so that Obama could get re-elected; and, Clinton could clear herself to run for President in the future. Of course, the narrative was kept up by others in the Obama Administration and the mainstream media. But Pat Smith, the mother of the State Department officer Sean Smith who was killed, wouldn't let Clinton off the hook so easily. She exclaimed,

"I blame Hillary Clinton personally for the death of my son. Personally."

The saga of the Benghazi hearings would conclude with the conclusion and addendum that,

"...the State Department's security measures in Benghazi were woefully inadequate as a result of decisions made by officials in the Bureau of Diplomatic responsibility..."

"The American people expect that when the government sends our representatives into such dangerous places, they receive adequate protection. Secretary Clinton paid special attention to Libya. She sent Ambassador Stevens there. Yet, in August 2012, she missed the last, clear chance to protect her people."

But Benghazi wouldn't end there. In 2017, Torres Advanced Enterprise Solution employees, Brad Owens and Jerry Torres, spoke to *Fox News*. They said that someone who reported to Hillary Clinton told them not to speak to the media about the fact that they knew there had been a lack of security at the Benghazi compound before the attack. They stated the government was haggling with their firm and another company, Blue Mountain U.K., for cheaper rates to secure the area in Libya. Although the U.S. government selected Blue Mountain U.K. for the security post, the government would realize this company had never been involved in "high threat areas" around the world before being hired. And, so, they rehired Torres Advanced Enterprise Solution. But during the transition between the two security companies, sadly, the Benghazi terrorist attack occurred. Owens said the people,

"...who made the poor choices that actually, I would say, were more responsible for the Benghazi attacks than anyone else, they're still in the same positions, making security choices for our embassies overseas now."

The bottom line is that an act of terrorism was responsible for the Benghazi attack, not some protests on an Internet video. Moreover, there wasn't adequate security present at the compounds during the time of the attack. But being that the 2012 Presidential election of Barack Obama was at stake, a false narrative was created by the Obama Administration, Clinton, and others. Then, the story was continued by the compliant mainstream media. Naturally, after Obama had been re-elected, John Kerry replaced Hillary Clinton as Secretary of State.

Then, in 2014, during the nine investigations into the Benghazi scandal, the House Select Committee uncovered something which was very troubling. Evidence had arisen that Hillary Clinton had been using an unauthorized private email server to perform her business at the State Department. This would mark the moment in time when all the inquiries about the Clinton email server began.

Secret email server - UNDER INVESTIGATION

After reports to newspapers leaked information that Clinton had an "unsecure" private email server, Congress would issue subpoenas. Then, Clinton IT staffers and lawyers searched through emails on her server with no security clearance. A total of roughly 33,000 emails were erased with a program called BleachBit, which made all her deleted emails unrecoverable. In addition, members of her staff destroyed mobile devices (with hammers) and turned in other devices to the FBI without SIM cards. This was *after* these items were *subpoenaed* by Congress. Also, while the email server investigation was taking place,

Bryan Pagliano, a Clinton staffer, Cheryl Mills, her lawyer, and others were given immunity by the FBI. Therefore, they were absolved of obstruction of justice charges, and admitted to destroying devices. But why would the FBI not press them before giving them immunity from criminal charges - especially after Congress subpoenaed many to bring forth the email server and other devices with the original data on them?

Others under fire, such as the IT staff and lawyers that deleted the emails, pleaded the 5th amendment to Congress. They did not desire to disclose information which would incriminate them. It would have exposed what type of emails and data were on the server, why it was created, who gave instructions to destroy emails, and more. Clinton said the emails deleted were about "wedding invitations", "yoga", and other things. But did she expect the public to believe there was nothing in those 33,000 emails other than personal information? If so, then why was a sophisticated computer program used to erase them?

The most plausible reason these emails were eradicated from her server was that it may have shown *classified* exchanges of emails between her and other Obama Administrative officials. It may have also revealed meetings with foreign entities who would inevitably contribute donations to the Clinton Foundation while she was Secretary of State – which was unlawful. Of course, this is just speculation because those emails have not been recovered - yet. Some foreign entity, however, may have breached her server and emails, as was admitted when former FBI Director James Comey gave Congressional testimony.

But while Hillary Clinton was still under investigation the infamous *tarmac meeting* occurred. Attorney General Loretta Lynch met with Bill Clinton on a private plane a week before Hillary was called into the office of FBI. Bill Clinton and Loretta Lynch said they talked about golf and grandchildren. Then, over the July 4th weekend of 2016, during her Presidential campaign, Hillary was allegedly interviewed for about 3 hours by the FBI. Within two days, FBI Director James Comey took an unprecedented step and made a public announcement about the email investigation. He opened by saying that nobody else knew of the decision he was about to make to the people of this country. He outlined a clear case of criminal negligence and other crimes. Then, he stunned many. Comey stated that although Clinton was "extremely careless" and it may have been "probable" foreign entities had accessed her email server, he recommended no indictment or charges be brought against Hillary Clinton. Obviously, some were ecstatic over her exoneration. Yet, others who knew the laws of this country were outraged, including some current and former FBI agents. Of course, Attorney General Lynch upheld his decision, and no trial was pursued. Clinton had gotten a free-pass; and ran for the highest office in our land.

What has been recently found, however, regarding Clinton's email server investigation and her exoneration letter is noteworthy. There are many potential criminal implications for the many who were involved in this obvious cover-up. In the first place, Clinton said there were no classified or work-related emails on the server. Former Director James Comey testified that this was false. He also stated the classified emails found were *marked* and *unmarked*. When Clinton was questioned about the emails with a "C" on them, meaning Confidential, she supposedly pleaded ignorance, and also blamed about 300 others who had sent her those emails. In addition, despite FBI Director Comey announcing to America that nobody knew about his final decision in the Clinton email case, AG Loretta Lynch *did know* Clinton was to be exonerated. As was previously mentioned, we know this because on July 1st, 2016, Lisa Page, who worked with FBI Deputy Director Andrew McCabe, had tweeted to her lover FBI agent Peter Stzrok,

"It's a real profile in courage (sic), since she knows no charges will be brought."

Moreover, before, during, and after the famous tarmac incident and email scandal Loretta Lynch was found to have used an alias, "Elizabeth Carlisle". But she was not the only one using an alias while working under the Obama Administration.

It was revealed that even President Obama used a pseudonym when exchanging emails, including with Hillary Clinton. As reported, when Huma Adebin, Clinton's close aide, was interviewed by the FBI she was shown emails between Clinton and someone she didn't recognize. She was allegedly shocked to discover that the other person was Obama.

Therefore, Obama must have known about Clinton's unsecure email server - another reason for the deletion of those emails.

Also, it has come to light that Clinton received *special treatment* from the FBI. In the FBI document, the wording was changed about Clinton to read "extremely careless" instead of "<u>negligent</u>" which is a prosecutable offense. Moreover, within the letter, the word "probable" was changed from the initial "<u>highly likely</u>" with respect to foreign entities accessing Clinton's unsecure server with classified information on it. Her exoneration letter was written several months before the announcement. This exoneration letter was written and collaborated by FBI Director James Comey, FBI agent Peter Strzok, and others *before* Clinton and 16 other key witnesses were to be interviewed by the FBI. Why? Some wanted and anticipated Hillary to be the next President.

Seemingly, a very extensive cover-up during the Clinton email investigation may have taken place with the aid of the Obama Administration's Department of Justice (DOJ) and Federal Bureau of Investigation (FBI). Many are implicated, including former Deputy Director Andrew McCabe, former Director James Comey, Attorney General Loretta Lynch, and FBI agents Lisa Page and Peter Stzrok. Furthermore, in 2018, there is new undeniable evidence alleging Strzok knew Clinton's email server was hacked and said nothing.

Given my personal knowledge and affiliation with transcribing, viewing, and delivering classified information while I was in the armed forces, felonies were committed. Classified material was haphazardly available to foreign actors who could access her unsecure email server. There were 33,000 emails erased on her server by IT staffers and lawyers. Other devices, like blackberries, which had classified emails on them, were destroyed with hammers although under subpoena by the U.S. Congress. At minimum, some should have been charged with the Espionage Act and Obstruction of Justice. But even more charges apply.

In contrast, General Petraeus was fined $100,000, with two- years' probation, for transmitting classified information to his mistress in 2015. Then, in 2016, U.S. navy sailor Kristian Saucier was sent to prison for one year, dishonorably charged, and was to do 100 hours of community service. He had taken photos inside a nuclear submarine and admitted to his mistake of disclosing classified information. And, there are many others who been convicted for exposing classified material. But Clinton is exonerated for having *marked* and *unmarked* classified emails on her unsecure server, so she could run for President? It's a travesty of justice. Another double-standard for the political elites.

So, did Hillary Clinton commit a crime? For any rational individual, the answer is obvious. It also appears very likely the DOJ, FBI, and other intelligence agencies had become politicized under the Obama administration. Therefore, Clinton was treated differently during her email investigation. Also, in 2018, a small number of her emails were recovered; and, yes, *some were classified.* Moreover, there is new evidence to suggest she was probably involved in many other unseemly acts as well. So, Hillary is not free from any indictments or charges yet.

2016 Presidential campaign

Before she challenged the billionaire and real estate mogul from Queens, New York in the 2016 Presidential election, Hillary Clinton ran against another in the Democratic Primaries - Senator Bernie Sanders. During the very competitive campaign Senator Sanders kept stating the process of the Democratic primary was "rigged" because Clinton was getting the majority of the super delegates. These delegates added to the overall count at the end of the primary. Everyone ignored him. But Sanders would be proven right because when the Democratic National Committee emails were hacked into there were several important points that were discovered from *Wikileaks*.

The emails confirmed the outright bias against Sanders and for Clinton. For instance: 1) The DNC began to target Sander's religion, or whether he believed in God or his Jewish faith; 2) The DNC chairwoman Debbie Wasserman-Schultz criticized Sanders about his lack of understanding about the Democratic Party, because he was an independent before running for President; 3) The Sanders' campaign would be maligned for their accusations about the DNC by a Clinton lawyer; 4) People wished Sanders would just end his bid for the presidency; 5) Sanders wanted to debate more with Clinton, and proposed California. They had no intention of giving him one. 6) A certain radio show host wanted to Clinton about her fund-raising controversy. But some in the DNC didn't want her to go on radio because the host was an alleged "Bernie Bro." And, besides disparaging Sanders, other emails showed clear partiality toward Hillary Clinton.

The emails that favored Clinton also revealed unethical funding of her campaign by the Democratic National Committee (DNC) and its contributors. Given these revelations of clear financial partisanship, DNC Chairwoman Debbie Wasserman-Schultz would have to resign. So, Donna Brazile became the new DNC chairwoman. Then, months later, after the Presidential election, Brazile admitted in a tell-all book that the emails which showed biased donations were accurate. Yet, even Donna Brazile, who had been a *CNN* pundit and contributor, was not clean. *Wikileaks* also revealed Brazile had helped Clinton by giving her the *CNN* network debate questions in advance to go against Sanders.

Brazile would also concede the primary was rigged in Clinton's favor for one main reason. There was a Joint Fund-Raising Agreement with Hillary for America, Hillary Victory Fund, and the Democratic National Committee. Therefore, the DNC allowed the Clinton campaign control over the Democratic Party's "finances, strategy, and all money raised." In addition, the Clinton campaign was in charge of "staffing, budgeting, data, analytics, and mailings" for the DNC. Not even a news release could be made without going through the Brooklyn Office - Clinton campaign headquarters. The large amounts of cash (billions) being raised by the Clinton campaign was a boon for a Democratic Party which was in deep debt. They didn't need Sanders small contributions.

After the nomination of Hillary Clinton for the Democratic Party's nomination for the U.S. President, she was both lauded and chided at the Democratic National Convention in July 2016. Sanders sat there hunched over with a brooding face. He looked like someone who had been unfairly screwed but was forced to watch the phoniness that would follow. Of course, Sanders would hesitantly support Clinton on her Presidential run. But, although there seemed to be no question in the mind of Clinton Democrats and the biased mainstream media that Hillary would be the next President, one man and his supporters stood defiantly and unapologetically in their way.

Undoubtedly, everyone knows the outcome of the 2016 U.S. Presidential election. Some hate the result, while others love it. But the reasons why he beat Clinton were many and were apparent. Her unlikeability, untrustworthiness, and past scandals were part of the equation. The "basket of deplorable" comment played a role. And, Bill Clinton chipped in by insinuating that her opponent's supporters were also "rednecks". Then, there were all those *Wikileaks* email dumps, exposing much about Hillary and her campaign. They are very telling. Here are some samples of the email contents:

- In a paid speech, Clinton admitted having a public and private position.
- Clinton was paid for a speech to bankers, telling them how the U.S. captured Osama bin Laden. But when someone else wrote a book about his involvement shooting Osama Bin Laden, he was fined millions of dollars for writing about this. Why the double-standard?
- In 2013, during a speech to bankers, Clinton said refugees can't be properly vetted. But publicly she wanted to increase refugee influx to 550% more than Obama – allowing more than 500,000 refugees. Yet, the FBI Director stated that ISIS would hide amongst refugees.
- In a speech to Goldman Sachs, Clinton said she was skeptical of the idea of a no-fly zone in Syria. But now she wanted it.
- In a speech, Clinton was unsure about keystone pipeline and praised fracking. Now she is against it because of environmental concerns. Bernie Sanders was against this from the beginning.
- Speaking on Wall Street Clinton praised and supported bankers. But then changed her mind, stating she wanted to go after them.
- In speech to bankers, Clinton wanted Open Borders and Free Trade and open global hemisphere.
- Clinton campaign used the Benghazi terror attack as a diversion from her private email server.
- In 2015, John Podesta to Cheryl Mills: "Think we should hold emails from Potus? (Obama) That's the heart of his exec privilege. We could get them to ask for that. They may not care, but it seems like they will."
- The Associated Press (AP) reported that 55% of non-government people who met with Clinton as Secretary of State ended up donating or pledging money to the Clinton Foundation (pay-to-play).

- ABC News reported after 2010 earthquake in Haiti (150,000 people died) that 10 billion dollars of relief aid was to go to Haiti. But special treatment was given to Bill Clinton's billionaire friend.
- Clinton's campaign team had awful remarks against evangelicals and Catholics, such as, "They must be attracted to the systemic thought and severely backward gender relations." And, "I imagine they think it the is the most socially acceptable, politically conservative religion – their rich friends wouldn't understand if they became evangelicals."
- The Clinton campaign made racist comments about Hispanics. In an email, they used the subject line: "Needy Latinos and 1 Easy Call."
- There was a false job ad on Craigslist by the Clinton campaign that stated her opponent had job openings indicating you "can't gain weight" and "must be open to public humiliation".
- CNBC's John Harwood offered advice to Clinton campaign, praised Hillary, and bragged about confronting her opponent during the Republican primary debate.
- *The New York Times* reporter allowed Clinton to check what they were going to write about her and edit quotes before they published story.
- Boston Globe pumped up Clinton campaign while battling Bernie Sanders during the primary.
- Univision pressured Clinton campaign into attacking her opponent about immigration.
- After a trip to Michigan, the Clinton campaign bragged that the media favored her instead of Sanders.
- Donna Brazile (from CNN and former DNC chair) leaked the exact questions to Clinton (death penalty) that she would be getting during a Town Hall during the primary against Bernie.
- Clinton hated using the term "everyday people" in speeches about American people. She was "far removed from the struggles middle class" because of her "fortunes" Bill and her now enjoy.
- The richest man in Mexico, who is major stock holder of New York Times, donated millions of dollars to Clinton Foundation.
- Huma Abedin said Clinton was "still not perfect in the head".
- Podesta and his aide criticized Clinton's instincts.
- A Clinton aide wrote "there is just no good answer" on server scandal. Obama knew about Hillary's private email server (just two interviews Mar. 8th, 2015 and October 11, 2015).
- Podesta said Obamacare premium increases were "politically deadly".

- Basically, they knew Obamacare would die so that Hillary could implement single payer Health care system.
- Cheryl Mills wrote "we need to clean up" about Obama comments on Clinton's server. The emails received don't say state.gov. They are from Clinton email.com.
- Podesta called Clintons email scandal a "hot mess".
- Journalists (65) who covered Clinton were invited to her campaign managers house (Podesta).
- Staff raised questions about Clinton's health.
- Campaign feared a potential 2016 Joe Biden Presidential run.
- Co-chair of transition team said "They wanted to get away with it" on server scandal.
- Miss Universe attack on Trump was planned for months.
- John Podesta was having dinner with justice department officials while FBI investigating Hillary.
- Money ($650,000) flowed from Clinton's best friend (Terry McAuliffe) to the wife of Deputy FBI Director Andrew McCabe. She was running for office while he was investigating the Hillary email server scandal.
- Clinton solicited $12 million donation from King of Morocco.
- Clinton ally raised questions about Bill Clinton's conflicts of interest.
- Clinton had different positions on Single-Payer Healthcare system.
- Podesta's daughter thought Clinton's "with a cloth" comment was scary. This was after Clinton affiliates deleted emails from her server.
- Doug Ban memo (13 page): Showed Bill Clinton getting rich while Hillary was Secretary of State. "Since 2001, President Bill Clinton's business arrangements have yielded more than $30 million for him personally, with $66 million to be paid out over the next nine years should he chose to continue with the current engagements." Chelsea Clinton was worried of a pay-for-play scheme between the Clinton Foundation and others getting favors in the State Department.
- Chelsea accused Taneo (Doug Ban) of making money off Bill Clinton's speeches for Clinton Foundation. Ban called Chelsea a "spoiled brat".

And, still there were other events which may have contributed to Clinton's defeat. Several Project Veritas videos exposed that: 1) Bob Creamer and Brad Woodhouse admitted to conspiring with the Clinton campaign and DNC to start violence at her Presidential opponent's campaign rallies, 2) there was someone dressed as Donald Duck, hired by Clinton affiliates, who had a sign reading "Donald Duck Releases His Taxes" – so why doesn't her opponent, and, 3) voter fraud had been used during the primaries by busing people across state lines.

After her loss Hillary Clinton wrote a book, *"What Happened"* and went on a tour blaming everyone for her defeat including (are you ready?): sexism, racism, misogyny, xenophobia, former FBI Director James Comey, Vladimir Putin, Wikileaks, Democratic National Party, Joe Biden, Barack Obama, Bernie Sanders, Guccifer, Anthony Wiener, the electoral college, polling data, cable news, *New York Times*, *Fox News*, fake news, Bots, *Facebook*, *Twitter*, *Netflix*, anti-American forums, low information about voters, people wanting change, people assumed she would win, Republican Party, *Citizens United*, farms, suburban women, Macedonia, white people, voter ID laws, chief Justice John Roberts, Steve Bannon, her husband Bill, Ivanka Trump, Jason Chaffetz (ex-Republican politician), her campaign, and much more.

Yet the blame should fall solely on her shoulders because she 1) didn't campaign in Wisconsin, 2) setup an ill-advised secret (classified) unsecure email server, 3) lied about the Benghazi scandal, 4) had an alleged pay-for-play with the Clinton Foundation while being Secretary of State, 5) called her Presidential opponent's supporters *"deplorable"* and *"irredeemable"*, and 6) thought the presidency was owed to her. She had been blinded by power and couldn't overcome her past, awful personality, and untrustworthiness many Americans had discovered.

The Russian (or Steele) dossier - UNDER INVESTIGATION

Since this subject was discussed in more detail within a previous chapter, its origins, use, and so forth shall only be summarized here. But it's worth some reiteration.

During the Presidential debates Clinton's opponent was asked during a debate he if would accept the results of the 2016 election. He stated that he would think about it. Of course, Hillary Clinton, Obama, Democrats, most of the mainstream media, and some Republicans went into their usual feigned outrage. But, then, ironically, after her grandiose defeat for the presidency, Clinton didn't accept the election results. So, she and many others became bitter and spiteful.

There would be recounts of the Electoral College. There was considerable anger, frustration, and tantrums projected on television, radio, and social media by many Democratic supporters, celebrities, and the mainstream media. These people were shocked they had gotten it wrong about Clinton. There was one dirty trick, however, that awaited the newly elected President – the infamous Steele (or Russian) dossier. She and her supporters now sought retribution for her *"huge"* loss.

The history leading to the Russian dossier is short. A Republican backed publication hired a shady international propaganda firm called *Fusion GPS* to obtain political ammunition that could be used against the would-be-President of the United States in the 2016 Republican primaries. Then, after his nomination, the publication stopped working with *Fusion GPS*. But in April 2016 the Clinton campaign and DNC (Democratic National Party) used the same scandalous firm, *Fusion GPS,* to get dirt on their Presidential opponent. The Clinton campaign and DNC lawyer funneled about twelve million dollars to *Fusion GPS* for unverified information which had been obtained from Christopher Steele, an ex-British secret agent. It has been reported and confirmed that Steele hated the would-be President. Then, after OUR President was elected, the phony and unsubstantiated document came to light in a big way. It was and has been pushed as truth by Democrats, Hillary supporters, so-called establishment Republicans, and those who hate our 45th President of the United States. They professed, and still do, that the new President and his campaign colluded and conspired with the Russians to the win the presidency. It was and is all a fabricated lie.

But this Steele (or Russian) dossier would be the basis for a Special Counsel investigation against OUR President. The dossier was also used as a reason to obtain FISA warrants to spy on the political opponent of an opposition party. Not only were the FISA warrants unethically obtained, but there were four sources connected with Hillary Clinton that were involved with the dossier. They were:

- Ambassador Alexander Downer: He contributed $25 million to the Clinton Foundation.

- Christopher Steele: He knew the Clinton campaign and DNC paid for his phony dossier.
- Michael Isikoff (Yahoo News): He had the same information from Steele – circular reporting.
- Sydney Blumenthal and Cody Shearer: These aides worked as smear artists and private intelligence operatives for the Clinton's. Shearer was composing a second phony dossier.

All roads would lead back to Hillary Clinton when it comes to this phony Russian dossier. And, in time, as the investigation unfolds, this scandal may turn out to be more massive than "Watergate" (when President Nixon and his political operatives sought to illegally gain opposition research from the Democratic Party during his re-election campaign). It may be that this was the biggest example of scandalous behavior, cover-up, and abuse of power by a previous Presidential Administration against a new President in American political history. But we'll have to wait to find out who did what, when, how, and why.

Regardless, on February 28, 2018, even though U.S. Secretary of State Hillary Clinton failed with the Russian reset button years ago, the Uranium One scandal was being investigated, and the phony Russian dossier was bought by her campaign, she had the audacity to tweet out something ridiculous about the 45th U.S. President. It read:

"I say this as a former Secretary of State and as an American: the Russians are still coming. Our intelligence professionals are imploring Trump to act. Will he continue to ignore & surrender, or protect our country?"

Yet let's consider who the real enemies to democracy and the world are in 2018. Is Russia the biggest threat? The Democrats believe so because they have an agenda to impeach OUR American President. But China steals U.S. intellectual properties, their economy is far-reaching, and its military is building up on South China Sea islands. Russia is a minor threat compared to China. Also, there are rogue regimes like North Korea and Iran who are attempting to manufacture a nuclear arsenal that can be used to annihilate western civilization, especially the U.S. So, quite frankly, Russia is the least of our worries.

Staying on the Asian continent, and getting back to the blunders of Hillary Clinton, in March 2018, she added to her insults from the past. At the *India Today Conclave* in Mumbai, Hillary used more identity politics to try and divide America again.

"So, I won the places that are optimistic, diverse, dynamic, moving forward, and his whole campaign, Make America Great Again, was looking backwards...You don't like black people getting rights, you don't like women getting jobs, you don't want to see that Indian-American succeeding more than you are, whatever your problem is, I'm going to solve it...We do not do well with white men and we don't do well with married, white women...And part of that is an identification with the Republican Party, and a sort of ongoing pressure to vote the way that your husband, your boss, your son, whoever, believes you should."

Ironically, one can't forget Senator Clinton's ignorant joke in 2006 when speaking about Mahatma Gandhi. She said,

"...He ran a gas station down in St. Louis for a couple of years. Mr. Gandhi, do you still go to the gas station? A lot of wisdom comes out of that gas station."

This statement was just as bad as Senator Joe Biden's comments in 2006, in which he insulted Indian-Americans, saying,

"You cannot go to a 7-Eleven or a Dunkin' Donuts unless you have a slight Indian accent. I'm not joking!"

Anyway, what rings truer than true about Hillary is another quote from Shakespeare: *"The lady doth protest too much, methinks."* (*Hamlet*). And, some should recall a profound old proverb that reads, *"...those who live in glass houses should not throw stones"*. Or, maybe <u>those that stand under glass ceilings should not throw stones</u> is better. You decide. By the way, it was reported that after her speech in India, Clinton slipped in her hotel bathroom and broke her wrist. Karma?

Chapter 14

FALLING LEFT:
STARS AND ACTIVISM

Why does Hollywood align left?

Everyone knows Hollywood is situated in California. Since most of the voters in this state vote for the Democratic Party it's why the stars align left. Right? Well, that is only partly true. It's correct to assume liberal policies of the state and some of its cities are supported by Hollywood stars. But the 1960's anti-war protests, hippie motto of "sex, drugs, and rock-n-roll", civil rights movements, and the declarations of being a gay man or women undoubtedly may have moved many celebrities in this industry toward a more liberal ideology. These Hollywood stars have gravitated toward left-leaning political movements because its essential for their professions. Sensationalized news coverage of societal changes in large populations like California and New York is good for them. They use these hooks of change to their utmost advantage by producing, directing, and performing in television shows, movies, and musicals which blaze unique trails and conform to the cultural evolutions in America. But did Hollywood elites always bend toward liberalism?

The stars of Tinsel town, or Hollywood, were *not always* left-leaning liberals. In the 1920's and 1930's, during the silent movie era and as films began using voice, many of the studio executives, like Cecil B. DeMille, had more conservative views. Moreover, *The Screen Actor Guild, Moving Picture Machine Operators,* and *International Alliance of Theatrical Stage Employees* were being overseen by conservatives.

But Hollywood was hit with some scandals in its early years. For example, 1) Mary Pickford, a silent film superstar, divorced from her husband to marry another actor Douglas Fairbanks; 2) there were rumors that silent film actor, comedian, and Director Roscoe Conkling "Fatty" Arbuckle raped and murdered an actress at a party; 3) actor

Wallace Reid died of a morphine overdose; and, 4) it was discovered that William Desmond had many love affairs with well-known actresses at the time. But this was revealed after Desmond had been murdered. All these scandals prompted the *Motion Picture Producers and Distributors of America* to hire Will Hays, the post master general of Warren G. Harding – the 29th American President and Republican.

It was suggested by Hays that industry heads should consider cutting back on sexual content and criminal activity in films and lean toward projecting an even more wholesome and conservative view to America. This would help avoid heavy censorship laws to be enforced in Hollywood by 'Democrats' controlling Congress at the time. But even with less carnality and crime shown on the silver screen for a few years, the 1940's and 1950's brought sex and violence to the spotlight again.

During the 1940's, some intellectuals in Hollywood would become communist sympathizers. Actors like Ronald Reagan, Robert Taylor, and Gary Cooper would expose these subversive communists to the *House Un-American Activities Committee*. In addition, there were soviet sympathizers such as Edward G. Robinson who turned over other communists. But being a government informant still wouldn't help him. After information was gathered from Robinson, he would be blacklisted with other actors. They were known as the *Hollywood Ten*.

In the 1950's, after the Supreme Court ruled that movies were a form of free speech, Hollywood took advantage and began to revolt. This prompted many in the industry to stand up and fight for the types of movies they wanted to produce, direct, write, and perform in – which included more sex and violence. So, by the 1960's and 1970's a counter-culture emerged in films. A more liberal approach of presenting race, gender, marriage, equality, and politics, including socialist views, became the norm. Now, in the 21st century, the freedom to act, direct, produce, and discuss liberal social and political issues are unrestrained.

The mockery

In 2011, President Obama mocked a would-be-President because he had fanned the flames of a so-called *birther* movement. The billionaire from Queens had accepted the notion that Barack Obama was not a natural born citizen for two reasons. In 2008, Hillary Clinton's campaign had insinuated then-Senator Obama was not American born; and, so, he couldn't be President. And, during the same time, Malik Obama, the half-brother of Barack, showed Obama's Kenyan birth certificate with the legitimate masthead reading: "Coast Province General Hospital, Mombasa, British Protectorate of Kenya". So, at the 2011 White House correspondence dinner, Obama showed a sarcastic animated video with a long-form Hawaiian birth certificate to mock the successful businessman (although we can't be certain who has the *true* birth record). Regardless, at the event, Obama said in a ridiculing tone,

"No one is happier, no one is prouder to put this birth certificate matter to rest than the Donald...that's because he can finally get back to focusing on the issues that matter, like: Did we fake the moon landing? What really happened in Roswell? And where are Biggie and Tupac?"

Then, the host, comedian Seth Meyers, really laid into him with,

"Donald Trump has been saying that he will run for President as a Republican — which is surprising, since I just assumed that he was running as a joke."

Of course, many in the room foolishly laughed at *The Apprentice* star. But, then two years later, late night television host John Oliver from *Comedy Central* taunted the then-citizen, by saying,

"Do it. Do it...I will personally write you a campaign check now, on behalf of this country, which does not want you to be President, but which badly wants you to run."

So, with all these people mocking and egging him on, what do you think a proud man would do? Assuredly, the ridicule aimed at this man spurred the New York real estate tycoon to run for the presidency. But all these buffoons and many others didn't see it coming!

In 2016, the image of the billionaire and his wife going down the escalator of his building, the Trump Tower, and his statements to the press solidified the fact that this man was serious about running for President of the United States. But the mainstream and celebrities unwisely continued to taunt him. On *Real Time with Bill Maher*, a questioned was posed to Anne Coulter, Republican writer, lawyer, and radio show commentator. She was asked by Bill Maher,

"And, which Republican candidate has the best chance of winning the general election?"

Ann Coulter didn't hesitate and replied,

"Of the declared ones? Right now, Donald Trump."

Maher laughed. Joy Reid from *MSNBC* laughed. Congressman Luis Gutierrez laughed. And, many others in the mainstream media and celebrities thought it was funny. They hoped that he would run because, of course, Hillary Clinton would beat him. They were all wrong and made to look like utter fools. Now, many, including those who laughed and derided him, are not laughing so hardily anymore.

Some celebrities, however, are crazily unyielding and persist to defame, disparage, and criticize every word, action, or tweet by the 45th President of the U.S. They still can't accept that someone who was part of their world during his hit television series, *The Apprentice*, has ascended to the highest office in the land. They are angry, envious, and afraid their celebrity statuses will be diminished, and messages will not be heard or trusted as it once did. It's because this new President knows the inner workings of Hollywood and they fear exposure at all levels. But these stars also know that they can shine brightly under his light.

Hypocrisy and hate

In Hollywood and throughout the entertainment world some celebrities exude hypocrisy. Their rants insinuating the 45th American President is a racist for building a wall fall on deaf ears. It's because those shouting the loudest and longest about this legitimate national security issue live behind gated communities or walled houses. The stars also speak about gun control, and not forcing schools to have security in them. Yet they have body guards with them 24 /7. Also, there may be more security at their *Academy Awards, Emmy Awards,* and *Grammy Awards,* as well as other star-studded events, than at political summits where world leaders meet. They make violent and racy films that adults, teenagers, and young children watch, which may influence shootings, underage sex, racial divide, chaos, and hysteria to take place in our world. Moreover, there are big stars flying in jets and driving in vehicles which are gas guzzlers, or who live in mansions using huge amounts of electricity. And, they are worried about climate change? So, these stars are very hypocritical about the way they live, view, and speak about life. That is why some celebrities shouldn't expect the public to respect them and their work after they stand on their stages of egregious sanctimony.

Celebrities talk about equal rights and sexual abuse to women – *now.* Yet they stayed silent for years about producer Harvey Weinstein. Some even praised the Director/Producer Roman Polanski's work, *The Pianist,* with a standing ovation at the Oscars. But they knew very well this man raped a 13-year child years ago. Still, these are not the only two in Hollywood who have abused women. Assuredly, there have been others through the years that have mistreated women in that industry, while giving them positions, roles, and pay for sexual favors. The new *#Metoo* movement is an acknowledgement by Hollywood of how they treated women in the past. And, regarding equal pay, even actress Natalie Portman emphasized how women make less than men there.

"Compared to men, in most professions, women make 80 cents to the dollar," she added. "In Hollywood, we are making 30 cents to the dollar."

Then, we have reliable confirmation about what many have long thought about most of the Hollywood celebrities. In January 2018, Rob Reiner, American actor, director, producer, writer, and liberal activist, surprisingly admitted to *Fox News* host Laura Ingraham that,

"...actors are the biggest narcissists in the world. They want attention. They want to be loved..."

So, there it is; a confirmation from someone in the business that celebrities crave recognition. That's why they all try to outdo each other, as does the mainstream media when attacking the President and his policies. They love the spotlight – bad or good!

Sadly, these stars tend to live in a bubble and willingly ignore the blatant facts about the wrongdoings and scandals of Hillary Clinton, President Obama, and other highly touted Democrats. But of the many celebrities, there are some in the entertainment and sports industries which have been extremely vocal about the 45th American President, his administration, Republicans, and those who support him. For example, below are just a few who have openly opposed the President.

> Kathy Griffin, Rosie O'Donnell, Chelsea Handler, Robert De Niro, Madonna, Cher, Lena Dunham, Johnny Depp, Tom Hanks, Meryl Streep, Jim Carey, George Clooney, Olivia Wilde, The View (Whoopi Goldberg, Joy Behar), Alec Baldwin, John Oliver, Stephen Colbert, Jimmy Kimmel, Bill Maher, Seth Meyers, Ellen DeGeneres, Sara Silverman, Bette Midler, Ashley Judd, Miley Cyrus, John Legend, Barbara Streisand, members of Hamilton (the Broadway Play), Shakespeare In the Park (Julius Caesar), George Clooney, LeBron James, Stephen Curry, Lindsey Vonn, Colin Kaepernick, Jemele Hill (ESPN), Tom Brokaw, Morning Joe (MSNBC), and many others.

Late-night host Jimmy Kimmel may be one of the fiercest critics of the 45th American President. But, in 2018, actress and comedienne Roseanne Barr came on his show and put Kimmel in his place.

Kimmel: "I'm shocked, because I know you were a very socially liberal person in general."

Barr: "I'm still the same — you all moved. You all went so f---ing far out you lost everybody...A lot of us, no matter who we voted for, we don't want to see our President fail."

Kimmel reminded Barr that she had called Hillary Clinton a "murderer" on twitter some time ago. But Barr replied with the usual sarcastic response she is known for on her past hit television show,

"I deleted it, f— you!" (as she flipped him the bird).

Regardless, what is quite disturbing is a long list of more than 100 celebrities vowed to work against this 45th U.S. President. They formally joined a *MoveOn.org Political Action's #UnitedAgainstHate* campaign during the Presidential election of 2016. A few of these individuals even tried to give their *lame* Peoples State of the Union speech the night before the *real* Presidential State of the Union in January 2018. The President's speech had a 75% approval by the 50 million people who watched. But their speeches were filled with hate, bias, mockery, and bigotry toward the President, his policies, and those who support him. Do these celebrities really believe that everyone in America adheres to the hostility of their progressively left-wing ideology? Not all Americans identify with what the west coast and north eastern seaboard states of America preach. Sadly, they "can't see the forest through the trees". Many of them have lost their way on the road to making a better, safer, and fairer America for all our citizens. Again, some of these so-called celebrities *were* initially part of the *#UnitedAgainstHate* movement, made public on the Internet. But only a few of them will be identified for brevity's sake.

> Shonda Rhimes, Ryan Murphy, Michael Moore, Samuel L. Jackson, Mark Ruffalo, Lena Dunham, Rashida Jones, Abbi Jacobson, Ilana Glazer, Adam McKay, Russell Simmons, Julianne Moore, Olivia Wilde, Taylor Schilling, Bryan Cranston, Kerry Washington, Chloë Grace Moretz, Mark Ruffalo, Neil Patrick Harris, Macklemore, Moby, Michael Stipe, Third Eye Blind, Kathleen Turner, Julia Stiles, Patricia Arquette, Meg Ryan, Michael Mann, Paul Haggis, Woody Harrelson, Jane Fonda, Tig Notaro, Rashida Jones, Maggie Gyllenhaal, Alyssa Milano, Rebecca Woolf, Cynthia Nixon, Laura Dawn, Neve Campbell, Jesse Tyler Ferguson, and others.

In this open letter, it had stated they wanted to bring to light the "dangers" of OUR President. They declared the 45th U.S. President's "rhetoric and policy proposals exclude, degrade, and harm" Mexicans, Latinos, blacks, Muslims, LGBTQ people, women, Asians, refugees, people with disabilities, working class people, and prisoners of war. But they are way off-base with their feigned assessments. In just over a year, millions of American citizens are already better off economically with tax breaks, bonuses, and pay raises. The U.S. unemployment rate is the lowest it has been in decades for African-Americans, Hispanics, and women under this President. Many in the U.S. armed forces love him;

and, there is much more he has achieved. Yet that doesn't stop the haters from endlessly expressing their dishonest, pathetic, and petulant criticisms about the President. The reasoning for their acted outrage is simple. Some of these entertainment stars seek to regain relevancy and attention because the lights are dimming on their careers.

It depends upon how much the mainstream media can drive fear, division, and hatred during the day that inevitably will spark some of these celebrities to become more vocal. The caricatures they draw of this President are not accurate. In many instances, they need to take the brush out of their hands and stop trying to imitate real artists who don't paint pictures with such broad and ugly strokes. When they do this in vulgar manners it cheapens their profession. And, yet, some celebrities do not seem to care about the backlash of negative press on social media. They shamefully seek the attention and act in irrational manners. And, sometimes, they go further and threaten the President.

Star bursts - top threats by celebrities

What is most disconcerting about the lengths these celebrities will go to scorn OUR President is their lack of realization that they have been promoting extreme hate to the public. By vocalizing or depicting threats against a U.S. President, tells others in society they too may follow suit. It's not right, morally or ethically, to make these threats - no matter who sits in the Oval Office. In some cases, these celebrities state they are using artistic expression and comedic license. Hog-wash! It's a veiled way to blatantly express their real emotions or phony outrage toward the President. But, whether intentional or unintentional, a threat to the President of the United States should be treated as such. The U.S. Secret Service and other law enforcement agencies should make inquisitions into any dangers the President faces, no matter how minor they may seem. There should be no exceptions to this rule. It doesn't matter if one is a star actor, athlete, singer, dancer, host, or news anchor. These persons should be treated like everyone else in society. To insinuate personal harm, injury, or death to a President must be taken seriously.

Unfortunately, many celebrities have gone way too far, and some continue to indulge and express their untethered animosity toward the

45th President of the United States. These individuals may or may not have been visited by the U.S. Secret Service or other law enforcement agencies. But if they weren't visited, maybe they should have been. Anyway, some obvious threats along with some very troubling remarks celebrities have spewed against the 45th American President will follow.

1) Kathy Griffin displayed a graphic video of a bloody beheaded the President, like those depicted by ISIS. She admitted it went too far. But she was visited by the secret service, got fired from *CNN*'s New Year's Eve show, and had her upcoming performances cancelled by venues.

2) Madonna was reportedly going to be investigated by the U.S. Secret Service because at the Women's March rally she shouted out,

"Yes, I'm angry. Yes, I'm outraged. Yes, I have thought an awful lot about blowing up the White House, but I know that this won't change anything…"

3) Snoop Dogg created a music video that showed the President as a circus clown. In a scene, Dogg shot a prop gun with a "Bang!" flag popping out of its barrel. Regarding the video, the rapper said,

*"I feel like it's a lot of people making cool records, having fun, partying, but nobody's dealing with the real issue with this f*cking clown as President, and the sh*t that we dealing with out here."*

4) Johnny Depp made a very flippant, unwise, and incendiary remark (although he apologized the next day) at a European music festival.

"It is just a question—I'm not insinuating anything. By the way, this is going to be in the press. It will be horrible. I like that you're all part of it. But when was the last time an actor assassinated a President? I want to clarify, I'm not an actor. I lie for a living. However, it's been a while and maybe it is time."

5) Robert De Niro ranted during the 2016 Presidential race that,

*"He's a punk, he's a dog, he's a pig, he's a con, he's a bullsh*t artist, a mutt who doesn't know what he's talking about, doesn't do his homework, doesn't care, thinks he's gaming society, doesn't pay his taxes......He's an embarrassment to this country....He talks [about] how he wants to punch people in the face... I'd like to punch him in the face."*

*6) A *Shakespeare in the Park* production of "Julius Caesar" in Central Park, N.Y. depicted the President as Caesar (in a business suit, tie, and blonde wig). He was stabbed violently to death by Senate members.

*7) *Mickey Rourke* told TMZ in April 2016 before the nomination,

*"Donald Trump can go f*ck himself," His wife said that he said, 'Oh, he's a tough guy.' He's not a tough guy, he's a bully and a bitch and he can suck my f*cking dick. I'll meet him in a hotel room any motherf*cking day of the week and give him a Louisville slugger. Kiss my motherf*cking ass you bitch punk c*cksucker."*

*8) *Michael Black,* a lesser known Democratic comedian, made a gross comment as Russian President Vladimir Putin and the President met. He said that since they were in a long two-hour meeting, the President

*"...must be terrible at bl*wjobs if it's taking this long."*

*9) *Steven Colbert* made a sickening joke after the President met with Russian President Vladimir Putin. The late-night host remarked,

*"The only thing your mouth is good for is being Vladimir Putin's c*ck holster."*

*10) *Larry Wilmore* (comedian) un-tastefully joked,

"Anyway, since we're talking about bigotry, we have to mention Donald Trump. Sorry everyone, I don't want to give him any more oxygen. That's not a euphemism by the way; I mean it literally. Somebody get me the pillow they used to kill Scalia, and I'll do it. I'll do it!"

*11) *Rapper YG and Nipsy Hussle* threatened the President-to-be in a song called "F*ck Donald Trump". Below are some of the lyrics.

*"I like white folks, but I don't like you/All the n*ggas in the hood wanna fight you/Surprised El Chapo ain't tried to snipe you/Surprised the Nation of Islam ain't tried to find you/Have a rally out in L.A., we gon' f*ck it up."*

**12) Marilyn Manson,* a shock rocker, released a music video depicting him killing the President. First, he rips out the pages of a Bible. Then, a knife's in his hand, as the President lies decapitated in a pool of blood.

Its unfortunate celebrities have succumbed to these tactics to be heard. Since some are fading out of the public limelight, they seek more exposure through outrageous comments or acts. They want the people to watch their films, listen to their songs, or attend their concerts or sporting events. But they are not helping their cause. For example, in 2017, the American box office attendance for movies declined by about 3%. Also, the *Academy Award* ratings dropped because viewers are sick and tired of the political rhetoric on a show which is supposed to be fun for the audience. But the only audience being pleased is their peer audience. Then, in 2018, this award show garnered only 26.5 million viewers, down from 32.9 in 2017. This trend will continue until American celebrities stop trying to be politicians and start acting again.

Stars that have the "right" idea

There are some stars who don't conform to celebrity "group think". They speak their own mind and stand up for what is right in America. Some voted for the 45th U.S. President or are registered Republicans.

Clint Eastwood, John Voight, Kid Rock, Willie Robertson, Chuck Norris, Scott Baio, Mike Tyson, Ted Nugent, Gene Simmons, Hulk Hogan, Lou Ferrigno, Jean-Claude Van Damme, Bruce Willis, Mariano Rivera, Johnny Damon, Paul O'Neill, Jim Brown, Caitlyn Jenner, Misty-May Treanor, Britt McHenry, Teresa Giudice, Charlie Sheen, Gary Busey, Dean Cain, Gary Sinise, Kelsey Grammer, Roseanne Barr, Patricia Heaton, Tim Allen, Antonio Sabato Jr., Stephen Baldwin, Derrick Rodman, Stacy Dash, Tila Tequila, Wayne Newton, Kayne West, Loretta Lynn, Kenny Rogers, Kayne West, Bill Belichick, Tom Brady, Bobby Knight, Mike Ditka, Natalie Gulbis, Aissa Wayne, Dana White, Paris Dennard, Diamond & Silk, etc.

Left-wing activism

Hollywood, stars of other industries, and the mainstream media don't acknowledge activist groups seeking to destroy the American society. There exists anarchist, communist, and socialist organizations which have websites, bookstores, and radical movements. These groups have shifted *progressively far-left*. Some have established a strong foothold in the U.S. to disperse false propaganda at every opportunity. In doing so, they divide the nation, while yearning to entice more liberal and independent thinkers to adopt their extreme ideologies. And, they engage in ethnic, racial, religious, sexual, and political intimidation, as well as arson and violence. Still others are anti-police, such as *Black Lives Matter*. All these types of organizations are tearing the fabric of American society apart - sometimes while messaging righteous hatred.

It's quite shocking to see this happen in a nation founded upon just democratic principles. "Life, liberty, and the pursuit of happiness" should be adhered to through peace, strength, and security. Americans can't permit the laws and Constitution protecting our freedoms to be trampled upon by activists which practice lawlessness. Civility, truth, and respect need to become instilled in the nation's citizens once again.

Of course, the mainstream media is complicit in supporting many liberal groups, no matter how radical. They only condemn groups such as the Klu Klux Klan, Neo-Nazis, and white supremacists, while declaring that these hate groups are backed by conservatives and Republicans in the U.S. This is utterly untrue rhetoric used to incite Democratic Party agendas. These hateful groups mentioned, such as the KKK, are, now, neither right nor left. They are un-American groups which should be denounced, as the President has done numerous times.

But, still, some extreme liberal banter and leftist groups have been propped up by politicians like Hillary Clinton. She supports some of their tactics because they coincide with her personal ideologies. As evidence of this, we know Clinton labeled those who supported her Presidential opponent, deplorable, irredeemable, sexist, homophobic, Islamophobic, xenophobic, and racist. It's the modus-operandi of her and many liberal activists. Sadly, through 2018, she continues to insult individuals and groups of people in America by using identity politics to the utmost. It's just one of many reasons she is not President.

Clinton, the mainstream media, celebrities, and activist groups remain filled with shame, hate, envy, sorrow, and disappointment for having been personally and financially involved with one of the greatest election defeats in history. Many of the liberal activists who supported Clinton were funded by the European billionaire George Soros. Still other activists continue being backed by Clinton, Obama, Democrats, celebrities, and liberal political operatives like David Brock. The sheer number of activists is shocking. But some notable ones can be shown.

ANTIFA is a very radical left-wing organization which proclaims to be against fascism. But they advocate violence, while practicing anarchist and fascist tactics. They are an extremist hate group with branches named Antifa Seven Hills, Antifa Unite, Four Corners Antifa, Rocky Mountain Antifa, Rose City Antifa, Torch Antifa, and WND Antifa.

Black Lives Matter (BLM) is a movement group which attempts to promote itself as being a racial civil rights group for African-Americans. But this organization is primarily founded upon the principal of seeking retribution for blacks, mostly men, who had been accidentally, wrongly, or lawfully killed or injured by the police in America. In protests against police, they have cried out: "What do we want?' The crowd responded, "Dead cops". The leaders continued, "When do we want it?" The crowd replied, "Now". They also said, "Pigs in a blanket! Fry em' like bacon". Is that how those who risk their lives and protect us should be treated?

Center for America Progress is a large group funded by George Soros. It has many affiliated advocacy organizations, such as *Think Progress* which transforms "progressive ideas into policy through rapid response communications, legislative action, grassroots organizing and advocacy, and partnerships with other progressive leaders throughout the country and the world." The Center for American Progress was led by John Podesta, the chief of staff of Hillary Clinton's Presidential campaign. He worked very closely with Clinton and her sympathizers.

Campus Progress is a project of Center for American Progress. It's backed by the European billionaire George Soros. Its overall unseemly objective is to "strengthen progressive voices on college and university campuses, counter the growing influence of right-wing groups on campus, and empower new generations of progressive leaders."

MoveOn.org is a massive liberal George Soros funded group, with many affiliates. Their partner activist groups include the *New Organizing Institute* ("trains young technology-enabled political organizers to work of progressive campaigns and organizations"), *Vote for Change* (consists of musicians and bands performing in concerts for key states during elections) and *Rebuild and Renew America Now.*

Media Matters for America is an organization promoting and aiding the mainstream media (i.e. television, radio, and publications) as being truthful and trusted outlets. They attack and attempt to discredit the conservative news and their media personalities (i.e. *Fox News*, Rush Limbaugh, Sean Hannity, Mark Levin, and Laura Ingraham) as being opinionated and fabricated. The group has apparently tried and been somewhat successful at lobbying for conservative speech to be shutdown. It seems they are ultra-protective of the mainstream media and play down major liberal scandals which are real news (i.e. Clinton scandals, Obama failures/scandals, real Russia collusion, and more).

Planned Parenthood is the largest abortion provider in the U.S. It has been caught selling illegal body parts to corporations for research and providing abortions beyond the law's provisions. But it annually lobbies for and receives taxpayer funded dollars to support these atrocities.

ACLU (American Civil Liberties Union) is not an activist group per se. But this organization should be mentioned. The group gives off the appearance of being fair in political ideologies, but it seems they lean a bit more left. On their website they declared, "Protecting free speech means protecting a free press, the democratic process, diversity of thought, and so much more. The ACLU has worked since 1920 to ensure that freedom of speech is protected for everyone." But, in 2017, the organization announced it would no longer defend the constitutional rights of any group which publicly demonstrates with loaded firearms. Also, the *John Adams Project* was hired by the ACLU to investigate "terrorists" who had been exposed to advanced interrogation methods for information. This was allegedly given to the lawyers of terrorist and al-Qaeda suspects. The ACLU also advocates for open borders.

Southern Poverty Law Center is an organization like the *ACLU*, which insists it's non-partial, but leans a bit left. They provide lists of so-called "hate groups". But it seems to exaggerate white racism, and ignores racism, bigotry, and hates from key left-wing groups. They don't recognize *Antifa, Black Lives Matter, New Black Panther Party, La Raza, MS-13,* and other anarchist groups, as hate groups. The hate groups it does list, however, are under the titles such as: Anti-Muslim, Anti-Immigrant, Anti-LGBT, Black separatist, Hate Music, Holocaust Denial, Ku Klux Klan, Neo-Confederate, Neo-Nazi, Racial Skinhead, Radical Traditional Catholicism, and White Nationalist. But what about hate groups which are Anti-Christian, Anti-White, or Anti-Latino?

Then, there are the many thousands of radical or passive liberal groups declaring that they support righteous causes. These organizations can be broken down into categories of liberal agendas they tend to promote. Again, there are thousands, but only some of them shall be presented.

Anti-Capitalism or Anarchist Groups

The Anti-Capitalist Initiative, Antifa, Burning River Anarchist Distro, Center for Progressive Leadership, Center for Constitutional Rights, Chicago Anarchist Black Cross, CrimetheInc., Democratic Socialists of America (DSA), Denver Anarchist Black Cross, Flatirons Anarchist Alliance, Hispagatos, Hackernol, Hudson Valley Anarchist Network, Institute for Policy Studies,), LeftSec/Anon Anarchist Action, New York Anarchist Action, NYC Anarchist Book Fair, NYC ANARKOARTLAB, NYC Anarchist Black Cross, Public Citizen, Wildfire Anarchist Prison Newsletter, and more...

Anti-Semitic

Al-Haq, Arab American Institute, Gish: Center for the Legal Protection of Freedom Movement, Hamas, I'lam, J Street, Jewish Funds for Justice, Nation of Islam, New Israel Fund, Palestinian Center for Human Rights, Palestinian Liberation Org., etc.

Democratic Party Get-Out-The Vote Groups

America Coming Together, America Votes, Association of Community Organizations for Reform Now, Ballot Initiative Strategy Center, League of Young Voters, Sentencing Project, Voter Participation Center, Voto Latino, We Are America Alliance, and more...

Left-Wing Education, Student, or Teacher Groups

American Federation of Teachers, Free Exchange on Campus, Pittsburgh Autonomous Student Network, Pitt Students for a Democratic Society, Coalition, Students Without Borders, Students Against State Violence, US Action Education Fund, and more...

Liberal Media Groups

ABC, CBS, CNN, CSPAN, NBC, MSNBC, Mother Jones magazine, Newsweek, PM Press, Politico, Rolling Stone magazine, TIME magazine, New York Times, Washington Post, American Independent Institute, Code Pink, Fairness and Accuracy in Reporting, Dropfox, Free Press, Independent Media Institute, Indivisible Project, Media Fund, Media Matters for America, New America, NewsCorp Watch, Pacifica Foundation, Progressive Media USA, Shareblue, The American Prospect, True Blue Media, etc.

Open Borders or Pro-Illegal Immigrant

America's Voice, American Immigration Law Foundation, American Immigration Council, Casa de Maryland, Fair Immigration Reform Movement, Four Freedoms Fund, Immigrant Defense Project, Immigrant Legal Resource Center, Immigrant Workers Citizenship Project, Immigration Policy Center, LatinoJustice PRLDF, League of United Latin American Citizens, Massachusetts Immigrant and Refugee Advocacy, National Council of La Raza, National Immigration Law Center, and more...

Pro-Socialized Medicine or Pro-Choice Groups

Campaign for Better Health Care, Center for Reproductive Rights, Families USA, Healthcare for America Now, Institute for America's Future, NARAL Pro-Choice America, National Abortion Federation, National Organization for Women, National Partnership for Women and Families, National Women's Law Center, Planned Parenthood, Universal Healthcare Action Network, Urban Institute, and more.

Miscellaneous Liberal Activism Groups

Advancement Project, Alliance for Justice, American Bridge 21st Century, American Constitution Society for Law & Policy, American Friends Service Committee, Amnesty International, Bill of Rights Defense Committee, Black Alliance for Just Immigrants, Black Rose Book Distro St. Louis, Black Lives Matter, Bloomington Solidarity Network, Brennan Center for Justice, Catalist, Center for Wisconsin Strategy (COWS), CopWatch Patrol Unit, Democracy 21, Democracy Now!, Earth First! Journal, Energy Action Coalition, Equality Matters, Feminist Majority, Gamaliel Foundation, Green For All, Its Going Down, KilledbyPolice, L.I.F.E.E. Organization, MADRE, Malcolm X Grassroots Movement, Morgantown Ultra Left Network, Mutiny Antarsya Tempe, New Wave Army, Onward Together, Organizing For Action, People Improving Communities

Through Organizing, Presidential Climate Action Project, Progressive Accountability | The Nation, Progressive Change Campaign Committee, Progressive Talent Initiative, Proteus Fund, Proletarian Liberation Front, Redneck Revolt, Revolutionary Security Corps, Sword of Spartacus, Stand Up Fight Back, Solidarity Houston, South Florida Smash HLS, subMedia, Revolutionary Communist Party, Revolutionary Love Project, The Roosevelt Group, Tides Center, Uncontrollables, Words as Weapons, and more...

Note: These groups were found on DiscoverTheNetworks, Breitbart, and Wikipedia.

Again, the organizations mentioned in the categories above are only a few of the thousands that may have formed, are forming, or will form. Some may have already dismembered. But it must be pointed out that only some of these groups are aggressive. Others work through protests, media outlets, community organizers, and relatively peaceful means which are protected by the laws in the U.S. Constitution.

Politicians

Of course, most celebrities, mainstream media types, and liberal activists support Democratic politicians and reflect their agendas through rhetoric or action. Some of these Democrats, however, are a bit more moderate than the rest of their party. Yet, when it comes to votes for bills or policies, they can't vote their mind or stand-up for what they really believe in. If they did, those in Democratic leadership positions, like Representative Nancy Pelosi and Senator Chuck Schumer, would ensure their demise in the Democratic Party. Therefore, these more-fair-minded politicians must cater to the liberal mob rather than expressing their individual thoughts and beliefs. But these Democrats need to gain a backbone. They need to step forward again and begin to take back their party from an abomination. If this was to occur, there might be a chance that the next Democratic President would <u>not</u> have a radical progressive agenda in mind which would inevitably hurt Americans. Anyway, some elected Democratic politicians with radical liberal views are apparent. They seek to keep and gain power by exuding animus toward the 45th President of the United States. Often, we see them in the news or speaking with television anchors in the media bashing and talking nonsense about the President. Here are just a few.

Minority House Leader Nancy Pelosi (California), Senator Dianne Feinstein (California), Eric Swalwell (California), Senator Kamala Harris (California), Governor Jerry Brown (Governor of California), Representative Adam Schiff (California), Senator Kamala Harris (California), Representative Brad Sherman (California), Representative Maxine Waters (California), Senator Chuck Schumer (New York), Senator Kirsten Gillibrand (New York), Governor Andrew Cuomo (New York), Representative Jerrold Nadler (New York), Mayor Bill DeBlasio (New York City), Representative Luis Gutierrez (Illinois), Senator Dick Durbin (Illinois), Mayor Rahm Emanuel (Chicago), Senator Cory Booker (New Jersey), Senator Bob Menendez (New Jersey), Senator Patrick Leahy (Vermont), Senator Bernie Sanders (Vermont), Senator Tim Kaine (Maine), Senator Mark Warner (Maine), Senator Christopher Coons (Delaware), Senator Ron Wyden (Oregon), Senator Elizabeth Warren (Massachusetts), Senator Richard Blumenthal (Connecticut), Senator Mazie Hirono (Hawaii), Representative Elijah Cummings (Maryland), Representative John Lewis (Georgia), Representative Keith Ellison (Minnesota), Representative Beto O'Rourke (Texas), Representative Al Green (Texas), etc.

What do these politicians have in common? Their constituents have been swayed to vote Democrat; and they must keep their liberal base happy by denouncing the 45th President of the U.S. It's Politics 101. Some are extremely hypocritical and have even at one time gladly taken donations from the former billionaire businessman when he had been a registered Democrat. Years before running for President, many times he had rubbed elbows with Senators Kristen Gillibrand, Cory Booker, Chuck Schumer, and Hillary Clinton, as well as President Bill Clinton and Governor Andrew Cuomo. But now that this man has adopted the Republican Party, and regardless of mixed conservative and liberal views, these individuals vigorously contest him. It's because politics is a very dirty business - in which you can be a friend one day and an enemy the next. Yet whether he has friends or enemies beside or around him, this President will always do what is right for the people.

President John F. Kennedy said it best regarding those who may openly dislike you, confront your beliefs, or question your way of life.

"Forgive your enemies, but never forget their names."

Chapter 15

OUR FOUNDING FATHERS' DOCUMENTS

The Declaration of Independence was signed on July 4th, 1776 by fifty-six brave men intent on forming a new nation. But it wasn't as easy as just putting signatures on a newly created document. These men were putting their lives, families, and properties at grave risk. After all, they were challenging King George III, who ruled over Great Britain, Ireland, and 13 colonies of the New World (America).

The British empire had been existence for about two centuries and had recently won two wars: The Seven Years' War with France (1756 – 1763) and French and Indian War in the U.S. colonies (1754 – 1763). But, these wars strained the British economy and resulted in taxes being imposed upon the colonies. This was known as the Stamp Act of 1765. The act stated all printed materials were to be produced on stamp paper which would be taxed. It ignited the colonies' Congress to secretly begin the process of fighting for independence against its motherland. In this congressional meeting, Patrick Henry culminated his spirited speech by uttering the famous phrase,

"Give me liberty or give me death".

Led by Samuel Adams and John Hancock in the Boston Tea Party, and other groups like The Sons of Liberty, some openly strived for independence in Massachusetts Bay. In 1774, Britain responded by passing the Coercive Acts. But, it was better known as the 'Intolerable Acts' by the colonists. Then, in 1775, the British parliament sent King George III a letter partially finding that,

"...a part of your Majesty's subjects, in the Province of the Massachusetts Bay, have proceeded so far to resist the authority of the supreme Legislature, that a rebellion at this time actually exists within the said Province..."

And so, the Battle of Lexington and Concord (April 1775) and Battle of Bunker Hill (June 1775) erupted in Massachusetts Bay. They were bloody battles. Yet, even after a semblance of victories by Bay State colonists, some colonies were opposed to the idea of independence. All that changed after Virginia statesman Richard Henry Lee gave a very inspirational and rousing congressional speech, partly stating,

"That these united colonies are, and of right ought to be, free and independent states; that they are absolved from all allegiance to the British crown; and that all political connection between them and the State of Great Britain is, and ought to be, totally dissolved."

The 13 colonies of Virginia, Georgia, Maryland, North Carolina, South Carolina, Maryland, Massachusetts Bay, Pennsylvania, New York Delaware, New Jersey, New Hampshire, Connecticut, and Rhode Island would agree. It was time to separate from Great Britain. So, Thomas Jefferson was elected to write a document to declare independence. Then, the colonies would join to form a new nation.

The initial document by Thomas Jefferson was edited by many, including Benjamin Franklin. The first paper was signed by 12 colonies in 1776. Eventually, it was approved and signed by the 13th colony, New York, later that year. Within the final document, the most poignant paragraphs to ring out are at its beginning, middle, and end.

<u>Beginning:</u> *"When, in the course of human events, it becomes necessary for one people to dissolve the political bands which have connected them with another, and to assume among the powers of the earth, the separate and equal station to which the laws of nature and of nature's God entitle them, a decent respect to the opinions of mankind requires that they should declare the causes which impel them to the separation."*

<u>Middle:</u> *"We hold these truths to be self-evident, that all men are created equal, that they are endowed by their Creator with certain unalienable Rights, that among these are Life, Liberty and the pursuit of Happiness."*

<u>End:</u> *"...And for the support of this declaration, with a firm reliance on the protection of divine providence, we mutually pledge to each other our lives,*

our fortunes, and our sacred honor."

Again, it must be noted that those bold men who signed this manuscript put themselves at great peril. They were willing to give up everything – their lives, fortune, and honor. This is evident if you read the last sentence carefully. Therefore, the battles for American freedom continued, and General George Washington's strategies led victories at Saratoga (1777), Valley Forge (1777), and Yorktown (1781). But these triumphs were only possible because of Frenchmen like Marquis De Lafayette and Comte de Rochambeau. Then, by 1783, John Adams, Benjamin Franklin, and John Jay would sign the Treaty of Paris with Britain to formally declare the long-awaited independence of America.

This U.S. history is extremely important because it shows the hardships, struggles, and battles that took place in order to form a nation. We should be thankful to the founding fathers and others who fought to gain our independence and shaped our nation. They blazed a path forward to give the natural God-given rights to Americans, provide protection under laws, institute a government of democracy, and infuse us with insight and resourceful pride to build a new home.

After the Declaration of Independence

On March 1, 1781, the *Articles of Confederation* were ratified by all 13 states, becoming the first American Constitution. It basically preserved the sovereignty and independence of each state. But the limited influence over national matters by the Confederation Congress spurred the inevitable creation of our current United States Constitution.

This new Constitution, The Bill of Rights, as well as other ratified Amendments, were documents that originally governed and have influenced our democratic way of life. Without these important manuscripts the United States of America would be a lawless nation. Therefore, becoming familiar with them will benefit each American because it will establish a foundation for understanding the rights and laws of each citizen, a state, and our federal government.

These documents have also been misrepresented to the public. They are rarely mentioned unless it's politically expedient to do so. This is especially true when the mainstream media cites the 1st Amendment to claim their "freedom of the press" rights or when expressing outrage over the 2nd Amendment – gun rights. Regardless, the intention of sharing information regarding these documents is to show the public that we have rights and laws which need to be upheld. And, a more poignant purpose is to spark a common vision of American patriotism.

In the polarized environment we live in, with the threats we face from within our own country and from those who wish us ill-will from abroad, a bond of unity will strengthen our resolve to go forward in the future. We need common sense, patience, and love in finding the truths that bring a union to humanity. A good start is via our U.S. documents.

Civil disagreement is good for the spirit, so that we may learn from one another. But we must also show a sense of respect for another person's opinions and ideals. By one not willing to participate in non-violent debate to further one's knowledge about another aspect of a specific subject acknowledges a person's desire and failure to grow. Shutting down free speech is just as bad because not engaging in worthwhile discourse to expand one's mental horizons shows an innate stubborn ignorance to comprehend another's feelings and beliefs. If we truly believe in a democracy, where people are free to choose what to do, think, and speak to advance in education, status, and prosperity, then we should desire coming to some type of agreement on certain issues. The only way to do this is to have private or communal dialogue with one another without flagrant animosity.

All peaceable communication and lawful action within our democratic society enforces an inevitable goal for every American. That objective is to benefit from "life, liberty, and the pursuit of happiness". It's what *we the people* have been given by our founding fathers and God. Everyone should be grateful that we have the choice to live as or become American citizens. Therefore, that is why we should adhere to and know the laws of this nation which make our freedoms possible.

The major issues like immigration, health care, abortion, and gun laws are often fought long and hard in Congress and on the streets between citizens without much resolution. There will never be a result which will be satisfactory to some. But those with a reasonable outlook on life in America can come to a compromise. The answer, as Buddhists call it, is the *middle-way*. It is not being obsessed or complacent about certain issues which bring disagreement but rather becoming involved and open to solutions when addressing difficult problems. As was mentioned, limitation and <u>not</u> elimination is the key to much in life.

Additionally, Americans can't be satisfied with the lawlessness certain sections of this nation have adopted. Citizens are entitled to be safe from criminals, have a fair shake at employment and education, while also being able to express their faith without fear of animosity or discrimination. Being American citizens, we have "inalienable" rights and should not tolerate those yearning to re-write or destroy our history to fulfill their personal and political satisfaction. To counteract this, we need to better comprehend the laws and rights in our founding documents, such as the U.S. Constitution and The Bill of Rights. Then, these presented documents can become an inspiration to citizens, and those who want to become citizens of America.

The United States Constitution

The United States Constitution was signed on September 17, 1787, by delegates to the Constitutional Convention in Philadelphia. There were 13 states recognizing this important document at the time of its creation. They were Georgia, Virginia, Delaware, Maryland, Rhode Island, New York, New Jersey, Pennsylvania, North Carolina, South Carolina, New Hampshire, Massachusetts, and Connecticut. Since these states were basically autonomous and had governed themselves for the most part, the Constitution provided more clarity about the laws of the federal government and the basic rights of its citizens. This manuscript also distinguishes the duties and rules of the executive, legislative, and judicial branches of the U.S. government. In addition, it enforces a scheme of checks and balances, so any one branch can't hold too much power. That is contained in the *Articles of the Constitution*.

The Bill Rights in the U.S. Constitution is made up of the first ten amendments. These amendments gave citizens guaranteed rights and limited the laws of the states and federal government. As years passed, more amendments were added. As of this writing in 2018, there are a total number of 27 amendments.

The U.S. Constitution consists of Articles, Sections, The Bill of Rights, and subsequent amendments. It's long and complex. So, for easier reading, only a summary of this key document shall be given.

Article 1 - The Legislative Branch

- Section 1:   Establishes the U.S. Congress, which consists of a Senate and House of Representatives. There are two Senators for each of the 50 states. The House of Representatives is based on the number of districts, which is based upon the population in each State.
- Section 2:   Rules for the House of Representatives
- Section 3:   Rules for the Senate
- Section 4:   Procedures for Elections and Meetings
- Section 5:   Membership Rules and Journals
- Section 6:   Pay and Protection for Congress Men and Women
- Section 7:   Bill to Raise Revenues, How the Process Works, and Veto
-              Power of the President
- Section 8:   Congressional Powers
- Section 9:   Congressional Limitations
- Section 10: Limits the Powers of the State

Article 2 - The Executive Branch

- Section 1:   The Presidential Voting Process (Electoral College) and Oath of Office
- Section 2:   Duties of the President (Cabinet, Appointments, Pardon Power, and Military)
- Section 3:   President's State of the Union
- Section 4:   Impeachments of the President, Vice-President, or Civil Officers

Article 3 - The Judicial Branch

- Section 1:   Powers of the Judiciary

- Section 2:   Modified by 11th Amendment (trials by jury must move from lower to upper courts)
- Section 3:   Penalties for Treason

Article 4 - The States

- Section 1:   Each State Must Honor "Public Acts, Records, and Judicial Proceedings of Every Other State"
- Section 2:   State Citizen Privilege and Protection
- Section 3:   Process of New State
- Section 4:   Guaranteed Republic Form of Government

Article 5 - The Amendment Process

Article 6 – Validity of Debts, Judges Bound to Laws of Constitution, Elected Officials Oath of Office

Article 7 – Ratification of the Constitution

....

The Bill of Rights (1791): These are the "God-given" rights of the people.

- Amendment 1:   Freedom of Religion, Speech, Press, and the Right to Assemble
- Amendment 2:   Right to Bear Arms
- Amendment 3:   Homeowners Obliged to Quarter Soldiers
- Amendment 4:   Unreasonable Legal Search and Seizure
- Amendment 5:   Trial, Due Process, Double Jeopardy, No Witness Against Self, and Just Compensation
- Amendment 6:   Right to Speedy and Public Trial, Impartial Jury, Witness Confrontation, and Defense
- Amendment 7:   Common or Civil Trial by Jury
- Amendment 8:   Excessive Bail and Fines, Cruel and Unusual Punishment
- Amendment 9:   Constitution Shall Not Be Constructed to Disparage or Deny Other Rights to People
- Amendment 10:   Powers Not Delegated to the Constitution Given Back to the States and People

Ratified After 1791:

- Amendment 11 (1795): Limitations of Judicial Law on Citizens of Another State, or Foreign State
- Amendment 12 (1804): Presidential and Vice-Presidential Elections
- Amendment 13 (1865): Slavery Not Allowed (Abolishment)
- Amendment 14 (1868): Citizenship for Slaves
- Amendment 15 (1870): Illegal to Deny Voters Based on Race or Color
- Amendment 16 (1913): Income Taxes by Federal Government
- Amendment 17 (1913): Elections of Senators by Popular Vote
- Amendment 18 (1919): LAW REPEALED IN 1933: Banned Sale and Consumption of Liquor
- Amendment 19 (1920): Women's Right to Vote (can't deny voting based on gender)
- Amendment 20 (1933): President and Congressional Terms of Taking Office
- Amendment 21 (1933): Repeal of 18th Amendment
- Amendment 22 (1951): Presidential Term Limits in Office (two-term maximum – 8 years)
- Amendment 23 (1961): Washington, the District of Columbia, Allowed to Vote as State
- Amendment 24 (1964): No Voting Poll Taxes
- Amendment 25 (1967): Chain of Authority and Succession if President Unable to Perform Duties
- Amendment 26 (1971): Voting Age Lowered from 21 to 18 Years Old
- Amendment 27 (1992): Congressional Pay Raises and Limitations

The Declaration of Independence, United States Constitution, Bill of Rights, and other amendments are the documents we should be proud of, fully comprehend, and respect as American citizens. To live freely in this country is, again, owed to the inalienable rights and laws granted within these documents. We should be cautious with idealisms that aim to eradicate these foundational principles of our nation. There is no utopia which we can strive for at this time in our humanity. This is an impractical mindset of social and political reform. We can add amendments to our laws which can enhance our way of life. But we shouldn't trounce on the rights of American citizens and the laws of our nation in the process of forging minor reformations.

Some people don't recognize that radical forms of progressivism which pushes for equality of prosperity, not of social means, will lead to a centralized government which is akin to a harsh form of socialism. Once under these socialist doctrines, the government can evolve negatively forward, and our laws will diminish. Then, all that shall remain is a totalitarian or communist regime.

The American people must understand that the principles of Marxism, and similar ideologies, are not beneficial to any nation which desires to live in a free democracy. If we bend toward socialist concepts in this country, we will inevitably give up our freedoms. The original equality that people sought and fought for will come to fruition in a form they did not hope for or expect. This variety of equality will bring poverty to all and abuse by the ruling elites. People will not be able to work from the bottom and work upwards to the top while obtaining more knowledge, wealth, and status. In an idealist achieved state of unconformable hard-lined socialism or communism, people will be told what not to say, how to think, if they can pray or not, be given pittances to live upon, and not be able to advance in profession unless it benefits the state. Those in power will look down upon the masses and dictate the circumstances of the people. It's an end scenario our nation must avoid at all costs. Americans must be vigilant in our stand against this.

Comprehending the rights and laws of our founding documents while confronting those willing to dictate our way of life, such as the mainstream media and political elites with their minions, allow us the chance to keep our freedoms and democracy intact. Therefore, we should be strong in union and opposition, via peaceful acts and speech, against those wishing to denigrate and destroy our history and way of life. Through these documents, people who respect and love our young nation, can find credence and cause to save America from foes within and outside its borders. It's our right to do so in a civil manner.

And, yet, our borders are being breached every single day. Illegal immigrant criminals are being harbored in over 500 *sanctuary cities* in our nation. The local jurisdictions where they hide in America are run by defiant representatives who seek to usurp federal laws for political gain. They set illegal immigrants free, regardless of the number or types (many of them felonies) of criminal acts they had committed, while at the same time putting Americans citizens at grave risk.

That is why we should give honor to those who have and wish to protect our people and country from injury or death. We should also thank those who created, uphold, abide by, and serve to defend our laws. They embrace and embolden our true spirit, defend the multiple colors of our patriotism, and reinforce the goodness of our humanity.

But be leery of those desiring to accept lawlessness as the norm or disregard the sanctity of life – especially those sworn to give or protect it. These persons lack the courage or will to implement their God-given sensibilities. Life is extremely precious. It should not be cut short with inconsideration, pretentious ignorance, or callous without serious rational and civil contemplation. Each life needs to flourish with love and be protected from those who lack the spiritual, moral, or ethical insight or knowledge of how the universe and its Creator work.

In the end, whether of a conservative, liberal, or independent mind, we do need bodies of government to create and oversee our laws so evil and chaos do not take hold on this planet. But, simultaneously, through prayer and meditation, we could also look to the heavens for some guidance to resolve our differences for the betterment of each society and the world. Then, we can live and work together under that guidance and those laws, from Heaven and Earth, to discover a more plausible and sustainable peace for each coming day.

"If we ever forget that we are 'one nation under God', then we will be a nation gone under." – Ronald Reagan

AFTERWORD

The writing of this book has been an absolute labor of love. The idea for it probably began during the elections in early 2016. To keep informed with what had been transpiring, I flipped back and forth between different news channels. But what I started to discover were shocking anomalies and truths. It seemed as if most news channels were echoing the same messages during the Presidential primaries and the general elections. They all were very transparent with their biases for one Presidential candidate. Negative news against *her* was either being spun in a positive narrative or not covered at all. Negative news concerning the other candidates, however, were making headlines. Something seemed amiss. The only channel that seemed to give fair and balanced coverage, and both sides of the political story, was *Fox News*.

I had never watched *Fox News* before 2016. But, although more than half of this broadcast news channel's analysis seemed to slant more toward a conservative viewpoint, there was nothing I uncovered which was inaccurate or fabricated. As a matter of fact, it was unfiltered and told more about what was really happening in the news than any other news channel. So, I started to scribble down notes about what I heard on *Fox News* and compared my notes with what was being broadcast as news on other channels. I had uncovered a stunning revelation. The other news channels and newspapers were not telling Americans all the facts. Furthermore, and most importantly, they were creating stories which were untrue regarding the political world.

Since I was battling the crux of an illness during this time, and still am to some degree, I had to put aside writing notes. But as months passed, I slowly began to convert those memos into a legible document on my computer. Then, I jotted down notes again while watching *Fox News,* and perused the Internet to find out more about a specific topic.

I discovered more truths about what was happening in our communities and around the world from *Fox News* and through research on the Internet than maybe any other time in my life. But I was alarmed, frustrated, and sad to see the rampant bias and hate being spread on all the other major news networks and some newspapers.

Therefore, in late 2017, a spark was lit inside me. I felt it my duty as a proud American citizen to share what I had found with the public. I wanted to bring back veracity to anyone who wanted to listen and uncover the real facts about the past and present. Ironically, and unwittingly, the dubious stories, biased insinuations, negative assaults, and flat-out lies from the mainstream media pushed me forward. They ignited old pistons which had been idle and dormant and gave me needed fuel to rev-up my engines of writing once again.

Once I started this ride, it was hard to put on the brakes. The mainstream media gave me an excess of inaccurate news I could follow so I was not bored on my journey. I diligently navigated through all of it, climbing up steep obstacles, moving over many holes, while also twisting and turning with the high beams on through much darkness and fog. Ultimately, I arrived at my destination after a very precarious, illuminating, and even comical trip. The information gathered while on that long ride, trip, or journey are what has been presented in this book.

Through that arduous journey, I saw and heard a tremendous amount of animosity, disgust, jealousy, and untruths coming from the mainstream media and others aimed at the 45th President of the United States. It solidified the assumptions I had about the mainstream media for months. Now, my views about them have become unshakeable.

The "lame"-stream media has predisposed opinions, over-the-top rhetoric, and negative sensationalism about anything or anyone that doesn't fit into their little bubble or narrative. It's exceedingly apparent. Their insatiable appetite for recognition, ratings, and high status overshadows the true objectives of journalists, reporters and news anchors. They should be informing the public with absolute honest, unfabricated, and straight-forward news. To do less and manufacture stories insults the intelligence of many; and, it undermines the integrity of their profession. These deceitful people have placed the art of journalism temporarily or permanently in a deep cold dark grave.

What has been spewed from their mouths about this President has been and continues to be unfathomable and unprecedented. Their determined fervor of hostility cannot be overstated. Therefore, I reject these elites in the mainstream media who propagate falsehoods and bend lies into truths. They are modern day myth and fable tellers!

Regarding the hot topics and issues in America, first-and-foremost, being a veteran, I believe the rule of law and OUR U.S. Constitution should be upheld. The problem of gun violence is akin to other problems we have in America, and around the world. When drugs, cigarettes, alcohol, and cell phones are abused they can be dangerous and cause death too. To state a fact, drug overdoses kill more people than guns do. "Cigarette smoking and second-hand smoke cause one in every five deaths" in America, as reported by the CDC (Centers for Disease and Control Prevention). And, there is no doubt that the over consumption of alcohol may lead to death over-time, provoke fatal accidents (i.e. car, boat, train) or domestic violence assaults, and incite the use of a deadly weapon. Even cells phones can lead to death because people are not paying attention to what they are supposed to be doing. Of course, all these items are harmless by themselves. But, it's the intent of a person abusing them that is harmful to self and others.

People need to know how to use these items much less and moderately, if possible. This will unquestionably lessen the number of deaths experienced in America, and throughout the globe. But can or should we remove all these vices from people's lives? Can we survive without these items in our lives? That is a question we must ask ourselves. But, although we play a role in answering these questions, Congress will make the decisions for us. To me, as discussed, the abuse of anything can best be remedied by understanding *limitation not elimination*. This may be the best inevitable answer.

In addition, I believe in the "right to die". But at the same time, I don't believe this should be a haphazard decision, and should be discussed, reevaluated, and seen from every possible angle. That is why I also adhere to the notion that we have the "right to try". With today's technology there are many new breakthroughs on the horizons to *try*, if available, before we *die*. Life is precious and should be treated as such. Therefore, again, I believe in limits and only certain conditions should prompt the harsh judgment about ending a life prematurely without just moral, ethical, physical, and spiritual consideration.

As an independent thinker and truth seeker, I now welcome what may come of new populist movement that has been invoked and brought to the American people by OUR new President. Yes! His unconventional style of speaking, whether it's candidly or jokingly, as well as the way he tackles the major and minor issues facing America is like no other politician or President that has served before him. Yes! He is brash and honest. But, this President carries himself with great confidence and, regardless of the mainstream media's impression, has a big and good heart. They have loudly and wrongly misrepresented him as uncaring and having a lack of empathy. It's another falsity that has been perpetuated to those willing to listen to their absurdities.

This President takes an excellent pulse of the American people because he too knows what it's like to be a citizen and be disappointed with how the government is being run by the so-called *political elites*. Although running as a Republican, his ideologies are his own. What he brings to the table is an unorthodox, and surprisingly middle-off-the-road approach to resolving the issues in the U.S.A. and abroad. Being a businessman, this President, with little political experience, brings a fresh look at how our country can: 1) best protect itself from rogue countries like North Korea, Iran, and others 2) fight against terrorists organizations such as ISIS and Al-Qaeda, 3) support our veterans at home and overseas, 4) craft fair trade deals to benefit America, 5) provide economic stability to individuals, families, and all businesses with more jobs and tax cuts, 6) embrace the availability of additional choices for education and healthcare, 7) reinforce the laws of this land, 8) support our constitutional rights, and 9) secure our borders and tackle immigration reform.

Moreover, the President has already kept most of the promises he made from the 2016 Presidential campaign trail in only about 16 months as Commander-in-Chief. For these reasons and many others, his message resonates with millions. It's also my unapologetic rationale for becoming a supporter of this man. Therefore, I will break my own rule in this book by recognizing him by name, OUR 45th President of the United States of America – Donald J. Trump.

I thank you for reading my book, and hope your life is filled with much happiness. Keep your faith! God bless you and your family.

HISTORICAL QUOTES TO PONDER

Some historical quotes one may have been heard many times, such as "The only thing to fear is, fear itself" (Franklin D. Roosevelt) or "And so my fellow Americans, ask not what your country can do for you; ask what you can do for your country" (John F. Kennedy). But there are lesser known historical quotes that may give one pause to ponder.

George Washington: *"Guard against the impostures of pretended patriotism."*

Queen Elizabeth: *"True patriotism doesn't exclude an understanding of the patriotism of others."*

Ronald Reagan: *"The future is best decided by ballots, not bullets."*

Andrew Jackson: *"You must pay the price, if you want to secure the blessing."*

Martin Luther King Jr.: *"If a man is called to be a street sweeper, he should sweep streets even as Michelangelo painted or Beethoven composed music or Shakespeare wrote poetry. He should sweep streets so well that all the hosts of heaven and earth will pause and say, "here lived a great street sweeper who did his job well."*

Eleanor Roosevelt: *"A woman is like a tea bag - you can't tell how strong she is until you put her in hot water."*

Margaret Thatcher: *"Being powerful is like being a lady. If you have to tell people you are, you aren't."*

Thomas Jefferson: *"Advertisements contain the only truths to be relied on in a newspaper."*

Eleanor Roosevelt: *"We are given in our newspapers and on TV and radio exactly what we, the public, insist on having, and this very frequently is mediocre information and mediocre entertainment."*

Nikita Khrushchev: *"Politicians are the same all over. They promise to build a bridge even where there is no river."*

Evita Peron: *"In government, one actress is enough."*

Theodore Roosevelt: *"Order without liberty and liberty without order are equally destructive."*

Margaret Thatcher: *"The problem with socialism is that you eventually run out of other people's money."*

Mahatma Gandhi: *"The Roots of Violence: wealth without work, pleasure without conscience, knowledge without character, commerce without morality, science without humanity, worship without sacrifice, politics without principles."*

Pope Francis: *"Every economic, political, social, or religious project involves the inclusion or exclusion of the wounded lying on the side of the road. Every day, each of us faces the choice of being a Good Samaritan or an indifferent bystander."*

Mother Teresa: *"The greatest destroyer of peace today is abortion, because it is a war against the child, a direct killing of the innocent child, murder by the mother herself. And if we accept that a mother can kill even her own child, how can we tell other people not to kill one another?"*

Princess Diana: *"Everyone of us needs to show how much we care for each other and, in the process, care for ourselves."*

Reverend Desmond Tutu: *"We are made for goodness. We are made for love. We are made for friendliness. We are made for togetherness. We are made for all of the beautiful things that you and I know. We are made to tell the world that there are no outsiders. All are welcome: black, white, red, yellow, rich, poor, educated, not educated, male, female, gay, straight, all, all, all. We all belong to this family, this human family, God's family."*

Winston Churchill: *"Truth is incontrovertible. Panic may resent it. Ignorance may deride it. Malice may distort it. But there it is."*

Dalai Lama: *"There is no religion higher than the truth."*

PUBLICATIONS & BOOKS TO CONSIDER READING

- Smear: How Shady Political Operatives and Fake News Control What You See, What You Think, and How You Vote (Sharyl Attkinson)
- American Pravda: My Fight for Truth in the Era of Fake News (James O'Keefe)
- Media Madness: Donald Trump, the Press, and the War over the Truth (Howard Kurtz)
- Old School: Life in the Sane Lane (Bill O'Reilly)
- Understanding Trump (Newt Gingrich)
- Let Trump Be Trump: The Inside Story of His Rise to the Presidency (Corey Lewandowski and David N. Bossie)
- The Making of the President 2016: How Donald Trump Orchestrated a Revolution (Roger Stone)
- Trump: The Art of the Deal (Donald J. Trump and Tony Schwartz)
- Fast and Furious: Barack Obama's Bloodiest Scandal and the Shameless Cover-Up (Katie Pavlich)
- The People vs. Barack Obama: The Criminal Case Against the Obama Administration (Ben Shapiro)
- Clinton Cash (Peter Schweizer)
- GUILTY AS SIN: Uncovering New Evidence of Corruption and How Hillary Clinton and the Democrats Derailed the FBI Investigation (Edward Klein)
- Hillary's America: The Secret History of the Democratic Party (Dinesh D'Souza)
- Crisis of Character: A White House Secret Service Officer Discloses His Firsthand Experience with Hillary, Bill, and How They Operate (Gary J. Byrne)
- The Truth About Hillary: What She Knew, When She Knew It, and How Far She'll Go to Become President (Edward Klein)
- The Clintons' War on Women (Roger Stone and Robert Morrow)
- Shattered: Inside Hillary Clinton's Doomed Campaign (Jonathan Allen and Amie Parnes)
- The Shadow Party: How George Soros, Hilary Clinton, and Sixties Radicals Seized Control of the Democratic Party (David Horowitz and Richard Poe)
- Deliver Us from Evil: Defeating Terrorism, Despotism, and Liberalism (Sean Hannity)
- Rediscovering Americanism and the Tyranny of Progressivism (Mark R. Levin)
- Shut Up and Sing: How Elites from Hollywood, Politics, and the UN Are Subverting America (Laura Ingraham)
- Race Pimping: The Multi-Trillion Dollar Business of Liberalism (Kevin Jackson)
- Time for a Turning Point: Setting a Course Toward Free Markets and Limited Government for Future Generations (Charlie Kirk)
- The Liberty Amendments: Restoring the American Republic (Mark R. Levin)

REFERENCES

Unfair and Unbalanced Journalism (Chapter 1)

http://www.americanthinker.com/articles/2017/12/cnn_declares_war_on_fox_news_.html
https://www.politico.com/blogs/on-media/2016/10/study-91-percent-of-trump-coverage-on-broadcast-news-was-negative-230297
https://ijr.com/the-declaration/2017/12/1034120-percentage-negative-coverage-trump-receives-media-staggering/
https://www.recode.net/2017/10/2/16401216/President-donald-trump-news-negative-pew-research-obama-bush-clinton
https://www.theepochtimes.com/media-give-trump-most-negative-Presidential-coverage-in-25-years_2327946.html
http://www.washingtonexaminer.com/harvard-study-as-trump-won-media-coverage-turned-sharply-negative/article/2596199
https://www.newsbusters.org/blogs/nb/rich-noyes/2018/03/06/tv-vs-trump-2018-lots-russia-and-91-negative-coverage
https://en.wikipedia.org/wiki/Media_bias_in_the_United_States
https://www.encyclopedia.com/history/culture-magazines/muckrakers-and-yellow-journalism
https://en.wikipedia.org/wiki/History_of_American_newspapers

Creating an Impeachment Angle (Chapter 2)

https://impeachdonaldtrumpnow.org/case-for-impeachment/
https://www.law.cornell.edu/constitution/articleii
https://www.law.cornell.edu/uscode/text/18/2381
http://academic.brooklyn.cuny.edu/history/johnson/rnimparticles.htm
https://www.law.cornell.edu/uscode/text/18/1519

Fake and Ignorant News (Chapter 3)

http://www.chron.com/news/nation-world/article/fake-news-stories-trump-real-rumor-2017-media-12451358.php#photo-12570594
http://www.fakehatecrimes.org/http://www.discoverthenetworks.org/summary.asp?object=Organization&category=
http://www.businessinsider.com/is-michael-wolffs-book-true-2018-1#many-of-wolffs-dialogues-likely-being-recreations-rather-than-factual-accounts-4
http://www.thesocialhistorian.com/fake-news/
https://www.wsj.com/articles/russia-the-nra-and-fake-news-1521761296
https://blogs.scientificamerican.com/anthropology-in-practice/three-historical-examples-of-fake-news/
https://www.politico.com/magazine/story/2016/12/fake-news-history-long-violent-214535

Hidden and Misrepresented Stories (Chapter 4)

https://www.washingtontimes.com/news/2017/jan/30/womens-march-three-times-more-coverage-march-life/
https://www.lifesitenews.com/news/pro-life-students-at-200-high-schools-to-stage-walk-out-protesting-abortion

http://www.doctorsonfetalpain.com/

https://www.nationalreview.com/2017/01/planned-parenthood-child-sex-trafficking-crimes-still-unreported/

https://www.washingtontimes.com/news/2017/aug/15/jake-tapper-on-media-bias-obama-said-things-that-w/

https://instituteforenergyresearch.org/analysis/u-s-outshines-countries-carbon-dioxide-emissions-reductions/

https://www.reuters.com/article/us-usa-epa-pruitt/epa-chief-wants-scientists-to-debate-climate-on-tv-idUSKBN19W2D0

 http://christiannews.net/2017/08/22/parents-feel-betrayed-after-teacher-reads-transgender-themed-books-to-kindergarten-class/

https://eaglerising.com/46697/first-grade-student-punished-for-misgendering-another-student

https://www.buzzfeed.com/uiekazoo/masculinity-is-actually-killing-men?utm_term=.eeMV2om5L#.fvEw5VyEm

http://dailyrollcall.com/california-muslim-imam-calls-for-killing-jews/

http://www.centerformedicalprogress.org/cmp/investigative-footage/

http://www.pewresearch.org/fact-tank/2015/11/20/40-of-millennials-ok-with-limiting-speech-offensive-to-minorities/

https://chicago.suntimes.com/news/at-major-northwest-side-bakery-labor-issues-pit-blacks-vs-hispanics/

https://nypost.com/2018/03/01/this-state-has-the-worst-quality-of-life-in-the-country/

http://wakeforestreview.com/wake-forest-declines-enforce-harassment-policies-conservative-student/

http://thefederalist.com/2016/10/13/voter-fraud-real-heres-proof/

https://www.campusreform.org/?ID=10614

https://www.factcheck.org/2008/03/Presidents-winning-without-popular-vote/

https://en.wikipedia.org/wiki/United_States_Presidential_election_in_California,_2016

http://www.foxnews.com/opinion/2018/03/22/children-with-down-syndrome-like-my-son-have-right-to-be-born-and-are-blessing.html

http://www.foxnews.com/entertainment/2017/08/15/patricia-heaton-blasts-cbs-over-abortion-report.html

https://www.today.com/health/mikayla-holmgren-becomes-first-woman-compete-miss-usa-state-pageant-t119492

https://www.americamagazine.org/politics-society/2018/03/21/elimination-down-syndrome-great-hate-crime-says-holy-see-conference-un

<u>Immigration – Guns – Law Enforcement (Chapter 5)</u>

http://www.washingtonexaminer.com/sen-dianne-feinstein-admits-daca-was-on-shaky-legal-ground/article/2633475

https://www.theatlantic.com/magazine/archive/2017/07/the-democrats-immigration-mistake/528678/

http://www.p2012.org/issues/platformimmig.html

https://www.cheatsheet.com/culture/dangerous-gangs-united-states.html/?a=viewall

https://crimeresearch.org/cprc-research/

https://www.telegraph.co.uk/news/2018/04/01/police-launch-murder-hunt-30th-stabbing-london-year/

https://www.realclearpolitics.com/video/2018/02/07/pelosi_my_grandsons_birthday_wish_was_to_have_brown_skin_the_face_of_the_future_of_our_country.html

https://www.usatoday.com/story/news/2017/12/28/number-officers-killed-2017-hits-nearly-

50-year-low/984477001/

http://www.breitbart.com/texas/2017/11/29/illegal-alien-shot-killed-assaulting-border-patrol-agent-arizona-say-feds/

https://www.washingtonpost.com/local/no-there-havent-been-18-school-shooting-in-2018-that-number-is-flat-wrong/2018/02/15/65b6cf72-1264-11e8-8ea1-c1d91fcec3fe_story.html?utm_term=.678d68a13ccb

http://www.breitbart.com/big-hollywood/2017/10/03/jimmy-kimmel-vegas-republicans-praying-god-forgive/

https://www.nationalreview.com/blog/corner/republicans-nra-money-critiques-ignore-planned-parenthood/

Presidential Criticisms and Insults (Chapter 6)

http://www.nytimes.com/1994/10/27/world/clinton-in-letter-assures-north-koreans-on-nuclear-reactors.html

http://dailycaller.com/2017/12/28/media-spends-2017-attacking-melania-trump/

http://www.foxnews.com/politics/2010/05/25/obamas-patience-wears-bp-struggles-contain-oil-spill.html

http://www.nytimes.com/2010/10/07/science/earth/07spill.html

http://www.washingtonexaminer.com/trumps-real-news-facebook-videos-alarm-media/article/2630817

http://thehill.com/homenews/administration/365068-exclusive-prominent-lawyer-sought-donor-cash-for-two-trump-accusers

https://www.cbsnews.com/news/obama-launches-site-to-debunk-rumors/

http://www.cnn.com/2008/TECH/11/10/obama.wired/index.html

https://townhall.com/columnists/johnhawkins/2017/04/15/the-7-worst-liberal-attacks-on-donald-trumps-family-n2313730

https://www.advocate.com/politicians/2018/2/13/omarosa-pence-believes-jesus-talks-him-would-be-worse-trump

https://townhall.com/tipsheet/mattvespa/2018/02/14/oh-my-did-the-views-behar-suggest-vp-pences-christian-faith-makes-him-mentally-ill-n2448994

Identity Politics & Political Correctness (Chapter 7)

https://www.merriam-webster.com/dictionary/political%20correctness

https://www.merriam-webster.com/dictionary/identity %20politics

http://www.weeklystandard.com/beware-linda-sarsours-harvey-hurricane-relief-fund/article/2009480

http://atlantablackstar.com/2014/04/09/5-native-american-communities-who-owned-africans-slaves/

https://www.prageru.com/videos/inconvenient-truth-about-democratic-party

https://blavity.com/black-pilgrims-plymouth-rock-researchers-think

https://www.snopes.com/fact-check/facts-about-slavery/

https://www.leoweekly.com/2017/08/white-people/

http://www.foxnews.com/us/2017/09/05/joel-osteen-tells-hurricane-harvey-victims-to-not-have-poor-old-me-mentality.html

https://www.theroot.com/6-historic-structures-in-america-that-were-built-by-sla-1790856172

https://www.epm.org/resources/2009/Dec/18/17-countries-where-christians-are-persecuted/

https://www.washingtonpost.com/news/fact-checker/wp/2016/03/01/donald-trump-and-

david-duke-for-the-record/?utm_term=.8d9834deab24
http://mediatrackers.org/2013/06/20/6-horribly-racist-comments-from-obama-admin-officials/

Achievements by the President (Chapter 8)

https://barbwire.com/2017/12/31/wnds-big-list-of-170-trump-accomplishments-in-340-days/
https://nypost.com/2017/12/04/this-is-armageddon-pelosi-trashes-gop-tax-bill/
https://en.wikipedia.org/wiki/Donald_Trump
https://www.washingtonexaminer.com/heritage-foundation-64-of-trumps-agenda-already-done-faster-than-reagan/article/2650141
https://www.insidephilanthropy.com/home/2015/9/29/a-quick-look-at-donald-trumps-philanthropy.html
https://www.whitehouse.gov/briefings-statements/the-inaugural-address/

Inspirational Speeches (Chapter 9)

http://thehill.com/blogs/pundits-blog/the-administration/334454-full-speech-President-donald-trump-address-in-saudi
https://www.whitehouse.gov/briefings-statements/remarks-president-trump-people-poland/
https://www.wsj.com/articles/donald-trumps-2018-state-of-the-union-address-1517375930

Cries of Russian, Russia, Russia!!! (Chapter 10)

https://www.washingtontimes.com/news/2017/jul/5/dnc-email-server-most-wanted-evidence-for-russia-i/
http://www.foxnews.com/politics/2017/07/07/hacked-dnc-servers-will-government-ever-be-given-access.html
www.thenation.com/article/a-new-report-raises-big-questions-about-last-years-dnc-hack
http://www.businessinsider.com/cia-pompeo-former-official-dnc-hack-trump-russia-intelligence-2017-11
https://nypost.com/2018/02/09/us-spies-reportedly-paid-100k-to-russian-operative-who-claimed-to-have-dirt-on-trump/
http://www.foxnews.com/politics/2017/10/17/trump-dossier-firms-smear-tactics-unveiled-fusion-gps-labeled-critic-pedophile-extortionist-and-drug-trafficker.html
http://dailycaller.com/2018/02/06/adam-schiff-pranked/
https://www.huffingtonpost.com/entry/exposing-the-man-behind-the-curtain_us_5877887be4b05b7a465df6a4
https://saraacarter.com/muellers-pit-bull-andrew-weissmann-busted-withholding-evidence-previous-case/
http://www.washingtonexaminer.com/byron-york-a-non-alarmist-reading-of-the-mueller-russia-indictment/article/2649445
https://spectator.org/obamas-meddling-in-foreign-elections-six-examples/
https://www.washingtonpost.com/news/worldviews/wp/2016/10/13/the-long-history-of-the-u-s-interfering-with-elections-elsewhere/?utm_term=.7a1637c16b7a
https://www.huffingtonpost.com/entry/conflicts-of-interest-and-ethics-robert-mueller-and_us_5936a148e4b033940169cdc8

The Real Obama Years: Failures (Chapter 11)

https://godfatherpolitics.com/farrakhan-is-only-a-tiny-part-of-womens-march-leaders-antisemitism/
https://fivethirtyeight.com/features/obama-granted-clemency-unlike-any-other-President-in-history
http://abcnews.go.com/Blotter/DemocraticDebate/story?id=4443788&page=1
https://ballotpedia.org/Obamacare_lawsuits
http://swampland.time.com/2013/10/24/traffic-didnt-crash-the-obamacare-site-alone-bad-coding-did-too/
http://thefederalist.com/2016/07/14/how-obama-has-bitterly-divided-america/
https://www.cbsnews.com/news/obama-explains-his-remark-about-punishing-enemies/
https://greatamericanpolitics.com/2017/09/obama-warned-violent-antifa-nothing/
https://www.frontpagemag.com/fpm/198280/how-obama-poisoned-race-relations-america-arnold-ahlert
https://offgridsurvival.com/obamas-legacy-chaos-chicago-gangs/
https://www.washingtontimes.com/news/2016/jul/12/obama-admin-sent-taxpayer-money-oust-netanyahu/

The Real Obama Years: Scandals (Chapter 12)

http://www.breitbart.com/big-government/2017/01/02/18-major-scandals-obama-presidency/
https://www.mediamatters.org/video/2016/04/10/how-many-times-do-i-have-say-it-chris-fox-cant-take-yes-answer-clinton-emails/209841
https://www.dailywire.com/news/24839/watch-joe-biden-falsely-claims-obama-never-had-any-ryan-saavedra
https://en.wikipedia.org/wiki/ATF_gunwalking_scandal
http://abcnews.go.com/ABC_Univision/News/things-operation-fast-furious/story?id=17362933
http://www.powerlineblog.com/archives/2016/04/documents-confirm-eric-holders-role-in-fast-and-furious-cover-up.php
https://www.thepostemail.com/2014/05/19/congressman-says-obama-knew-of-veterans-admin-scandal-but-ignored-it/
https://www.frontpagemag.com/fpm/225837/veterans-affairs-and-death-bureaucracy-arnold-ahlert
https://ballotpedia.org/Veterans_Affairs%27_secret_waiting_lists
https://www.forbes.com/sites/peterjreilly/2017/10/27/irs-scandal-ends-as-it-began-with-an-apology/#72299123fd4b
https://en.wikipedia.org/wiki/IRS_targeting_controversy
https://www.eff.org/nsa-spying/timeline
https://en.wikipedia.org/wiki/Edward_Snowden
https://www.americanthinker.com/articles/2013/06/pigford_the_unexamined_obama_administration_scandal.html
http://www.weeklystandard.com/private-citizen-sebelius-solicits-obamacare-donations/article/724523#!
https://www.americanthinker.com/blog/2015/08/media_covering_up_epas_responsibility_for_colorado_river_pollution.html
https://www.washingtonpost.com/news/post-politics/wp/2014/10/01/a-shortlist-of-recent-secret-service-scandals/?utm_term=.9d22f2c3d963

What Really Happened with Hillary? (Chapter 13)

http://www.dailymail.co.uk/news/article-5369935/FBI-informant-Russia-paid-influence-Clinton-uranium.html
https://en.wikipedia.org/wiki/Uranium_One
https://www.investors.com/politics/editorials/sorry-hillary-you-and-bill-not-tax-cuts-caused-the-financial-crisis/
http://planetxnews.com/2015/07/31/all-of-saul-alinskys-8-levels-of-control-are-now-operating-in-america/
http://www.wisegeek.com/what-was-the-whitewater-scandal.htm
http://www.foxnews.com/politics/2009/03/06/clinton-goofs-russian-translation-tells-diplomat-wants-overcharge-ties.html
http://thehill.com/policy/national-security/356323-bill-clinton-sought-states-permission-to-meet-with-russian-nuclear
https://www.washingtonpost.com/politics/1100-donors-to-a-canadian-charity-tied-to-clinton-foundation-remain-secret/2015/04/28/c3c0f374-edbc-11e4-8666-a1d756d0218e_story.html?utm_term=.db3307618306
https://www.vox.com/2015/10/12/9489389/benghazi-explained
http://www.washingtonexaminer.com/security-officers-who-survived-benghazi-say-clintons-team-silenced-them-report/article/2634234
https://www.nationalreview.com/2016/09/obama-email-alias-clinton-why-fbi-didnt-prosecute-hillary/
https://www.washingtonpost.com/news/the-fix/wp/2017/11/02/ex-dnc-chair-goes-at-the-clintons-alleging-hillarys-campaign-hijacked-dnc-during-primary-with-bernie-sanders/?utm_term=.3b3a6dab4e99
https://www.washingtonpost.com/news/the-fix/wp/2017/09/24/hillary-clinton-blames-many-things-for-her-loss-george-clooney-blames-her-frustrating-speeches/?utm_term=.ac5784df151b

Falling Left: Stars and Activism (Chapter 14)

http://www.discoverthenetworks.org/viewSubCategory.asp?id=1237
https://www.activistfacts.com/organizations/media-matters-for-america/
https://en.wikipedia.org/wiki/Anarchism_and_the_Occupy_movement
https://www.thewrap.com/roseanne-barr-kimmel-trump-pence/
https://www.thoughtco.com/how-conservative-hollywood-became-a-liberal-town-3303432
http://www.breitbart.com/big-hollywood/2017/06/14/15-times-celebrities-envisioned-violence-against-trump-and-the-gop/
https://www.rollingstone.com/politics/news/bryan-cranston-kerry-washington-sign-anti-trump-petition-w431136
http://www.papermag.com/100-celebrities-united-against-trump-1944786776.html
http://www.foxnews.com/entertainment/2017/06/23/entertainers-who-have-joked-about-harming-trump.html
http://www.breitbart.com/big-government/2017/01/19/here-is-the-list-of-75-leftist-groups-that-want-to-stop-donald-trump-from-taking-the-oath-of-office/

Our Founding Fathers' Documents (Chapter 15)

https://www.archives.gov/russia-docs/declaration-transcript
http://thehistoryjunkie.com/signers-of-the-declaration-of-independence/
https://www.history.com/topics/american-revolution/declaration-of-independence
http://constitutionus.com/
https://www.archives.gov/founding-docs